Troubleshooting

Microsoft®
Windows®

Stephen W. Sagman

PUBLISHED BY
Microsoft Press
A Division of Microsoft Corporation
One Microsoft Way
Redmond, Washington 98052-6399

Library of Congress Cataloging-in-Publication Data
Sagman, Stephen W.
     Troubleshooting Microsoft Windows / Stephen W. Sagman.
          p. cm.
     Includes index.
     ISBN 0-7356-1166-1
     1. Microsoft Windows (Computer file)   2. Operating systems (Computers)   I. Title.

   QA76.76.O63 .S34117   2000
   005.4'469--dc21   00-048685

Printed and bound in the United States of America.

1 2 3 4 5 6 7 8 9   QWT   6 5 4 3 2 1

Distributed in Canada by Penguin Books Canada Limited.

A CIP catalogue record for this book is available from the British Library.

Microsoft Press books are available through booksellers and distributors worldwide. For further information about international editions, contact your local Microsoft Corporation office or contact Microsoft Press International directly at fax (425) 936-7329. Visit our Web site at mspress.microsoft.com. Send comments to *mspinput@microsoft.com*.

Acquisitions Editors: Christey Bahn, Alex Blanton
Project Editor: Jenny Moss Benson

Technical Editor: Jack Beaudry
Manuscript Editor: Jennifer Harris

Quick contents

Contents

About this book

Troubleshooting Windows offers a new way to diagnose and solve the computer problems you encounter. It helps you quickly determine the source of the problem and leads you directly to the solution so that you can quickly get back to work (or play).

How to use this book

Although *troubleshooting* sounds like a task for a team of white-coated lab technicians, it's something you can accomplish yourself when you run into a computer problem. You don't need to be a computer scientist to fix a problem. But you do need to know which techniques are most likely to resolve the problem, and that's where this book helps. The step-by-step instructions tell you where to start and what to do to zero in on and fix a problem.

You don't have to go through this book from cover to cover or even read it in any particular order. It's designed so that you can jump in, quickly diagnose a problem, and then fix the problem using the information you find. The problems it covers are grouped into chapters that are presented alphabetically, like any good reference book. The chapter titles are simple so you'll know at a glance what kinds of topics the chapter covers.

In each chapter, you'll find two specific elements: a flowchart and a set of solutions.

The flowchart

Your first stop in each chapter is the helpful and easy-to-use flowchart. The flowchart asks carefully chosen questions and takes you through precise, yes-or-no answers to help you diagnose a problem. If the solution to a problem requires only a few steps, you'll find them in a *quick fix* right there on the flowchart. If the solution requires a little more explanation or a few more steps, you'll be directed to the specific page in the chapter that covers the problem. And if you don't find your problem on the flowchart, the list of related chapters that appears on each flowchart will lead you to another chapter that might have the solution you need.

The solutions

The solution topics are where you'll find the answers to the problems you've pinpointed in the flowchart. They tell you the source of the problem you're experiencing, and they show you how to fix the problem with clear, step-by-step instructions. The solutions provide plenty of screen shots, showing exactly what you should see on the screen as you move through the steps.

The solutions in this book are designed to give you just the facts so you can quickly fix a problem and be on your way. But you'll probably find yourself reading the additional information the solutions provide because it will help you understand why a problem has occurred and, more important, show you how to avoid similar problems in the future. Tips and sidebars offer additional related material.

The many versions of Windows

Troubleshooting Windows focuses on the current consumer versions of Windows—

Windows Millennium Edition (Windows Me), Windows 98, Windows 98 Second Edition, and Windows 95. If you use Windows 95, you'll still find plenty of helpful information because the topics in the book usually pertain to all versions of Windows. However, you might sometimes need to extrapolate slightly to account for minor differences in menus or dialog boxes, and to account for the fact that some features available in Windows 98 and Windows Me are missing from Windows 95.

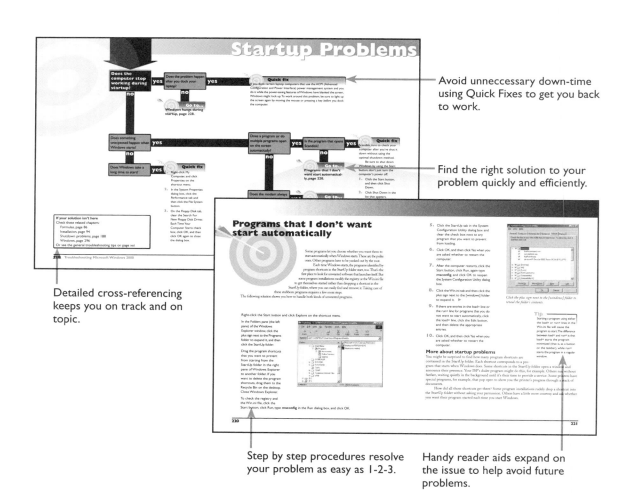

Avoid unneccessary down-time using Quick Fixes to get you back to work.

Find the right solution to your problem quickly and efficiently.

Detailed cross-referencing keeps you on track and on topic.

Step by step procedures resolve your problem as easy as 1-2-3.

Handy reader aids expand on the issue to help avoid future problems.

Troubleshooting tips

Troubleshooting a problem requires careful attention to all the circumstances surrounding the problem. If something has gone wrong, ask yourself when it began, what you were doing in Windows at the time, and what else might have been happening on the computer that might have been a contributing factor. Did the problem arise when you were trying to install a new device or program? Has someone else been using your computer? Having a handle on these questions will help you clearly define the problem so that you can narrow it down more effectively with the flowchart.

Consider how you would categorize the problem. Does it have to do with browsing the Internet? Sending e-mail? Playing games? Working with folders? Once you decide what category the problem falls into, you can turn to the chapter in the book that most likely has the solution.

Remember that computers are very consistent. If a problem with Windows happens once, it will probably happen again under the same circumstances. This makes

diagnosing problems easier. It also means there's no point in trying the same task again the same way. For example, if you try to copy a file to a different folder but you get a shortcut to the file instead, you can assume that dragging the file using that technique will always create a shortcut. (Using the Internet and e-mail is the exception to this rule because you're relying on outside resources whose services you can't control. For example, your Internet connection might be interrupted because of a problem at your Internet service provider.)

Keep in mind that millions of other people are using Windows just like you. If you run into a problem, the chances are good that many others have already encountered it, and the solution might be readily available in updated software. Frequently in this book, you'll be prompted to make sure you've downloaded and installed from the manufacturer's Web site or the Windows Update Web page the newest device drivers for your hardware and the latest updates for your programs.

If you're still stuck

This book does its best to anticipate the most common problems you're likely to run into when you're using Windows, but obviously it can't be exhaustive. Specific hardware devices and software programs can cause some of the problems that occur in Windows. There's even a chance that the solutions in this book won't solve your problem. If you run into a dead end, you can turn to Microsoft product support or to any of these recommended resources:

- **MyHelpDesk.com** (*www.MyHelpDesk. com*) A giant computer help site on the Web that offers extensive information about Windows.

- **ZDNet Help** (*www.zdnet.com/zdhelp*) Offers how-tos, expert advice, tutorials, guides, and other features.

- **Microsoft Knowledge Base** (*search. support.microsoft.com*) Offers technical support information for all Microsoft products. The best place to go to search for help with questions about problems with specific hardware devices and software programs.

Troubleshooting Web site

With the purchase of this book, you now have access to the Microsoft Troubleshooting Web site (*mspress.microsoft.com/troubleshooting*), which complements the book series by offering deeper, more extensive, and regularly updated troubleshooting information that will be posted monthly. So if you have a problem that wasn't addressed in this book, you can check the Web site to see if its solution is there. Although you can access the site at no charge, remember that your regular connection time charges may apply. Even if you don't have a specific problem you're looking to solve, you might discover information that you'll find useful anyway. To access the site, you need this code: *MSM0001*.

The Troubleshooting Web site is just as easy to navigate as this book, and it shares the goal of helping you quickly locate your problem and its solution without going into too much detail.

Acknowledgments

One of the great pleasures in professional life is the opportunity to work closely with the kind of talented and committed people who strived with me for many months to produce this book.

From the outset, my editors—Christey Bahn, Jenny Benson, Laura Sackerman, and Wendy Zucker—along with their associates at Microsoft Press conceived and shared a bright and clear vision for the *Troubleshooting* series, nurtured me and the other series authors, and worked intensively to bring their wonderful concept into being.

Also working shoulder to shoulder with me have been two very talented editors. Both Jennifer Harris, who untangled my text, and Jack Beaudry, who tested every procedure, made enormous contributions to the material and offered invaluable suggestions all along the way.

Two very skilled writers added excellent chapters to the book. Michelle Rogers contributed the "Sound" chapter and Don Gilbert contributed the "Backing Up," "The Screen," "The Taskbar," and "Window, Working with a" chapters. I'm grateful to them both.

As always, my charming friend, Sharon Bell of Presentation Desktop Publications, who's a fellow veteran of many of these projects, carefully created and professionally polished the pages you'll read. She's a champ, a trooper, and a pleasure to work with.

I'd also like to thank Judith Bloch at Microsoft Press for pitching in at the last minute, Jim Kramer and Joel Panchot for their delightful designs, and Matt Sullivan and his team for their inspiration. Go Matt!

Finally, my gratitude always to Eric and Lola, my home team, for their love and support, and to my friends and family who've heard about nothing but "the book" for a long time now. I couldn't have written this book without their forbearance.

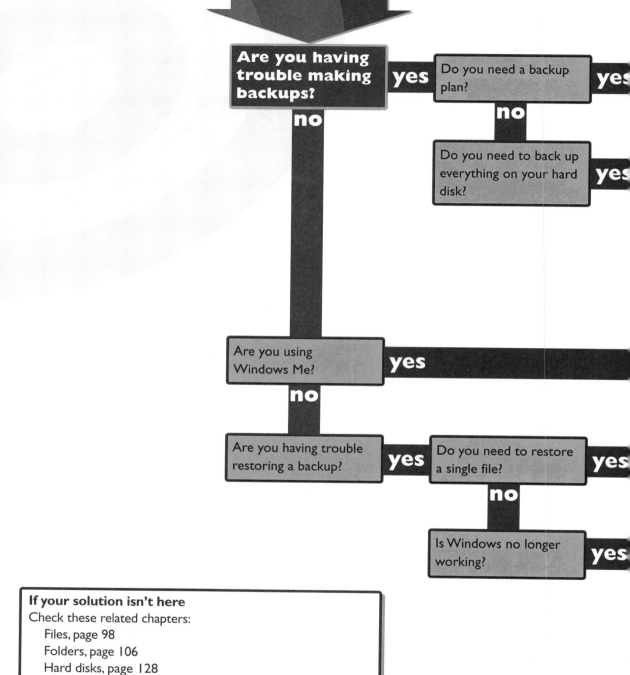

Are you having trouble making backups?

yes → Do you need a backup plan? yes →

no ↓

Do you need to back up everything on your hard disk? yes →

Are you using Windows Me? **yes** →

no ↓

Are you having trouble restoring a backup? yes → Do you need to restore a single file? yes →

no ↓

Is Windows no longer working? yes →

If your solution isn't here
Check these related chapters:
  Files, page 98
  Folders, page 106
  Hard disks, page 128
  Hardware, page 138
Or see the general troubleshooting tips on page xiii

Backing up

Go to...
I don't know how to create a backup routine, page 6

Do you have a tape backup drive?

yes

Do you know how to do a full system backup?

no

no

Go to...
I want to do a backup, but I don't have a tape drive, page 4

Go to...
I don't know how to protect Windows from a hard disk crash, page 10

Go to...
I deleted a file and need to retrieve it from a backup, page 12

Go to...
Windows is damaged, so I can't use Microsoft Backup, page 8

Quick fix

The Setup program for Windows Me doesn't install Microsoft Backup, and for some reason, upgrading from Windows 98 doesn't preserve the Start menu command for Microsoft Backup. You can install Microsoft Backup in Windows Me by following these steps:

1. Insert the Windows Me CD, and in the Windows Millennium CD-ROM window, click Browse This CD.

2. Double-click the Add-ons folder, and then double-click the MSBackup folder.

3. Double-click Msbexp to start the installation.

I want to do a backup, but I don't have a tape drive

Source of the problem

Using a computer without having a backup of your most critical files is a risk you shouldn't take. But if your computer doesn't have a tape drive, which would let you safeguard files on a tape cassette, you're not out of luck. You can still use Microsoft Backup to back up your data on floppy disks, or removable disks, such as Iomega Zip or Jaz disks. With Backup, you can even back up your data to a second hard disk or to a disk in a computer in your home or office network. Here's how to create a backup.

How to fix it

1. Click Start, point to Programs, point to Accessories, point to System Tools, and then click Backup. (In Windows Me, you'll have to install Backup by double-clicking Msbexp in the \Add-ons\MSBackup folder on the Windows Me CD.)

   If this is the first time you've run Backup, click No in response to the message telling you that no backup devices were found on your computer.

2. Click Close to close the Microsoft Backup dialog box.

3. On the Backup tab in the Microsoft Backup window, in the What To Back Up section, click the plus sign next to the drives and folders you want to open. ▶

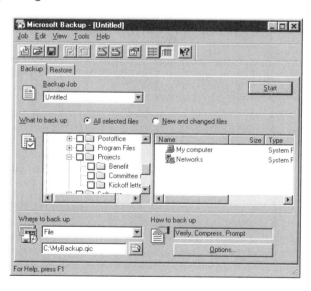

4. Select the check box next to each folder whose entire contents you want to back up, or click the folder in the left pane to open it, and in the right pane, select the check boxes next to the files or subfolders you want to back up.

5. In the Where To Back Up section, type a path or click the Browse button (next to the Path box) and select a drive, folder, and file name on your computer or on a computer on the network. Then click Open.

6. To include a backup of the Windows registry, which stores all the settings for Windows and the programs you run in Windows, click Options, and on the Advanced tab in the Backup Job Options dialog box, select the Backup Windows Registry check box and click OK.

    You should back up the registry only if you are also backing up the Windows folder because the registry references specific files in the Windows folder.

7. If you think you'll want to back up the same information in the future, click Save As on the Job menu in Backup, and then in the Save Backup Job As dialog box, type a name for the backup job and click Save.

    In the future, you'll be able to click Open on the Job menu and select the backup job, which will set the folders and files to be backed up and the destination for the backup.

8. Click Start.

    If you're using removable disks, be prepared to swap disks when you're prompted, and be sure to label the backup disks in numbered sequence, including the date and name of the backup job on each disk.

9. Click OK to close the message box telling you that the operation is completed, click OK to close the Backup Progress dialog box, and quit Backup.

Which type of backup medium is right for you?

Here are some alternatives to tape that you might consider for backing up your computer:

- **A second hard disk** Offers the greatest convenience among backup media. The cost of hard disks is now low, their storage capacity is large, and their speed is much greater than backup tapes. You can also use a second hard disk for program and file storage in addition to backed up data from the primary hard disk. Remember, though, that a lightning strike or a power surge could zap both hard disks in a computer that doesn't have a surge protector, so you might also want to use removable disks to create a backup that you can store away from the computer.

- **A network hard disk** No longer an option only for office networks. If you have a network at home, you can back up essential data by copying it to the hard disk of another computer.

- **Removable disks** Can be transported easily and reused hundreds of times. While the cost-per-MB for removable disks is greater than that of backup tapes, a removable disk is much faster and it lasts much longer without degrading.

- **Floppy disks** Convenient for backing up your most critical files. They're slow, and their capacity is small compared to other media, but they're inexpensive and easy to take along with you.

- **File storage Web sites** Including *www.driveway.com* and *communities.msn.com/filecabinets*. Convenient if you have a high-speed Internet connection, such as a cable modem, Digital Subscriber Line (DSL), or connection through an office network. These sites offer 25 MB to 100 MB or more of free storage. Although you can't use Backup to transfer files directly to these sites, you can use it to create a backup file (which is compressed, so it's small) and then copy the backup file to an online storage site.

I don't know how to create a backup routine

Source of the problem

You can back up your data whenever you happen to remember to, but unless you follow a specific backup scheme, backing up particular files at definite intervals, you might not be fully protected if your hard disk crashes, or a virus strikes, or someone inadvertently deletes your favorite folder. Fortunately, in Microsoft Backup you can use any of a number of time-tested systems for creating backups. Each backup you create is called a *backup job,* and here are some suggestions for creating, using, and organizing backup jobs.

How to fix it

A frequently used scheme for backing up files is to alternate between *complete backups* (backing up all your files) and *interim backups* (backing up only new and changed files). You can choose between these two backup styles by clicking either All Selected Files or New And Changed Files in the What To Back Up section on the Backup tab in the Microsoft Backup window. Because interim backups copy only the files that have changed since the last backup, they take less time to create and recover.

The best scheme for backing up your data most efficiently is this:

1. Create a weekly, complete backup of your entire hard disk by clicking All Selected Files and selecting the hard disk in the What To Back Up section on the Backup tab in the Microsoft Backup window.

    Save this backup job with a name such as *Full Backup.*

2. Between the weekly backups, create a series of daily backup jobs, clicking the New And Changed Files option in the What To Back Up section on the Backup tab in the Microsoft Backup window.

    Be sure to name these interim backups sequentially, and don't reuse any interim backup media until the next complete backup because the interim backups capture only the files that are new and changed since the last backup.

To completely restore your computer, you'll need to restore the last complete backup, followed in sequence by each of the interim backups you've made during the week. To help you implement a daily backup scheme that you'll repeat each week, permanently label each backup disk with the name of the backup job and the day to use it, such as *Sunday Full Backup* or *Tuesday Interim Backup.*

Other backups you might want to create

In addition to the system of complete and interim backups, which would allow you to fully restore your computer, you might want to make these backups, from which you can recover specific files:

- Create a backup job that backs up only the data created by your programs.

  As you work, you might want to store all your important data in subfolders within a single folder, such as the My Documents folder, so that you can easily back up one folder to preserve everything you can't live without.

- Create a backup job that backs up the Windows folder, its subfolders, and the registry. Run this job before you install new hardware and software so that you'll have a working version of Windows to which you can return should you encounter errors after you install a new component.

  In Windows Me, you can use System Restore to create a restore point to which you can return if something goes wrong with a software or hardware installation. For information about using System Restore, see "I Get a Message About a Windows Registry Problem," on page 46.

- Create a backup job that contains all the program files you've downloaded from the Internet. These are usually compressed files, so before you click Start on the Backup tab in the Microsoft Backup window, click Options. On the General tab in the Backup Job Options dialog box, click Never Compress The Data and then click OK, because trying to compress compressed files can actually increase their size, even though that sounds like a contradiction in terms.

How to find the files you should back up

Some programs don't make it clear where they're storing their data, so finding the files you need to back up can be a challenge. To help find these files, you can use the Find or Search command to determine which files have been recently modified. Follow these steps:

1. Click Start, point to Find, and then click Files Or Folders. (In Windows Me, click Start, point to Search, and then click For Files Or Folders.)

2. In the Find dialog box, click the Date tab, and click During The Previous x Month(s). (In Windows Me, click Search Options in the Search Results window, select the Date check box, and click In The Last x Months.)

3. Click Find Now. (In Windows Me, click Search Now.)

   If this search finds too many files, you can narrow the results to include only files of a single type. Click the Advanced tab in the Find dialog box, and then click the Of Type down arrow and click a file type in the list. (In Windows Me, select the Type check box, click the Type down arrow, and then click a file type in the list.) Search again by clicking Find Now (or Search Now in Windows Me).

Windows is damaged, so I can't use Microsoft Backup

Source of the problem

As long as you have a full backup of your hard disk, a Windows Startup disk, a CD-ROM drive, and your Windows CD, you can recover your computer even if you're no longer able to run Windows.

    The Windows CD includes a program you can run to reinstall Windows, recover your data, and restore your computer to the state it was in the last time you created a full system backup. To restore your computer when Windows won't work, follow these steps.

How to fix it

1. Insert the Windows CD in the CD-ROM drive.

2. Insert the Windows Startup disk, and reboot the computer.

3. At the Microsoft Windows Startup Menu, select the Start Computer With CD-ROM Support option. ▶

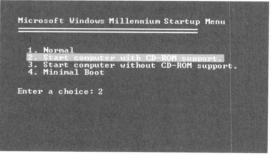

4. After the computer starts, at the MS-DOS prompt (C:\>), type the letter of the CD-ROM drive followed by a colon, and press Enter.

5. At the MS-DOS prompt, type **cd \tools\sysrec**, and press Enter.

6. Type **pcrestor**, and press Enter.
    Microsoft System Recovery reinstalls a working copy of Windows.

7. Remove the Windows Startup disk from the floppy disk drive.
    After Setup is complete, the System Recovery Wizard opens.

Windows Me

In Windows Me, you can use System Restore to restore Windows to an earlier state, when it worked properly. Restart your computer, and press and hold the Ctrl key while Windows starts. Select Safe Mode at the Microsoft Windows Startup Menu. In the Safe Mode Troubleshooter, which starts automatically, click the System Restore link and follow the steps of the wizard.

8. On the first page of the System Recovery Wizard, click Next.

9. On the next page of the wizard, type your name and your company name and click Next.

10. On the third page of the wizard, click Finish. Microsoft Backup starts.

11. In the Microsoft Backup dialog box, click Restore Backed Up Files, and click OK. ▶

12. If the backup is on a removable disk or tape, insert the most recent full system backup.

13. On the first page of the Restore Wizard, select the location of your backup, and click Next.

14. In the Select Backup Sets dialog box, select the most recent full system backup, and click OK.

15. On the next page of the Restore Wizard, select the check box next to each hard disk listed and click Next. ▶

16. On the next page of the Restore Wizard, leave Original Location selected and click Next.

17. On the last page of the Restore Wizard, click Always Replace The File On My Computer and then click Start to begin restoring files.

18. After the files are restored, click OK to close the message box telling you that the operation was completed, click OK to close the Restore dialog box, and then quit Backup.

19. If you've performed interim backups (you chose New And Changed Files in the What To Backup section of the Backup tab rather than All Selected Files) since your last full system backup, restore the interim backups in order, starting with the oldest first.

20. Restart the computer.

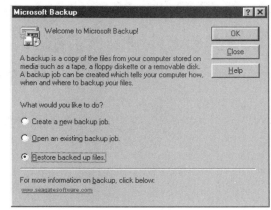

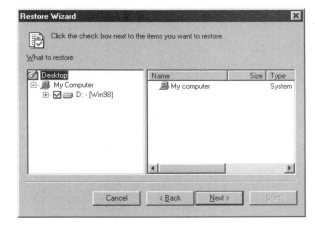

I don't know how to protect Windows from a hard disk crash

Source of the problem

Anyone who has experienced a hard disk crash knows the importance of having a full system backup on hand. A full system backup is a copy of everything on your hard disk, and it's the key to recovering your computer after a hard disk crash. As long as you have a full system backup, you can install a new hard disk and use the backup, along with the Windows Startup disk and the original Windows CD, to restore your computer to its precrash state. Here's how to go about creating a full system backup, starting with creating a Windows Startup disk.

How to fix it

1. Click Start, point to Settings, and click Control Panel.

2. In Control Panel, double-click Add/Remove Programs. (In Windows Me, you might be able to single-click the Add/Remove Programs link.)

3. On the Startup Disk tab in the Add/Remove Programs Properties dialog box, click Create Disk and follow the directions. ▶

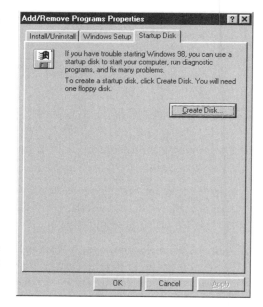

Perform a full system backup using the Backup Wizard by following these steps:

1. Click Start, point to Programs, point to Accessories, point to System Tools, and click Backup.

2. If this is the first time you've run Microsoft Backup, click No in response to the message telling you that no backup devices were found on your computer.

3. In the Microsoft Backup dialog box, make sure Create A New Backup Job is selected and click OK.

4. On the first page of the Backup Wizard, make sure Back Up My Computer is selected and click Next. ▶

5. On the next page of the wizard, make sure All Selected Files is selected and click Next.

6. On the next page of the wizard, click the Where To Back Up down arrow and click your media type in the list.

   Click File if you are backing up to another hard disk, to a removable disk, or to a hard disk in a network computer. To select an existing file, click the Browse button (next to the Path box), select a disk, folder, and file name for the backup file and click Open. ▶

7. Click Next.

8. On the next page of the wizard, make sure the verify the data and compress data check boxes are selected and click Next.

9. Type a name for the backup job, and click Start.

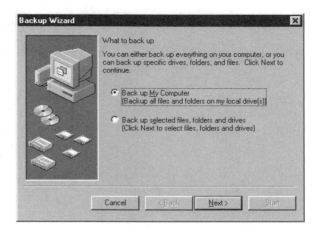

I have only floppy disks

If you have no removable disk, tape drive, second hard disk, or network computer to which you can back up, you should preserve your most irreplaceable data on floppy disks along with your personalized Windows settings. Use Backup to copy the following files to floppies:

● If the logon dialog box is not displayed when you start your computer, copy the \Windows\ Favorites folder, the \Windows\History folder, and the \Windows\Cookies folder. Also copy the \Windows\Desktop folder and the \Windows\Start Menu folder and subfolders.

   If you do log on to your computer, copy the \Windows\Profiles\<*logon*> folder, where <*logon*> is the name you log on with. For example, if you log on as Dale, copy the \Windows\ Profiles\Dale folder. This folder contains all of the above settings. You also might want to copy the entire Profiles folder because it contains the personal settings for everyone who uses the computer.

● Copy the files in the \Windows\Tasks folder to preserve your scheduled tasks.

● Copy all .pwl files in the Windows folder to preserve your password files.

I deleted a file and need to retrieve it from a backup

Source of the problem

You can only truly know how happy you'll be to have a backup after you've irretrievably deleted a critical file. Even with the protection afforded by the Recycle Bin, which stores deleted files so you can recover them gracefully, it's all too easy to permanently remove a file that you really wanted to keep. Fortunately, restoring files you've backed up is a snap in Microsoft Backup. You can restore an entire backup, or you can selectively restore files from among a large number of files you've backed up. Here's how to accomplish it.

How to fix it

1. Insert the disk or tape containing the backup to which you saved the file.

2. Click Start, point to Programs, point to Accessories, point to System Tools, and click Backup.

3. In the Microsoft Backup dialog box, click Restore Backed Up Files and click OK. ▶

4. On the first page of the Restore Wizard, select the backup file that contains the file you need and click Next.

5. In the Select Backup Sets dialog box, select the specific backup that contains the file and click OK. ▶

6. In the left pane of the next Restore Wizard page, click the plus sign next to the disks and folders you want to expand to find the folder that contains the file you need to restore.

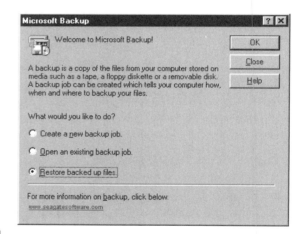

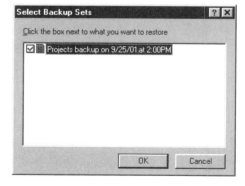

7. Click the folder containing the file, and then in the right pane, click the check box next to the file that you want to restore and click Next. ▶

8. On the next page of the wizard, click Next to restore the file to its original location. ▶ below

9. Click Start to retrieve the file.

10. In the Media Required dialog box, click OK.

11. Click OK when you see the *Operation completed* message.

If the Status box in the Restore Progress dialog box reads *Restore completed—No errors*, click OK. Otherwise, you can click Report to see what errors occurred, correct the problem, and try recovering the file again.

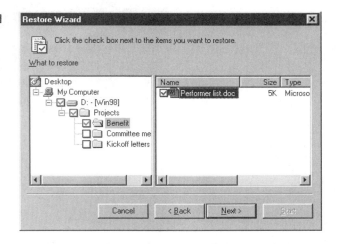

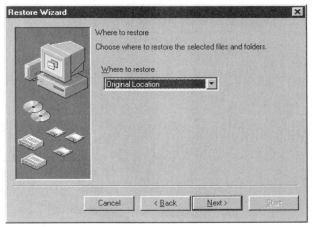

In Windows 98 or Windows Me, I can't restore a file I backed up in Windows 95

If you backed up a large enough set of files in Windows 95 that the resulting backup file spanned multiple disks, you won't be able to restore individual files from the backup in Windows 98 or Windows Me. If you try to restore just one file, you end up with a useless restored file that has 0 bytes.

The solution to this problem is not difficult—it's just annoying. To restore a file from a multiple-disk backup made in Windows 95, you'll need to restore all the files in the backup and then remove those files you don't need. If you have enough disk space, you can restore the entire backup to a temporary folder, copy the file you need out of that folder, and then delete the temporary folder.

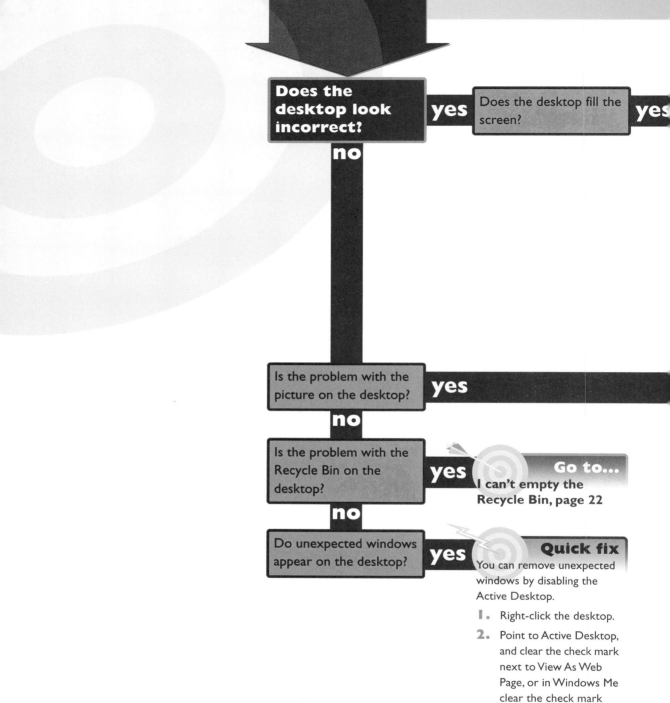

Does the desktop look incorrect?

yes → Does the desktop fill the screen? **yes**

no

Is the problem with the picture on the desktop? **yes**

no

Is the problem with the Recycle Bin on the desktop? **yes**

Go to...

I can't empty the Recycle Bin, page 22

no

Do unexpected windows appear on the desktop? **yes**

Quick fix

You can remove unexpected windows by disabling the Active Desktop.

1. Right-click the desktop.

2. Point to Active Desktop, and clear the check mark next to View As Web Page, or in Windows Me clear the check mark next to Show Web Content.

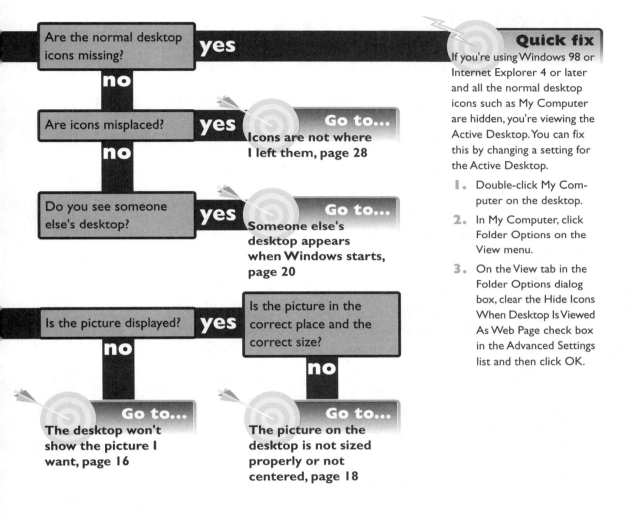

Are the normal desktop icons missing? **yes**

no

Are icons misplaced? **yes**

Go to...
Icons are not where I left them, page 28

no

Do you see someone else's desktop? **yes**

Go to...
Someone else's desktop appears when Windows starts, page 20

Is the picture displayed? **yes**

Is the picture in the correct place and the correct size?

no

no

Go to...
The desktop won't show the picture I want, page 16

Go to...
The picture on the desktop is not sized properly or not centered, page 18

Quick fix

If you're using Windows 98 or Internet Explorer 4 or later and all the normal desktop icons such as My Computer are hidden, you're viewing the Active Desktop. You can fix this by changing a setting for the Active Desktop.

1. Double-click My Computer on the desktop.

2. In My Computer, click Folder Options on the View menu.

3. On the View tab in the Folder Options dialog box, clear the Hide Icons When Desktop Is Viewed As Web Page check box in the Advanced Settings list and then click OK.

If your solution isn't here
Check these related chapters:
Or see the general troubleshooting tips on page xiii

The desktop won't show the picture I want

Source of the problem

Even though you've scanned your favorite picture, you can't put it on the Windows desktop unless it shows up in the list of pictures you can use for wallpaper. If your scanned images don't appear in this list, your scanning software is probably producing .tif or .jpg files. While this format is suitable for desktop publishing or Web pages, you'll need a .bmp file to use for wallpaper.

Similarly, a picture you've downloaded from a Web site or received in an e-mail message might not show up in the list because it's usually a .jpg file. You need to convert the file from .jpg to .bmp. See "How to Fix It (With a Downloaded Picture)," on the facing page, for help converting a downloaded image to a .bmp file.

How to fix it (with a scanned picture)

1. Position the picture in the scanner, and start your scanning software.

   In some programs, you choose the output file type before you scan, and in others, you scan a picture and then choose a file type when you save the picture.

2. On the File menu, click Save As, and in the Save As dialog box, click the Save As Type down arrow and click Bitmap Image, Windows BMP, or Windows Bitmap. Click Save to save the file. ▶

3. Close the scanning program, right-click an empty area of the Windows desktop, and click Properties on the shortcut menu.

4. On the Background tab in the Display Properties dialog box, click the Browse button, open the folder in which you saved the .bmp file, select the .bmp file, and click Open.

   If the picture is the wrong size or if it's not centered properly on the screen, see "The Picture on the Desktop Is Not Sized Properly or Not Centered," on page 18.

5. Click OK to close the Display Properties dialog box.

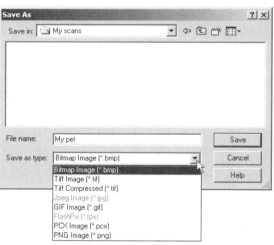

Saving a picture using the scanning software for Hewlett-Packard scanners.

How to fix it (with a downloaded picture)

If you copied a picture from a Web page (by right-clicking it on the Web page and clicking Save Picture As on the shortcut menu in Internet Explorer), or if you downloaded the picture from a file download site or got it from someone through e-mail, the file is probably a .jpg file, which is the most commonly used format for displaying images on the screen.

The easiest way to get a .jpg file onto the desktop as wallpaper is to follow these steps:

1. Double-click the file in My Computer to open it in Internet Explorer.

2. Right-click the image, and click Set As Wallpaper on the shortcut menu. ▶

   If you right-click the desktop, click Properties on the shortcut menu, and then inspect the Wallpaper list on the Background tab in the Display Properties dialog box, you'll see the image now listed as Internet Explorer Wallpaper. ▶

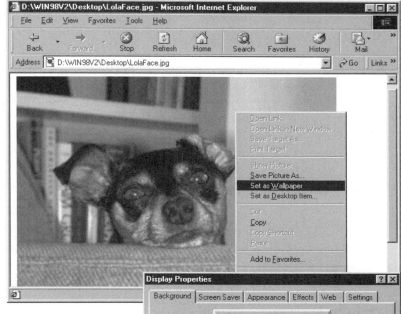

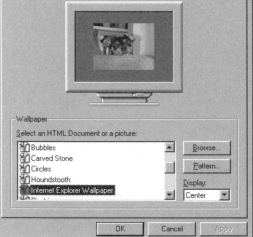

Another technique for producing a file that you can use for wallpaper is to use an image editing program such as Jasc Software Paint Shop Pro (a program that's available at *www.jasc.com*), Adobe PhotoDeluxe, Microsoft PhotoDraw, or the image editing software that came with your computer or scanner. Open the .jpg file in the image editing program, and then save it as a .bmp file by selecting the .bmp file format from the Save As Type list in the Save As dialog box. Before you save the picture, you can also tweak it in the image editing program to change attributes such as its brightness or contrast.

The picture on the desktop is not sized properly or not centered

Source of the problem

Windows won't adjust the size of a picture to fit the desktop—it leaves that job to you. Fortunately, resizing a picture for wallpaper requires just a few steps, as you'll learn in the solution below.

If the background picture is already the correct size but it's not in the middle of the screen, look for a border on the picture that's wider along one of the picture's edges. When you scan a picture but don't fit the area to be scanned closely enough to the picture edges, the background that you've included can act as a border on one side and push the image off center. If you still have the picture, the easiest option is to rescan it without the border. Otherwise, you can remove the border by following the instructions in "Chopping Off a Border to Center a Picture," on the facing page.

How to fix it

1. To determine the size of the desktop, right-click an empty area of the desktop, click Properties on the shortcut menu, and in the Display Properties dialog box, click the Settings tab. ▶

   The Screen Area section shows the desktop size in *pixels* (screen dots). Typical sizes are 800 by 600 pixels (800 dots horizontally by 600 dots vertically) or 1024 by 768 pixels.

2. Open the picture you want to use on the desktop in an image editing program, such as Microsoft PhotoDraw.

   If you don't have an image editing program, see "Resizing the Background in Microsoft Paint," on the facing page.

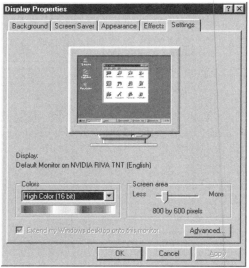

3. In the image editor, find the command that lets you change the overall size of an image, often called *Resize*. (Microsoft PhotoDraw lets you easily resize an image by dragging its corners.)

4. Enter dimensions in pixels that are the same as your screen area dimensions, or if you want to leave a border around the image as a space for desktop icons, enter a size that's about

150 pixels smaller horizontally and about 200 pixels smaller vertically (leaving extra vertical space for the taskbar).

5. In the image editor, click Save on the File menu and save the image as a .bmp file.

Chopping off a border to center a picture

Most image editing programs (including Microsoft Paint, a built-in accessory in Windows for working with picture files) let you *crop* a picture—that is, chop off excess around the edges. If a picture you've placed on the background is off center, try opening the picture in your image editor and cropping everything outside of the actual image area. In Microsoft Paint, you can drag a handle on the side of a picture toward the center of the picture. If you find there's more to crop on one side than the facing side, you've found the reason the picture was off center on the desktop.

Tip
If a background picture is not centered, right-click the desktop, click Properties on the shortcut menu, and on the Background tab in the Display Properties dialog box, make sure that Display is set to Center rather than Tile.

Resizing the background in Microsoft Paint

In Microsoft Paint, you don't have the precise control over image size that you get in many image editing programs. You can't resize an image to exact dimensions in pixels. But working in Paint can be even easier because the image in Paint is the same size it will be on the desktop.

1. Click Start, point to Programs, point to Accessories, and click Paint.

2. In Paint, open the picture file, and on the Image menu, click Stretch/Skew.

3. In the Stretch section in the Stretch And Skew dialog box, type percentages in the Horizontal and Vertical boxes, and click OK to see the newly resized image. ▶

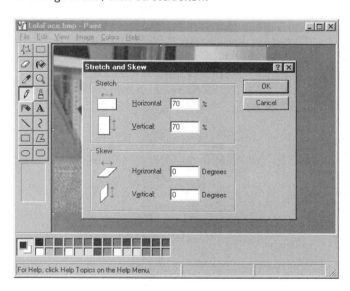

   To reduce the picture to half its current height, for example, type **50** in the Vertical box. If the result doesn't look correct, click Undo on the Edit menu to return to the original size, and try a different percentage. If you don't use Undo, the next percentages you enter will be percentages of the current size rather than the original size.

Someone else's desktop appears when Windows starts

Source of the problem

If you turn on your computer and the wrong background picture pops up along with unfamiliar icons on the desktop and a Start menu that doesn't list your programs, either you're in the wrong house or you're not looking at your own desktop. If you've skipped the logon dialog box by pressing Esc or clicking Cancel, Windows isn't using your personal settings, including your personalized desktop, because you haven't logged on properly with your user name and password.

Another possibility is that you haven't set up Windows for multiple users, which gives each person who uses the computer a user profile, including a personalized desktop. Someone might have made a few changes to the desktop without realizing that the changes affect everyone's desktop. On the other hand, if you do have multiple-user profiles, someone might have set Windows to automatically log on with a user name and password other than yours.

How to fix it

1. Click Start, point to Settings, click Control Panel, and then double-click Passwords. (In Windows Me, you might need to click View All Control Panel Options to see the Passwords option.)

2. On the User Profiles tab in the Passwords Properties dialog box, see whether the All Users Of This Computer Use The Same Preferences And Desktop Settings option is selected, and then click OK.

   If this option is selected, continue below. Otherwise, skip to "Disabling Automatic Logon" on the facing page. ▶

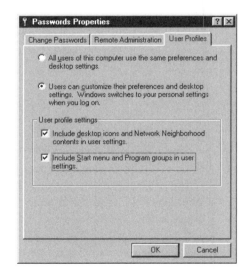

Turn on multiple-user profiles:

1. In Control Panel, double-click the Users icon.

2. On the first page of the Enable Multi-User Settings Wizard, click Next.

3. On the Add User page, type your user name, and click Next.

4. On the Enter Password page, type your password in the Password box and click Next.

5. On the Personalized Items Settings page, select the check boxes for the items you want to personalize and click Next. ▶

6. Click Finish, and when you are asked whether you want to restart the computer, click Yes.

After you enable multiple-user profiles, you can create additional users, each with a user name and password and personalized settings such as desktop icons, wallpaper, and Start menu commands.

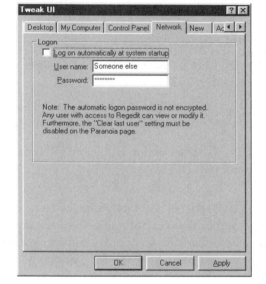

Disabling automatic logon

If a dialog box asking for a user name and password appears briefly and then disappears just before the desktop is displayed, someone else's user name and password are being sent to the logon dialog box. Fix this by double-clicking Tweak UI in Control Panel (see "What Is Tweak UI?" on page 32) and clearing the Log On Automatically At System Startup check box on the Network tab. ▶

Click OK, and then restart Windows.

Keeping order on the desktop

After you've set up multiple users and given others their own user profiles on your computer, you need to enforce a few rules so that no one messes with anyone else's settings. The first rule is that everyone (including you) must log off after using the computer by clicking the Log Off command on the Start menu. This forces the next person who uses the computer to log on with a user name and password. That, in turn, opens a user profile and displays the desktop stored in the user profile.

Rule number two: No using Tweak UI to log on automatically.

Rule number three is simple: No one presses Esc or clicks Cancel in the logon dialog box. Everyone enters a user name and password. No exceptions, and no substitutions.

> **Tip**
> If all else fails, kick everyone else off your computer and disable multiple users. Drastic, but it works.

I can't empty the Recycle Bin

Source of the problem

The Recycle Bin isn't fragile and it has lots of space for your deleted documents, but it sometimes can't let go of the files you've dropped into it. Sometimes when you try to empty the Recycle Bin, it displays an error message and doesn't fully clear itself of the files and folders you've deleted. This can happen if you try to delete a folder from the Recycle Bin while you're viewing its contents in Windows Explorer. It can also happen when you try to delete a folder for which you have enabled Thumbnail view. (Thumbnail view lets you see the contents of the files in a folder in the form of tiny pictures.)

How to fix it

1. Click a folder in Windows Explorer other than the one you are currently viewing.

2. Right-click the Recycle Bin, click Empty Recycle Bin on the shortcut menu, and click Yes to confirm the deletion. ▶

Another option is to close Windows Explorer altogether and then retry step 2.

Taming the Recycle Bin

Another Recycle Bin quirk is its constant nagging. It does so both when you delete a file and again when you try to empty the Recycle Bin of files you've deleted. "Are you sure? Are you sure?" it asks.

To fix this problem, drag files to the Recycle Bin rather than selecting them and pressing the Delete key. If you've gone to the trouble of dragging a file all the way to the Recycle Bin, the Recycle Bin seems to believe that you're serious about deleting the file and doesn't ask for confirmation.

You can also remove the confirmation message about deleting each file by following these steps:

1. Right-click the Recycle Bin.

2. Click Properties on the shortcut menu.

3. On the Global tab in the Recycle Bin Properties dialog box, clear the Display Delete Confirmation Dialog Box check box.

Tip

Files that you delete in a DOS session (in an MS-DOS Prompt window) don't go to the Recycle Bin—they're deleted instantly. This is another way to get around the nagging of the Recycle Bin, but it's a long way around.

Other Recycle Bin problems and solutions

The Recycle Bin doesn't work when you try to drag certain icons into it from the desktop. My Computer, Network Neighborhood, and other icons just won't go. In fact, when you drag one of these icons to the Recycle Bin, you see a prohibited symbol (a circle with a slash through it) in place of the mouse pointer. ▶

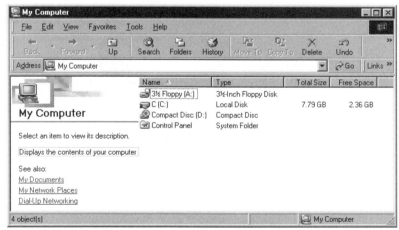

The prohibited symbol is how Windows tells you that certain icons are there to stay—the only way you'll get them off the desktop is to blast them off. (You can hide the desktop icons if you use the Active Desktop. You can also use Tweak UI to remove these icons if you must have a clear desktop at all costs. See "What Is Tweak UI?" on page 32.)

Keep in mind that if you drag a floppy disk to the Recycle Bin, the files on the disk are deleted without being moved to the Recycle Bin. (You do see a warning message before any files are removed.) You can't delete the files on a hard disk by dragging the hard disk to the Recycle Bin—a good thing too, because inadvertently wiping your hard disk clean would be tragic.

The Recycle Bin thinks my drive is only 2 GB

Ignore what the Recycle Bin in Windows 98 tells you when you view the Recycle Bin Properties dialog box. At least ignore the part about the size of your disk drive if it is larger than 2 gigabytes (GB) in size. No matter how many GB of storage space you have on your hard disk or in a partition on the hard disk (a section of the disk that has its own drive letter), the Recycle Bin in Windows 98 reports that the drive is only 2 GB in size (or 1.99 GB, to be exact). The Recycle Bin in Windows Me recognizes drives that are larger than 2 GB.

To determine the true size of a disk or a partition on the disk, double-click My Computer, and click Details on the View menu. The Total Size column accurately reports the size of each drive or partition on your computer. ▶

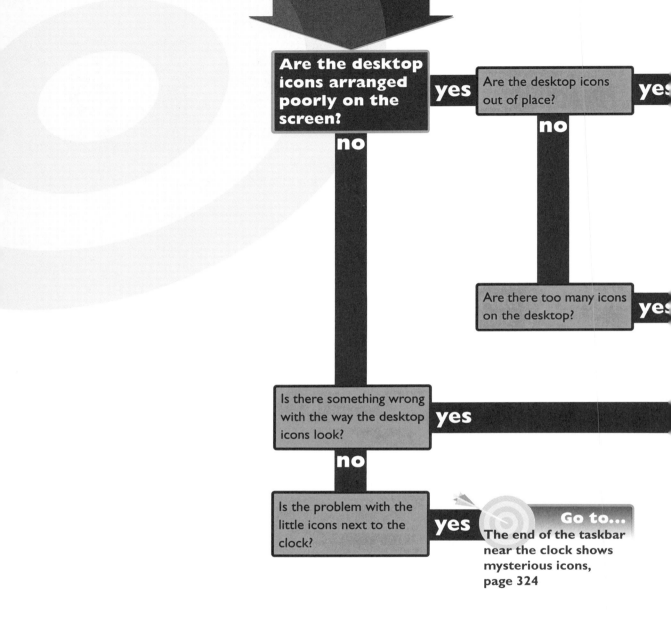

Are the desktop icons arranged poorly on the screen?

yes → Are the desktop icons out of place?

yes

no

no

Are there too many icons on the desktop?

yes

Is there something wrong with the way the desktop icons look?

yes

no

Is the problem with the little icons next to the clock?

yes

Go to...

The end of the taskbar near the clock shows mysterious icons, page 324

Desktop icons

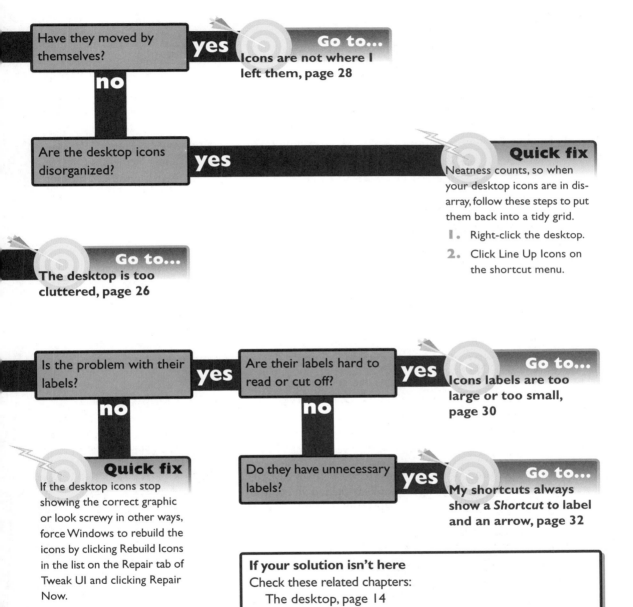

Have they moved by themselves?

yes → **Go to...** Icons are not where I left them, page 28

no

Are the desktop icons disorganized?

yes → **Quick fix**

Neatness counts, so when your desktop icons are in disarray, follow these steps to put them back into a tidy grid.

1. Right-click the desktop.
2. Click Line Up Icons on the shortcut menu.

Go to... The desktop is too cluttered, page 26

Is the problem with their labels?

yes → Are their labels hard to read or cut off?

yes → **Go to...** Icons labels are too large or too small, page 30

no

Quick fix

If the desktop icons stop showing the correct graphic or look screwy in other ways, force Windows to rebuild the icons by clicking Rebuild Icons in the list on the Repair tab of Tweak UI and clicking Repair Now.

no

Do they have unnecessary labels?

yes → **Go to...** My shortcuts always show a *Shortcut to* label and an arrow, page 32

If your solution isn't here
Check these related chapters:
The desktop, page 14
Programs, page 252
The screen, page 264
The taskbar, page 318
Or see the general troubleshooting tips on page xiii

The desktop is too cluttered

Source of the problem

The Microsoft Windows desktop is a convenient place for you to drop everything, from documents you want to keep handy, to shortcuts, to project files and programs. As time goes by, though, the desktop becomes more and more cluttered. It's just too easy to leave documents lying around the Windows desktop, just as you might on a real desktop.

In addition, many software setup programs drop shortcuts onto your desktop without even asking. Remember, it's your desktop and your workspace, not an advertising billboard. Here are some ideas for cleaning up not only your own desktop icon mess, but also clutter produced by extraneous wallpaper, trash deposited on your desktop by other users, and the Active Desktop, which displays Web content on the desktop.

How to fix it

1. Check to see whether the programs that have desktop icons also have commands on the Start menu. Most do.

If you don't mind the slight extra step of using the Start menu to access programs, you can delete the desktop icons by right-clicking desktop shortcuts that are present primarily to advertise software products and clicking Delete on the shortcut menu.

2. Delete desktop icons for programs and services you don't need.

For example, you can delete the Online Services folder if you've already set up an Internet service provider (ISP) to access the Internet. You can also delete the Setup MSN Internet Access icon if you have MSN installed or if you're using a different ISP. In Windows 98, delete the Internet Connection Wizard icon if you have an Internet connection working.

3. Drag the desktop icons of the two or three programs you use most to the Quick Launch toolbar, located just to the right of the Start button, to get them off your desktop. ▶

4. If the Channel bar is visible on your screen (in Windows 98—Windows Me doesn't have a Channel bar), turn it off to free up some desktop space. Right-click a blank area of the desktop, point to Active Desktop, and then click Customize My Desktop. On the Web tab of the Display Properties

Quick Launch toolbar

dialog box, clear the Internet Explorer Channel Bar check box and click OK. ▶

5. Right-click the desktop, point to Active Desktop, and see whether a check mark appears next to View As Web Page (in Windows 98) or Show Web Content (in Windows Me). If so, choose the command again to turn off the Active Desktop. You'll lose the Channel bar and possibly other windows that are part of the Active Desktop, but you can always reenable the Active Desktop by reselecting the check box.

6. Drag loose documents on the desktop into the My Documents folder, or create folders on the desktop for groupings of documents and programs and drag documents and programs into these folders. ▶

   Group documents and programs by project, by task, or by type, or use whatever sorting scheme makes sense for your needs. Create a new folder by right-clicking a blank area of the desktop, pointing to New, clicking Folder on the shortcut menu, and then typing a folder name.

7. Turn off that wallpaper by right-clicking the desktop, clicking None in the Wallpaper list in the Display Properties dialog box, and clicking OK. Yes, it's a picture of your adorable little pooch, but it's taking up valuable screen space and making it harder to see the icons you want.

8. Drag icons to the far corners of the desktop rather than leaving them all bunched up against the left edge.

9. Increase your screen area by right-clicking the desktop, clicking Properties on the shortcut menu, clicking the Settings tab, dragging the Screen Area slider one notch to the right, and clicking OK. This gives you more desktop area to work with.

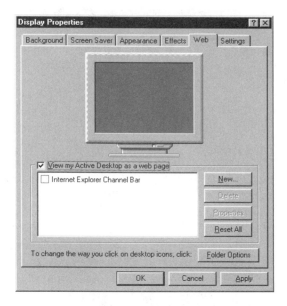

Tip
You can instantly clear your desktop at any time by clicking the Show Desktop icon on the Quick Launch toolbar that's just to the right of the Start menu. Every window that's open is minimized down to a button on the taskbar, so you can see the desktop shortcuts and the documents that were hidden beneath open windows. Your programs aren't closed, though. You can click the taskbar buttons to reopen their windows.

Icons are not where I left them

Source of the problem

One of the nifty aspects of using Windows is that you can customize the desktop so that it looks just the way you want. You can change the desktop's color, change the font and size of the labels under icons, and put the desktop icons wherever you like them—or so you'd think.

If the icons on your desktop seem to have a mind of their own and won't stay where you put them, several causes might be to blame. You might have Windows set to automatically arrange the desktop icons. There's an easy fix for that. Another possibility is that you have Windows set to display different desktops depending on who logs on. Maybe you're looking at someone else's desktop! Or maybe someone else has inadvertently modified your user profile while trying to customize the desktop. Here's how to fix all these possibilities.

How to fix it

1. Right-click an empty area of the Windows desktop and point to Arrange Icons on the shortcut menu.

2. If there's a check mark next to Auto Arrange, click Auto Arrange to clear the check mark. ▶

   Now you can drag icons wherever you want them and they won't scoot back into a grid at the left edge of the desktop.

3. Click Start, and look for the Log Off [*name*] command on the Start menu. ▶

   If someone else's name is there, you're looking at someone else's desktop. That explains why the icons are missing or rearranged. If you don't see the Log Off command at all, someone else must have messed around with your desktop. Follow the rest of these steps to set up multiple user profiles.

4. Click Start, point to Settings, and then click Control Panel.

5. In Control Panel, double-click the Users icon. In Windows Me, you might need to click View All Control Panel Options to see the Users option.

6. In the Enable Multi-User Settings Wizard window, click Next.

7. In the Add User page, type the user name you entered when you set up Windows.

8. In the Personalized Items Settings page, select the items you want to personalize. Make sure you select the Desktop Folder And Documents Menu check box, because the desktop folder contains your desktop icons. ▶

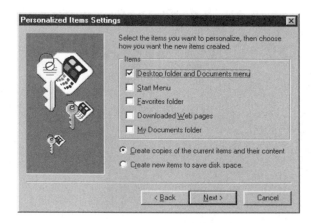

9. Click Next, and then on the last page of the wizard, click Finish. When you are prompted to restart Windows, click Yes.

10. Click Start, point to Settings, and click Control Panel.

11. In Control Panel, double-click Users. In Windows Me, you might need to click View All Control Panel Options to see the Users option.

12. In the User Settings dialog box, click New User. ▶

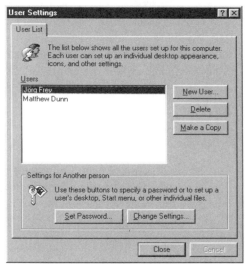

13. Follow the steps of the Add User Wizard, which asks for the person's user name, password, and the items that the individual can personalize. Be sure to select the Desktop Folder And Documents Menu check box for each new user so that everyone can have individual desktop arrangements.

Managing multiple users

Now that you've enabled multiple users who can each have a personal set of desktop icons, you need to enforce a few simple rules to maintain a little order around the desktop. Anyone who wants to modify how the desktop looks must sign on by entering a user name and password. That way, the changes will be part of that person's user profile, not yours. If you're already signed on, you must log off before someone else can sign on. (Click Start and then click the Log Off [*your name*] command.)

Tip

Saving documents on the desktop makes them handy, but it contributes to desktop clutter. One useful alternative is to drag documents to the My Documents folder on the desktop, where they'll be nearly as easy to get to.

Icon labels are too large or too small

Source of the problem

An obvious way to save desktop space is by resizing the text labels under the icons. But it's easy to make that text the wrong size. If you make the labels too small, they can be hard to read. Conversely, if you make them too big, they can get truncated, which is an impress-your-friends term for chopped off. Here's how to resize icon labels so they'll fit well on the desktop.

How to fix it

1. Right-click an empty area of the Windows desktop and click Properties on the shortcut menu.

2. On the Appearance tab of the Display Properties dialog box, click the Item down arrow and then click Icon. ▶

3. Choose a new size from the Size list to the right of the Font list. (The Display Properties dialog box has two Size options, so take care to choose the correct one.)

4. Click Apply and take a look at the icon text. If it's not the size you want, repeat steps 1 through 3 and try a different size. Click OK when the size is correct.

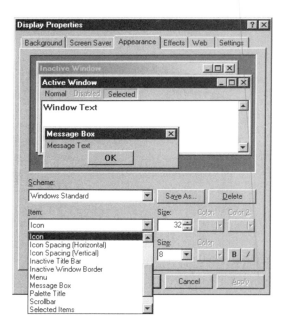

My icon labels are getting cut off like th...

You can't tell when the end of the label under an icon will be chopped off and replaced with an ellipsis (...)—at least, you can't tell until it's too late. ▶ But when you see it happen, you can try two methods for fixing things. One is to reduce the text size, as described above, and the other is to increase the spacing between icons. Follow steps 1 and 2 in the procedure above, but in step 2, click Icon Spacing (Horizontal) rather than Icon in the Item list. Gradually increase the value in the item Size list, clicking Apply after each change, until the space surrounding each icon is large enough to contain the entire icon label.

Network Neighbo...

Changing other desktop items

Windows comes with dozens of schemes that let you personalize the look of your desktop. Each desktop scheme you choose from the Scheme list in the Display Properties dialog box customizes colors, sizes, and fonts for all the text on the Windows desktop. Windows refers to each part of its desktop—icons, menus, text in messages boxes—as an *item*. The trick to controlling the look of the screen is to know which item controls which part the screen. Here's some help:

Tip
You can't change the color of the icon labels. They're always black unless you choose a dark desktop color—in which case they switch to white.

● The Icon item controls the size and font of the text under icons, and it also controls the size of the text used for the file and folder listings in My Computer and Windows Explorer. This is good to know if the text in My Computer becomes too small when you try to reduce just the icon label size.

● The Menu item controls the size and font of the text on the Start menu (along with menus within My Computer, Windows Explorer, and other programs).

● This one is not so obvious. The size of the text on taskbar buttons is controlled by the size of the text for the Active Title Bar item. This makes sense if you think of a taskbar button as a shrunken title bar for a program that's running.

● One more thing: The Active Title Bar and Inactive Title Bar items are linked, so changing the size of one changes the size of the other (although you can make them different colors). The Menu and Selected items (the regular entries on menus and those that are selected) are linked similarly. You can give them different colors, but not different sizes. ▶

Controlled by
Active Title Bar item

Controlled by
Menu item

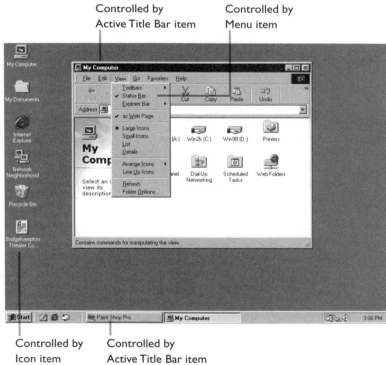

Controlled by
Icon item

Controlled by
Active Title Bar item

My shortcuts always show a *Shortcut to* label and an arrow

Source of the problem

The *Shortcut to* text and that little arrow at the lower left corner of a shortcut icon are there to remind you that the icon is just a link to a document rather than the document itself. A link is like an arrow that points to the file you want; it's not the actual file, but it takes you to it. You can delete the shortcut, but the document remains untouched.

Shortcut to
Scripts

But while the *Shortcut to* text and the shortcut arrow are handy, they also clutter the screen, and you almost certainly don't need both. You could delete the *Shortcut to* text for each icon, but you can't delete the arrow if you've already created the shortcut. You'll have to delete the shortcut and create a new one without an arrow. Here's a way to prevent the label (and the arrow) from appearing when you create new shortcuts.

How to fix it

1. Click Start, point to Settings, and then click Control Panel.

2. In Control Panel, double-click Tweak UI. If you don't see a Tweak UI icon, refer to "Where Do I Get Tweak UI?" on the facing page.

3. Click the Explorer tab in the Tweak UI dialog box.

4. On the Explorer tab, clear the Prefix "Shortcut To" On New Shortcuts check box to eliminate the words *Shortcut to* in new shortcut labels. ▶

5. In the Shortcut Overlay section of the Explorer tab, click None to get rid of the shortcut arrow altogether, or click Light Arrow for a smaller, less ostentatious version.

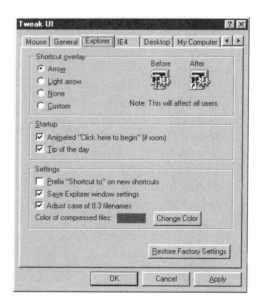

What is Tweak UI?

Tweak UI is a nifty little Microsoft utility that lets you change (tweak) a bunch of hidden settings in the user interface (UI)—the menus, dialog boxes, icons, and other items on the screen that let you interact with Windows. It lets you change internal settings within Windows that you can't otherwise modify without digging deep into the registry, the complex central file that holds all the settings for each computer. Tweak UI is easy to install, easy to use, and it's free. Now that's a great set of attributes.

Where do I get Tweak UI?

Windows
95

Windows 95 users can download Tweak UI version 1.33 from *www.microsoft.com/ NTWorkstation/downloads/PowerToys/Networking/NTTweakUI.asp*. You can also find Tweak UI at *www.download.com* and other file download spots around the Web.

Windows
98

Windows 98 users can find Tweak UI on the Windows 98 CD. If you are using Windows 98 (not Windows 98 Second Edition), insert the CD and click Browse This CD on the opening screen. In the \Tools\ResKit\PowerToy folder, right-click Tweakui.inf, and then click Install on the shortcut menu and follow the instructions. If the setup program seems to stop when the Help screen appears, close the Help screen so that the program can resume its task.

Windows 98 Second Edition does not include Tweak UI on the CD, but you can download the Windows 98 version of Tweak UI (Tweak UI 98) from *www.winmag.com/windows/win98/ software.htm* and other file download sites on the Internet. You'll need to follow one extra step when you install Tweak UI from the downloaded files because Tweak UI 98 thinks it's being installed from the CD. When the setup program asks you to insert the CD, disregard the message, click Browse, navigate to the folder in which the setup files are located on your hard disk, and then click OK. The installation will then finish properly.

Windows
Me

Windows Me users can download Tweak UI version 1.33 at *www.microsoft.com/ntworkstation/ downloads/PowerToys/Networking/NTTweakUI.asp*. Even though Tweak UI has not officially been updated to support Windows Me, it works fine. To install Tweak UI, follow these steps:

1. Right-click the desktop, click New on the shortcut menu, and click Folder.

2. Type a name for the folder.

3. Click the Download Now button on the Web page, and in the File Download dialog box that opens, click Save This Program To Disk, and click OK.

4. In the Save As dialog box, navigate to the folder you just created, and then click Save.

5. Open the folder and double-click the downloaded file.

6. In the WinZip Self-Extractor window, enter the path of the folder in which you downloaded Tweak UI.

7. Close the WinZip Self-Extractor window, right-click Tweakui.inf, and click Install on the shortcut menu.

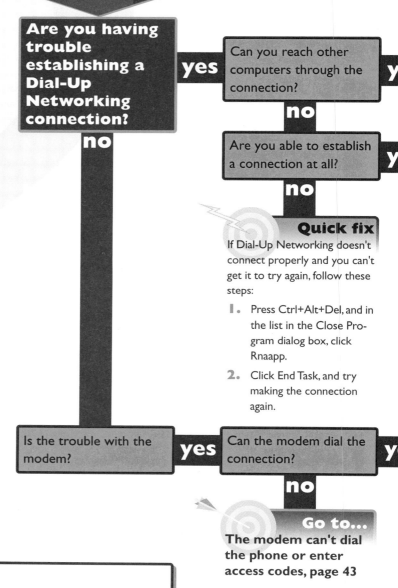

Are you having trouble establishing a Dial-Up Networking connection?

yes → **Can you reach other computers through the connection?** **yes**

no

Are you able to establish a connection at all? **yes**

no

⚡ **Quick fix**

If Dial-Up Networking doesn't connect properly and you can't get it to try again, follow these steps:

1. Press Ctrl+Alt+Del, and in the list in the Close Program dialog box, click Rnaapp.

2. Click End Task, and try making the connection again.

no ↓

Is the trouble with the modem? **yes** → **Can the modem dial the connection?** **yes**

no

Go to...
The modem can't dial the phone or enter access codes, page 43

If your solution isn't here
Check these related chapters:
Or see the general troubleshooting tips on page xiii

Is using the Dial-Up Networking connection awkward?

yes

Go to...
Connecting through Dial-Up Networking requires too many clicks and confirmations, page 39

no

Go to...
I can't reach other computers through a Dial-Up Networking server, page 36

Are you having trouble saving a password?

yes

Go to...
I can't save the password for a Dial-Up Networking connection, page 40

Are you having trouble receiving faxes?

yes

Quick fix

While you're running a Dial-Up Networking server, you can't receive faxes because your fax modem is busy waiting for a Dial-Up Networking connection. If you need to receive a fax, your only option is to temporarily disable the Dial-Up Networking server until the fax arrives.

1. On the Connections menu in the Dial-Up Networking window, click Dial-Up Server.

2. Clear the Allow Caller Access check box, and click OK.

I can't reach other computers through a Dial-Up Networking server

Source of the problem

Dialing a Dial-Up Networking server at home or in the office is not difficult, but what's the point if you can't communicate with other computers on the network and exchange files or check e-mail? If after you call a Dial-Up Networking server you see *Connected* next to the connection in the Dial-Up Networking window but you can't find other computers in the Network Neighborhood window, you probably need to install a network protocol called NetBEUI. You need NetBEUI to connect to a Dial-Up Networking server (whereas connecting to an ISP through Dial-Up Networking requires only the TCP/IP protocol). While you're at it, you should install the IPX/SPX protocol too. Having all three protocols is extra insurance for obtaining a good networking connection. Remember, protocols are like languages that networks use to communicate. Fortunately, you don't need to learn its language to use a network's services.

How to fix it

1. Make sure you have the Windows CD on hand before you continue.

2. Right-click Network Neighborhood on the desktop (in Windows Me, right-click My Network Places), and click Properties on the shortcut menu.

3. Click the Configuration tab in the Network dialog box.
   In the list of installed network components, you should see NetBEUI → Dial-Up Adapter. ▶
   If NetBEUI is not listed, you need to install it to communicate with the Dial-Up Networking server by following the rest of these steps.

4. Click Add.

5. In the Select Network Component Type dialog box, click Protocol and then click Add.

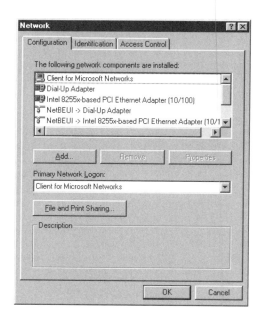

6. In the Select Network Protocol dialog box, click Microsoft in the Manufacturers list, click NetBEUI in the Network Protocols list, and then click OK.

7. Take a look at the list of installed network components. You should now see NetBEUI → Dial-Up Adapter and possibly a second entry linking NetBEUI and your network card.

8. Click Add again, click Protocol, click Add, click Microsoft in the Manufacturers list, and click IPX/SPX-Compatible Protocol in the Network Protocols list. Then click OK.

9. Click OK to close the Network dialog box. Windows adds the protocols and installs the files it needs from the Windows CD.

10. If you are asked whether you want to keep any files, click Yes.

11. Click Yes when you are asked whether you want to restart the computer.

Tip

If you have a full-time Internet connection, you might not use Dial-Up Networking to connect to an ISP, so you might not have it installed. To install Dial-Up Networking, go to Add/Remove Programs in Control Panel, click the Windows Setup tab, click Communications in the Components list, click Details, and then select Dial-Up Networking.

Fixing the Dial-Up Networking connection

To make sure that NetBEUI and IPX/SPX will be used by the connection you've created for the Dial-Up Networking server, follow these steps:

1. Double-click My Computer on the desktop, and then double-click Dial-Up Networking. In Windows Me, click Start, point to Settings, and click Dial-Up Networking.

2. Right-click the connection for the Dial-Up Networking server, and click Properties on the shortcut menu.

3. In the dialog box for the connection, click the Server Types tab (in Windows Me, click the Networking tab) and make sure the NetBEUI and IPX/SPX Compatible check boxes are selected. ▶
Make sure the Log On To Network and Enable Software Compression check boxes are selected also. (In Windows Me, click the Security tab to see these two check boxes.)

4. Click OK to close the dialog box, and then try connecting to the Dial-Up Networking server again.

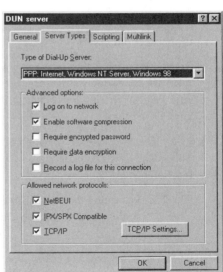

To continue with this solution, go to the next page.

I can't reach other computers through a Dial-Up Networking server

(continued from page 37)

I'm running the Dial-Up Networking server

If no one else can view network resources through your Dial-Up Networking server, you need to configure the server so that File And Printer Sharing is installed in the Network dialog box. To do so, follow these steps:

1. Right-click Network Neighborhood (in Windows Me, right-click My Network Places) and click Properties on the shortcut menu.

2. On the Configuration tab of the Network dialog box, click File And Print Sharing.

3. In the File And Print Sharing dialog box, select the I Want To Be Able To Give Others Access To My Files check box, and click OK. ▶
    You can also select the I Want To Be Able To Give Others Access To My Printer(s) check box in the File And Print Sharing dialog box if you want those who dial in to be able to use your printer.

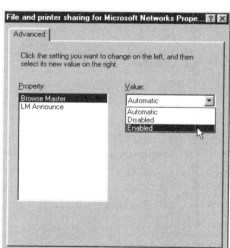

You also need to enable the Browse Master, which allows dial-up users to find other computers on the network.

1. In the Network dialog box, scroll through the list of network components that are installed, click File And Printer Sharing For Microsoft Networks, and click Properties.

2. In the File And Printer Sharing For Microsoft Networks Properties dialog box, click Browse Master in the Property list.

3. Click the Value down arrow, click Enabled in the list, click OK, and click OK again to close the Network dialog box. ▶

4. Click Yes when you are asked whether you want to restart the computer.

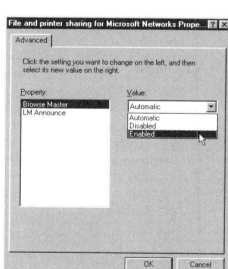

One last thing: Make sure everyone who dials up to your server has the correct workgroup name entered on the Identification tab in their Network dialog boxes.

Connecting through Dial-Up Networking requires too many clicks and confirmations

Source of the problem

Unless you change a few settings, Dial-Up Networking nags you every step of the way as you establish a connection. Before dialing, Dial-Up Networking tells you what it's going to do. After connecting, it tells you what it's done. And at each step, you need to click OK to confirm what you want and give Dial-Up Networking a pat on the back. Here's how to streamline Dial-Up Networking.

How to fix it

1. Double-click My Computer on the desktop.

2. In My Computer, double-click Dial-Up Networking. In Windows Me, click Start, point to Settings, and click Dial-Up Networking.

3. In the Dial-Up Networking window, click Settings on the Connections menu.

4. Clear the Show A Confirmation Dialog After Connected check box. ▶
   In Windows 95 and Windows 98, also clear the Prompt For Information Before Dialing check box, and click OK.
   In Windows Me, double-click the connection and make sure the Save Password and Connect Automatically check boxes are selected.

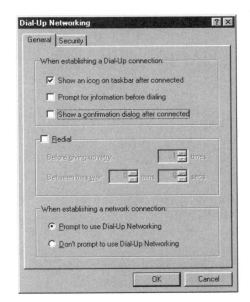

When you double-click any Dial-Up Networking connection from now on, Dial-Up Networking will place the call and make the connection without prompting for your user name and password in advance or displaying a confirmation dialog box after the connection is established. If you need to enter a different user name and password, you'll need to repeat steps 1 through 4, but select the Prompt For Information Before Dialing check box.

I can't save the password for a Dial-Up Networking connection

Source of the problem

For a multitude of reasons, you might find that either the password you carefully entered in a Dial-Up Networking connection dialog box just isn't there the next time you try the connection or the Save Password check box is unavailable so that you can't even save the password. Both problems can be an annoyance, and you'll need to try a few sets of corrective measures until you find one that works.

How to fix it

1. When you start Windows, be careful not to skip the logon dialog box by pressing Esc or clicking Cancel.

   If you log on without entering a user name, Windows can't open your passwords file for Dial-Up Networking passwords. (Each user on a computer can have a different passwords file.)

2. Right-click Network Neighborhood (in Windows Me, right-click My Network Places) and click Properties on the short-cut menu. On the Configuration tab of the Network dialog box, verify that Client For Microsoft Networks is included in the installed network components list. If the client is not installed, click Add, click Client, and click Add to open the Select Network Client dialog box. In the Manufacturers list, click Microsoft, and in the Network Clients list, click Client For Microsoft Networks. ▶

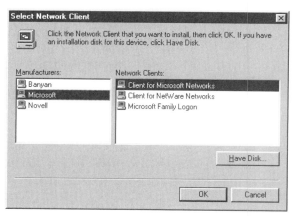

3. Click OK, and click OK again to close the Network dialog box. If you are asked whether you want to restart the computer, click Yes.

Try resetting your passwords by following these steps:

1. Click Start, point to Find (in Windows Me, point to Search), and then click Files Or Folders (in Windows Me, click For Files Or Folders).

2. In the Find All Files dialog box (the Search Results dialog box in Windows Me), type ***.pwl** in the Named box, click the Look In down arrow, click My Computer, and then click Find Now (in Windows Me, click Search Now).

3. In the list that appears at the bottom of the Find dialog box, or on the right in the Search Results dialog box, delete any .pwl files that are in the Windows folder or its subfolders. ▶

4. Restart Windows. You'll need to reenter all your passwords whenever you're asked for them, but at least you should now be able to save them.

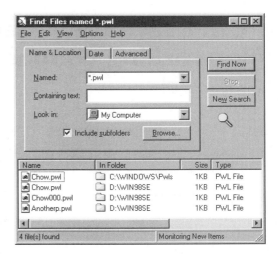

Make sure none of the Dial-Up Networking connections has the Save Password check box cleared by following these steps:

1. Open the Dial-Up Networking window, and then click Settings on the Connections menu.

2. Select the Prompt For Information Before Dialing check box, and click OK. (In Windows Me, double-click the connection and clear the Connect Automatically check box.)

3. Double-click the other connections in the Dial-Up Networking window. If any one of them has the Save Password check box cleared, they might all be failing to save passwords. It's not fair, but it happens.

Try removing and reinstalling Dial-Up Networking by following these steps:

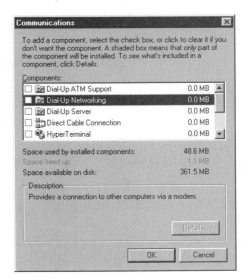

1. Double-click Add/Remove Programs in Control Panel, click Communications on the Windows Setup tab, click Details, and then clear the Dial-Up Networking check box. ▶

2. Click OK, and then click Yes when you are asked whether you want to restart your computer. Repeat the procedure, but this time select the Dial-Up Networking check box, click OK, and then restart the computer.

If this solution didn't solve your problem, go to the next page.

I can't save the password for a Dial-Up Networking connection

(continued from page 41)

Enable user profiles and recreate the Dial-Up Networking connection with these steps:

1. Double-click Passwords in Control Panel and, on the User Profiles tab of the Passwords Properties dialog box, click Users Can Customize Their Preferences And Desktop Settings.

2. Click OK, and restart your computer.

3. Delete the Dial-Up Networking connection, and then re-create it by clicking Make New Connection in the Dial-Up Networking window.

Finally, verify that password caching is not disabled, but hold onto your hat—these steps require editing the registry.

1. Click Start, and then click Run.

2. In the Run dialog box, type **regedit** in the Open box, and click OK.

3. In the left pane of the Registry Editor, click the plus signs next to these folders in sequence: HKEY_LOCAL_MACHINE, Software, Microsoft, Windows, Current Version, and Policies.

4. Click the Network folder.

5. If you see a DisablePwdCaching item in the right pane of the Registry Editor, double-click it and change its Value Data value from 1 to 0, close the Registry Editor, and then restart Windows.
  If you do not see this item, follow the rest of these steps:

6. Right-click anywhere in the right pane of the Registry Editor.

7. Point to New on the shortcut menu, and then click DWORD Value.

8. Type **DisablePwdCaching** and press Enter.

9. Double-click the new entry and make sure Value Data is set to 0.

10. Click OK, close the Registry Editor, and then restart Windows. ▶

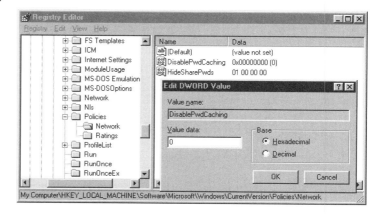

The modem can't dial the phone or enter access codes

Source of the problem

Sometimes, when you're traveling or not at your own desk, you might need to dial with the help of an operator, punch in a special access code by hand, or use the only phone nearby, which just happens to be an old rotary model from the late 1950s. In these cases, you need to do the dialing yourself, listen for the modem tones coming through the handset, and then have your modem pick up the line and establish the Dial-Up Networking connection.

How to fix it

1. Double-click My Computer on the desktop, and in My Computer, double-click Dial-Up Networking. (In Windows Me, click Start, point to Settings, and click Dial-Up Networking.)

2. Right-click the connection icon in the Dial-Up Networking window, and click Properties on the shortcut menu.

3. On the General tab of the Connection Properties dialog box, click Configure.

4. On the Options tab of the Modem Properties dialog box, select the Operator Assisted Or Manual Dial check box and click OK. Click OK again to close the connection properties dialog box.

5. When you're ready to place the call, double-click the connection icon and, if necessary, click Connect. A message box opens and prompts you to lift the receiver and dial the phone number. ▶

6. As soon as the modem at the other end answers, click Connect and hang up the phone.

> **Manual Dial** ☒
>
> You have selected Manual Dial. Lift the receiver and dial the phone number that you would like to connect to.
>
> Immediately after the call is answered, click Connect and hang up the phone.
>
> [Connect] [Cancel]

When you return home or to the office, you'll need to repeat steps 1 through 4, but at step 4, be sure to clear the Operator Assisted Or Manual Dial check box and click OK. Click OK again to close the connection properties dialog box.

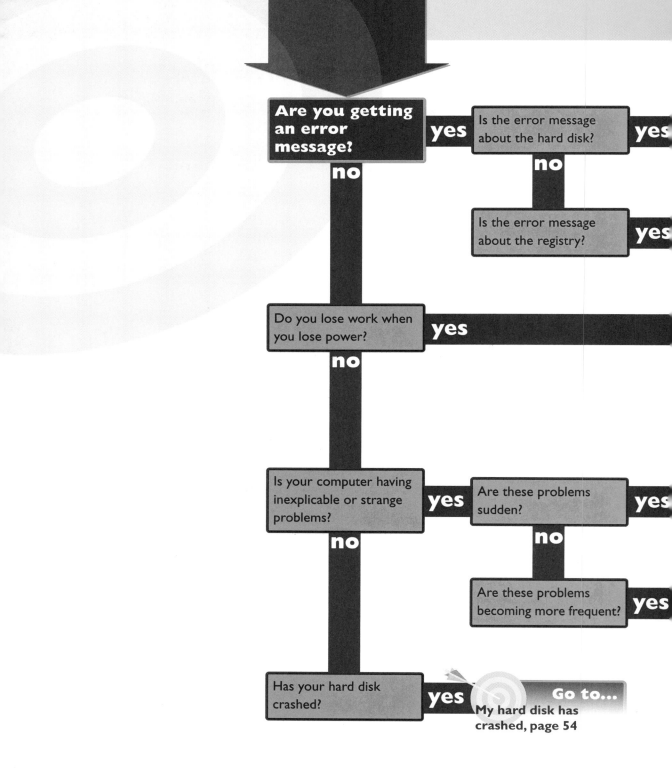

Are you getting an error message?

yes → Is the error message about the hard disk? → yes

no ↓

Is the error message about the registry? → yes

Do you lose work when you lose power?

yes →

no ↓

Is your computer having inexplicable or strange problems?

yes → Are these problems sudden? → yes

no ↓

Are these problems becoming more frequent? → yes

Has your hard disk crashed?

yes → **Go to...**
My hard disk has crashed, page 54

Go to...
My hard disk has crashed, page 54

Go to...
I get a message about a Windows registry problem, page 46

Quick fix
To keep your computer running for a short time even when the power fails, you can buy and install an uninterruptible power supply (UPS). You plug the UPS into the wall and plug the computer and monitor into the UPS. These devices are like giant batteries—they store power when it's available and then dispense power to your system starting the instant the lights go off. If the power just flickers, the UPS can keep your computer running so you won't lose any work. If the power goes off for longer, the UPS gives you the chance to save open documents, and then shut down the computer.

Go to...
My computer might have been infected with a virus, page 48

Go to...
Windows stops running, page 50

If your solution isn't here
Check these related chapters:
Backing up, page 2
Hard disks, page 128
Hardware, page 138
Setting up Windows, page 272
Or see the general troubleshooting tips on page xiii

I get a message about a Windows registry problem

Source of the problem

Because the registry stores the settings for absolutely everything there is to know about your Windows installation, Windows won't run if it detects a corrupt or damaged registry. Instead, it displays disheartening error messages about a corrupt registry, an error accessing the registry, or an insufficient amount of memory to load the registry.

All versions of Windows check the registry every time you start your computer. If the registry looks fine, Windows makes a backup copy of it for safekeeping. Windows keeps five days' worth of these backups. But if Windows detects that the registry is bad, it removes the damaged registry and replaces it with the most recent backup. Windows Me's System Restore program also backs up crucial system files every 10 hours of Windows running time. So if you suddenly encounter an error message about the registry, you can manually restore the last backup in Windows 95 and Windows 98 or use System Restore in Windows Me to restore your system to its previous good health. Here's how to do both.

How to fix it (in Windows 95 and Windows 98)

1. If you're still able to use Windows after encountering a registry-related error message, click Start, click Shut Down, click Shut Down again, and click OK.

If you're unable to use Windows, turn off the computer using its power switch.

2. Turn on the computer, and while the computer is starting up, press F8 repeatedly until the Microsoft Windows Startup Menu appears.

3. Choose Command Prompt Only. ▶

4. At the MS-DOS command prompt (for example, C:\>), type **scanreg /restore** and press Enter.

5. On the Microsoft Registry Checker screen, press Enter to restore the most recent of the five backups listed.

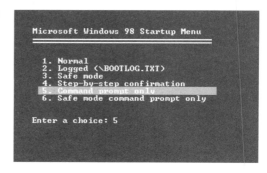

```
Microsoft Windows 98 Startup Menu


  1. Normal
  2. Logged (\BOOTLOG.TXT)
  3. Safe mode
  4. Step-by-step confirmation
  5. Command prompt only
  6. Safe mode command prompt only

Enter a choice: 5
```

6. If a message box appears, asking whether you want to restart the computer, click OK; otherwise, press Ctrl+Alt+Del to restart the computer.

How to fix it (in Windows Me)

1. If you're unable to use Windows Me after encountering a registry-related error message, turn off the computer, turn it back on, and while the computer is starting up, press F8 repeatedly until the Microsoft Windows Millennium Startup Menu appears.

If, on the other hand, you're able to use Windows, click Start, point to Programs, point to Accessories, point to System Tools, and click - System Restore. In the System Restore window, click Next, and then skip to step 5.

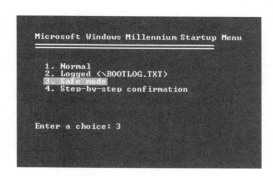

2. At the Microsoft Windows Millennium Startup Menu, type **3** and press Enter to choose Safe Mode, which starts the computer using a minimum of drivers, components, and programs. ▶

3. On the Safe Mode Troubleshooter page of the Help And Support window, click the System Restore link. ▶

4. In the System Restore window, click Next.

5. On the next page of System Restore, if there isn't a System CheckPoint listed for the current date, click the most recent date shown in boldface in the calendar (indicating a backup) and click Next. ▶

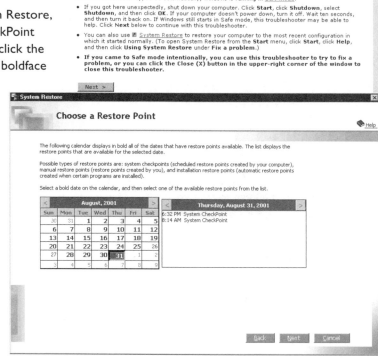

6. Click OK when System Restore warns you to close programs and files, and then click Next.

System Restore restores the crucial system files from the date you specified, including the registry, and then restarts the computer and shows a message saying that the system restore was completed.

My computer might have been infected with a virus

Source of the problem

A *virus* is a malicious program that infects your computer through a file you get across the network, from the Internet, or through an e-mail message. While some viruses are relatively benign, displaying a "gotcha" message on the screen, others are very harmful. They can't physically damage your computer, but they can damage or delete your data, and they can replicate and transfer themselves from your computer to other computers. One type of virus can even send itself to everyone in your e-mail address book.

Not every computer problem is a symptom of a virus, but these symptoms might indicate that your computer has been infected:

- Some files or programs are suddenly missing.
- A program doesn't work properly.
- Unusual messages appear on the screen, or you hear unusual sounds or music playing unexpectedly.
- Files that you haven't created appear on your computer.

The most important measure you can take to protect yourself is to obtain antivirus software that can both remove viruses from your computer and shield your computer from new viruses. Here's how to rid your computer of an existing virus and protect yourself from future attack.

How to fix it

1. Obtain and install an antivirus program.

   Buy an antivirus program from a well-known software manufacturer that will provide updates to the software as new viruses are discovered. The leading antivirus programs are always available on the Web in trial versions that you can download and use immediately until you have the full version of the software. Visit *www.symantec.com* and *www.mcafee.com,* for a start.

2. Run the antivirus program and use its scanning feature, which can detect viruses in the computer's memory and on the hard disk.

3. If the antivirus program detects a virus in a file, select the program's Clean or Disinfect option. If the file can't be cleaned or disinfected, delete the file and be sure to empty the Recycle Bin.

4. Contact any people with whom you've recently exchanged files, e-mail attachments, or Zip disks to let them know that you've found a virus and that they should check their computers for viruses too.

Protecting your computer from viruses

Even though your goal is to detect and remove viruses you might have already received, it's just as important to also protect yourself from new viruses by taking these steps:

- Run the antivirus program's real-time monitoring service, which scans incoming files and e-mail messages as they arrive.

- Scan floppy disks and removable disks, such as Zip disks, that you receive from others.

- Do not open attachments in e-mail messages from strangers, unless the attachments are .jpg pictures or .txt text files.

> ## Hoaxes
>
> Almost as widespread as jokes in e-mail messages are warnings from well-meaning friends about new viruses. Unfortunately, many rumors about viruses are hoaxes, and you'd be doing a disservice to other people by passing the warnings on. To determine which viruses are real and which are hoaxes, you can visit several sites on the Web that track hoaxes. Among these are: *antivirus.about.com/compute/antivirus/library/blenhoax.htm* and *www.symantec.com/avcenter/hoax.html.*

- Don't leave floppy disks or removable disks in your computer's drives—that way, they won't become infected with a new virus.

- Update your antivirus software frequently by visiting the software manufacturer's Web site and downloading updates that will eliminate new viruses.

    All antivirus software makers publish frequent updates that can identify and remove new viruses that have appeared since the last update of the program.

- After you've scanned your system and found it clear of viruses, back up all your important files to be sure you have spare copies in case your computer becomes infected later. For more information about backing up, see "I Don't Know How to Create a Backup Routine," on page 6.

- Create a startup disk that you can use to start your computer in case of a virus infection: Click Start, click Settings, and click Control Panel. In Control Panel, double-click Add/Remove Programs. (In Windows Me, you might be able to single-click the Add/Remove Programs link.) On the Startup Disk tab in the Add/Remove Programs Properties dialog box, click Create Disk and follow the instructions on the screen.

    Scan this disk for viruses, and then store it in a safe place.

Tip
Even though you've purchased and installed an antivirus program from a major manufacturer, you might want to download, install, and scan your system with a trial version of another manufacturer's antivirus program to get a second opinion. After you run the scan, you should uninstall the second program, as using both programs for ongoing monitoring can be too taxing on your system's resources.

Windows stops running

Source of the problem

Some people who use Windows heavily encounter a gradual and inexorable decay in its performance over time—and even hang-ups, when Windows stops running altogether. As they install and uninstall software, patches, updates, and devices, they begin to experience more hang-ups that require a restart of their computer, unusual error messages, or pauses or long delays as they work. Their computer becomes less dependable and feels more and more like the old model they retired instead of the snappy new model they bought as a replacement.

If the computer you're having trouble with is your own, the most reliable solution to this deterioration is to rebuild your Windows installation while preserving your personal settings and data. To accomplish this, you save all your essential settings and then remove and reinstall Windows. Before you begin, be sure to see "Windows Has Become Sluggish," on page 236, to determine whether a less drastic treatment can solve the problems you're experiencing.

Warning
Because this is an extreme step that will require reinstalling Windows, along with reinstalling all your programs and rebuilding your working environment, you should make sure that you have plenty of time and that you have your Windows CD and product key, along with all the disks you'll need to reinstall all the programs you use. You'll also need all the product keys or serial numbers for those programs.

How to fix it

1. Double-click My Computer on the desktop, and double-click your hard disk.

2. In the My Computer window, right-click in a blank area, point to New, and click Folder on the shortcut menu to create a folder to which you'll copy your essential Windows settings.

3. Type a name for the folder, such as *Essentials*, and press Enter.

4. Copy the C:\Windows\Favorites folder and the C:\Windows\Cookies folder to the new folder.

5. Copy the folder containing your Outlook Express e-mail folders to the new folder.
   For information about locating your Outlook Express folders, see "I Can't Back Up My Outlook Express 5 E-Mail Messages," page 73.
   If you are using Outlook rather than Outlook Express, copy the Outlook.pst file to the new folder. You can find the Outlook.pst file using the Find or Search command on the Start menu. When you find the .pst file, copy it from the search results list to the new folder.

6. Copy the Windows Address Book (.wab) file to the new folder.

To find this file, use the Find or Search command on the Start menu, and copy the .wab file from the search results list to the new folder.

7. Double-click My Computer and double-click Dial-Up Networking. (In Windows Me, click Start, point to Settings, and click Dial-Up Networking.)

8. Drag the connections listed in the Dial-Up Networking folder to the new folder.

9. If you use a full-time Internet connection, such as a Digital Subscriber Line (DSL), with a fixed IP address and DNS server addresses, make a note of these addresses.

You can find these addresses by right-clicking Network Neighborhood or My Network Places (in Windows Me), clicking Properties on the shortcut menu, and on the Configuration tab in the Network dialog box, clicking the entry for TCP/IP → *[network adapter connected to the Internet line]* and clicking Properties. The addresses are listed on their respective tabs in the Properties dialog box. ▶

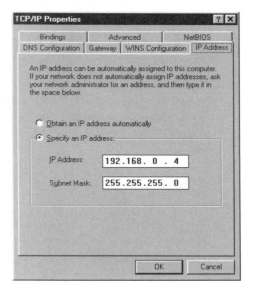

10. If you have backup software, use it to create a Complete, Full, or System backup.

You can use the Windows Backup accessory. For more information about backing up your computer with Windows Backup, see "I Don't Know How to Protect Windows from a Hard Disk Crash," on page 10.

11. Make notes about the organization of your Start menu if you want to re-create the same categories for shortcuts after you reinstall Windows.

12. From the Windows folder, copy the icons, wallpaper images, or sounds that you've customized to the new folder.

If you don't have a Windows Startup disk, create one now by following these steps:

1. Click Start, point to Settings, and click Control Panel.

2. In Control Panel, double-click Add/Remove Programs. (In Windows Me, you might be able to single-click Add/Remove Programs if it's an underlined link.)

To continue with this solution, go to the next page.

Windows stops running

(continued from page 51)

3. On the Startup Disk tab in the Add/Remove Programs Properties dialog box, click Create Disk and follow the instructions on the screen. ▶

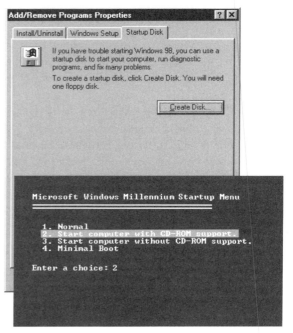

4. After you make the disk, click Cancel to close the Add/Remove Programs Properties dialog box.

5. Leave the newly created Windows Startup disk in the drive, insert the Windows CD in the CD-ROM drive, and restart the computer.

6. At the Microsoft Windows Startup Menu, choose Start Computer With CD-ROM Support and press Enter. ▶

Then make sure you can access the CD-ROM drive by typing its drive letter (you're told this drive letter at startup) and a colon (for example, *E:*) at the MS-DOS command prompt and then typing **DIR** and pressing Enter to see a listing of the files on the CD.

When the computer restarts, make sure that it reads the Windows Startup disk to start the computer. Some computers can be set to bypass the floppy disk drive and start the computer directly from the hard disk. If your computer bypasses the floppy disk drive, run the computer's configuration program and set the computer to try booting first from the floppy disk and then, if there's no disk in the floppy disk drive, to boot from the hard disk.

If you're unable to access the CD in the CD-ROM drive, you should restart the computer without the floppy disk in the drive, and then in Windows copy the Win95 or Win98 folder on the CD (or the Win9x folder on the Windows Me CD) to a newly created folder on the hard disk.

7. After booting from the Windows Startup disk, type **deltree c:\windows /Y** at the MS-DOS command prompt, and press Y to confirm deletion of the Windows folder, its subfolders, and all the files within. This may take some time to complete.

If your Windows files are located in a folder with a different name, substitute that name for *c:\windows*.

You should now reinstall Windows by following these steps:

1. At the MS-DOS command prompt, type **e:\setup**, replacing e with the drive letter of your CD-ROM drive if necessary, and press Enter.

If you've copied the Windows CD files to a folder on the hard disk, switch to the folder that contains the files by typing **CD** followed by a space, a backslash (\), and the name of the folder and pressing Enter. Then type **setup** and press Enter.

2. When Microsoft ScanDisk finishes checking your hard disk, press X to exit ScanDisk.

3. Follow the Windows Setup procedure, reinstalling Windows to its original drive and folder. ▶

4. In Windows, double-click My Computer on the desktop, browse to the folder you created to hold the important Windows files you wanted to preserve, and double-click the folder to open it. ▶

5. Double-click My Computer again, and double-click the C:\Windows\ Favorites folder.

6. Copy the files from the Favorites folder in the folder you created to preserve files to the C:\Windows\Favorites folder.

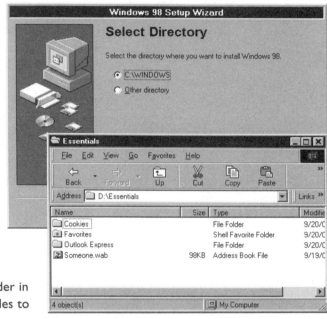

7. Open the C:\Windows\Cookies folder, and copy the files from the Cookies folder in the folder you created to preserve files to the C:\Windows\Cookies folder.

8. Open the Dial-Up Networking folder by double-clicking My Computer and double-clicking Dial-Up Networking. (In Windows Me, click Start, point to Settings, and click Dial-Up Networking.)

9. Copy the connections from the Dial-Up Networking folder in the folder you created to preserve files to the Windows Dial-Up Networking folder.

10. Copy the Outlook Express folders from the folder you created to preserve files and overwrite the new Outlook Express folders in your new Windows installation.

11. If you need to set up a fixed IP address for a full-time Internet connection, follow the instructions provided by your Internet service provider (ISP).

12. Use the installation disks to set up the programs you need and any devices that weren't automatically recognized and set up by the Windows Setup program.

My hard disk has crashed

Source of the problem

Usually a hard disk starts making odd sounds—grinding or banging noises—before it gives out. It also may become reluctant to start when you turn on the computer. You might need to flip the power switch a few times before you hear the whine of the disk as it begins to spin. This is your signal to immediately back up your data before you lose it. But occasionally hard disk problems manifest themselves as increasingly common error messages, such as *Sector not found*, when you try to open files or start programs.

If the problem with a disk is mechanical, there may be little you can do but replace the disk. Most computer manufacturers or disk drive manufacturers will replace a disk rather than repair it if it's still under warranty. But if the symptom is repeated error messages, you should use ScanDisk, the disk maintenance program in Windows, to repair the disk. If ScanDisk can't repair the problem, you may need to reformat the hard disk and restore Windows from your backed up data. These options are covered here.

How to fix it

1. Double-click My Computer on the desktop, and right-click the hard disk.

2. On the shortcut menu, click Properties, and on the Tools tab in the Properties dialog box, click Check Now in the Error-Checking Status section.

3. In the ScanDisk dialog box, click Thorough, select the Automatically Fix Errors check box, and then click Start. ▶

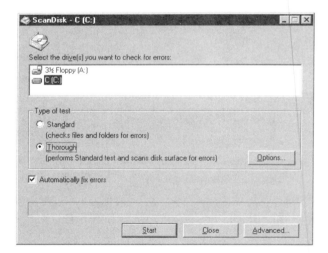

If ScanDisk can't fix it

If you still encounter errors even after running ScanDisk, you may need to reformat the hard disk and restore Windows from the most recent full system backup you have. Here's how:

1. Make sure you have the Windows Startup disk, the Windows installation CD, and a full system backup that you created with Microsoft Backup.

2. Insert the Windows Startup disk in the floppy disk drive, insert the Windows CD in the CD-ROM drive, and then start the computer.

3. At the Microsoft Windows Startup Menu, choose Start Computer With CD-ROM Support.

4. At the MS-DOS prompt (C:\>), type **format c: /s**. Replace *c* with the letter of your hard disk, if necessary. The hard disk will be formatted.

5. At the MS-DOS prompt , type **e:\tools\sysrec\pcrestor** and press Enter. Replace *e* with the drive letter of your CD-ROM drive, which is provided to you in the messages you see when Windows starts.

   The Pcrestor file starts an automatic version of Windows Setup. After setup is complete, the System Recovery Wizard starts.

6. Remove the Windows Startup disk from the floppy disk drive, and on the first page of the System Recovery Wizard, click Next.

7. Type your name and company name, and click Next, and on the last page of the System Recovery Wizard, click Finish. The Microsoft Backup program starts.

8. In the Microsoft Backup dialog box, click Restore Backed Up Files, and then click OK.

When the Restore Wizard starts, choose the following options on successive pages of the wizard. Click Next after you make each choice to go to the next page:

1. For Restore From, select the location where the full system backup is stored. For Select Backup Sets, select the most recent full system backup.

2. For What To Restore, select the check box for the hard disk. For Where To Restore, click Original Locations.

3. For How To Restore, click Always Replace The File On My Computer. Click Start.

Tip

If a drive appears to be dead and it contains essential data that you don't have backed up, you can contact a data recovery company, which may be able to recover your critical files. This service is extremely expensive, however, so it's really only an option for organizations whose critical data is at risk.

Are hard disks reliable?

Most components in your computer—the processor, the video adapter, the sound card, even the monitor—are electronic, without moving mechanical components. But the hard disk in your computer is both electronic and mechanical. The heads that read and write data move rapidly across the surface of disk platters that are rotating thousands of times per minute. So even though a hard disk is extraordinarily reliable, and rated to work for hundreds of thousands of hours before failing, it is the component in your computer that's most likely to break down and have a mechanical failure. One of the oldest adages in computing is: It's not *if* your hard disk breaks down, it's *when*. Take every precaution to back up your data so that you'll be prepared for that day.

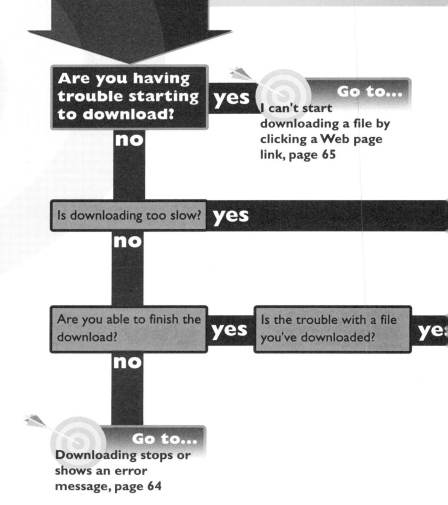

Are you having trouble starting to download?

yes → **Go to...** I can't start downloading a file by clicking a Web page link, page 65

no ↓

Is downloading too slow? yes →

no ↓

Are you able to finish the download? yes → **Is the trouble with a file you've downloaded?** ye

no ↓

Go to... Downloading stops or shows an error message, page 64

Downloading files

Quick fix
The same problems that cause Web pages to be displayed slowly on your screen affect the transfer rate of files you download. For information about getting the best possible transfer rate, see "Web Browsing Is Slow," on page 238.

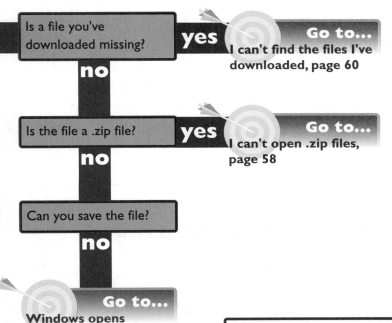

Is a file you've downloaded missing?

yes → Go to... I can't find the files I've downloaded, page 60

no

Is the file a .zip file?

yes → Go to... I can't open .zip files, page 58

no

Can you save the file?

no

Go to... Windows opens downloaded files before I can save them, page 62

If your solution isn't here
Check these related chapters:
   E-mail, receiving, page 66
   Files, page 98
   Folders, page 106
   Internet, connecting to, page 164
Or see the general troubleshooting tips on page xiii

I can't open .zip files

Source of the problem

Anyone who wants to make files available for downloading can compress an entire folder's worth of files into a single, small .zip file. The .zip file will be only a fraction of the size of the separate, uncompressed files, so it'll take much less time to download. But you can't open a downloaded .zip file unless you have a program that "unzips" .zip files. Without it, Windows doesn't know what to do with them.

Fortunately, you can download several popular programs that do nothing but unzip .zip files. These programs copy the files from within a .zip file, restore them to the exact state they were in before they were compressed, and place them neatly into any folder you choose. Among these programs, WinZip is the most popular, so it's covered here, but other unzipping programs work along the same lines.

How to fix it

1. Download and install WinZip. (See "Where Do I Get WinZip?" on the facing page.)
   WinZip's setup program associates .zip files with WinZip so that double-clicking a .zip file opens WinZip; you'll see each .zip file's icon change to the WinZip icon (a clamp compressing a file folder).

2. Click Start, and then click WinZip.

3. If WinZip opens in Wizard mode, click WinZip Classic.
   The WinZip Wizard takes you through the unzipping process step by step, but you'll get a better understanding of .zip files if you see how the Classic version works first.

4. Drag the .zip file's icon to the WinZip window, which then shows a list of the files within the .zip file. ▶

5. Double-click My Computer on the desktop and open the folder into which you want to copy the files you'll extract from the .zip file.

6. Drag the files you want to copy from the WinZip window to the folder you've opened.
   To drag all the files, click Select All on the Actions menu (or press Ctrl+A),

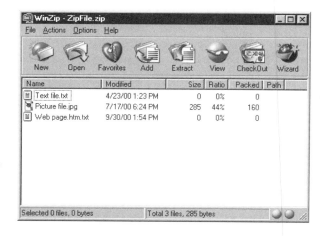

and drag the selection to the destination folder. ▶

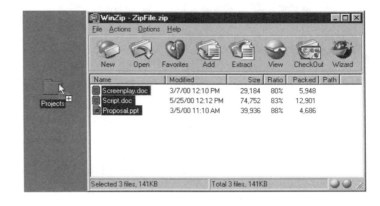

Where do I get WinZip?

WinZip is available at *www.winzip.com*. But because WinZip is so popular, it's also available at most file download sites on the Web, including *www.download.com* or *www.tucows.com*.

WinZip isn't free—it's shareware, which means that you can download it from anywhere, try it, and then buy it at the WinZip Web site. But it's inexpensive, absolutely reliable, and easy to use.

Variations on WinZip

WinZip may be the most popular program for working with .zip files, but other shareware programs—and even freeware programs (programs that are absolutely free)—perform the same tasks. Some programs even work so well with Windows that you can open .zip files from within My Computer without running a separate unzipping program.

But WinZip is still the tops because it's easy, quick, and flexible, and it has advanced features such as automatic disk spanning, which lets you save a .zip file that's too big for a single floppy disk onto multiple floppy disks. And WinZip is less likely to interfere with Windows than unzipping programs that modify how My Computer works.

Tip
WinZip adds commands to the shortcut menu you see when you right-click a file in My Computer. You can use these commands to add the file to an existing .zip file or to quickly create a new .zip file with the same name as the file you've selected.

Creating your own .zip files

Consolidating many files into a single, small .zip file solves all kinds of problems. A single .zip file is easier to track than a bunch of loose files. A .zip file is tiny compared to the original files, so it's easier to fit on removable media like floppy disks. And a single small .zip file is easier and faster to send via e-mail than many large files. You can send all the pictures from your latest vacation in a single file, for example.

Tip
Instead of dragging a .zip file into the WinZip window to open it, you can skip a few steps by double-clicking a .zip file to both start WinZip and open the .zip file.

To store multiple files in a .zip file, start WinZip, click the New button on the toolbar, type a name for the new .zip file, and click OK. Click the Add button on the toolbar, select the files you want to include, and click Add. You can also add files by dragging them from My Computer or the desktop to the WinZip window.

I can't find the files I've downloaded

Source of the problem

When you click a Web page link to download a file, Windows opens a File Download dialog box that asks whether you want to open the file or save it so that you'll have it on your hard disk for use later. Clicking the save option leads you to another dialog box, which asks whether you want to choose a different location for the file. Unless you specify a different folder, Windows uses the same folder you downloaded to last time. The hot new music file you download, for example, might end up in the folder to which you downloaded an updated driver for your video card. Unless you keep track of where your files are going, they might become as good as lost.

To avoid losing track of downloaded files on your hard disk, follow this rule: After you click a Web link to download a file and then click Save This File To Disk and click OK in the File Download dialog box, be sure to carefully choose a destination folder for the file in the Save As dialog box. If the file is already somewhere on your hard disk, here are a few ways to find it.

How to fix it

1. Click the same Web page link again, or if you've closed the Web page, click any link on a Web page that will start a file download.

2. In the File Download dialog box, click Save This File To Disk and click OK.

3. In the Save As dialog box, click the Save In down arrow and check to see which folder is open. The file you've downloaded is most likely in that folder. ▶

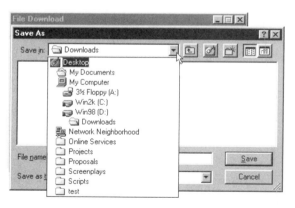

4. Click Cancel to avoid downloading the file again.

5. In My Computer, browse to and open the folder you located in the Save As dialog box.

6. Open the destination folder in another My Computer window, and then drag the downloaded file to the destination folder.

Using Find to locate a file you've downloaded

Another way to find a downloaded file that's hiding in an unknown folder on your hard disk is to use the Find command in Windows (in Windows Me, you use Search, instead). Ordinarily, you search for files by name, but you can also use Find or Search to look for files by date. In this example, you'll be looking for today's files—that is, the files you added to your hard disk today.

To search for today's files, follow these steps:

1. Click Start, point to Find, and click Files Or Folders. In Windows Me, point to Search, and click For Files Or Folders.

2. In the Find All Files dialog box, click the Date tab. In Windows Me, select the Date check box in the Search Results window.

3. Click the During The Previous *x* Day(s) option, and then click Find Now. ▶
   In Windows Me, click In The Last *x* Days, and click Search Now.

4. In a My Computer window, open the folder in which you want to put the file, and then drag the file you want from the search results list to the destination folder.

If you downloaded the file yesterday or a few days earlier in the week, you can change the number of previous days to search from 1 to 2 or 3, or to any other number you want.

Creating a download folder

To avoid losing the files you download, create a special folder for downloaded files on your hard disk. You can create it on your desktop so it'll always be easily available. Name it anything you like. ▶

If you always download files to this folder, you'll know where to find the files after the download is complete, and you can then drag the files you've downloaded from the download folder to their final destination in another folder on your hard disk.

Windows opens downloaded files before I can save them

Source of the problem

If Windows no longer displays the File Download dialog box to ask whether you want to open or save a downloaded file, you must have cleared the Always Ask Before Opening This Type Of File check box the last time you downloaded a file of the same type (such as .zip). If you choose not to be asked, Windows remembers the previous setting and uses it to determine whether to display the File Download dialog box when you download a file. For each file type you can download, you can change whether Windows will display the File Download dialog box or skip right over it.

How to fix it

1. Double-click My Computer on the desktop.

2. On the View menu (on the Tools menu in Windows Me), click Folder Options.

3. On the File Types tab of the Folder Options dialog box, click the file type that no longer causes the File Download dialog box to appear, and click Edit (or click Advanced in Windows Me).

4. In the Edit File Type dialog box, select the Confirm Open After Download check box, and click OK. ▶

5. Click OK to close the Folder Options dialog box.

If the file type is executable (.exe)

If the File Download dialog box won't open when you download an executable file (.exe), you can't use the Folder Options dialog box to fix the problem. Instead, you need to make a change in the registry.

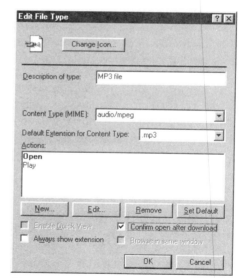

The Edit File Type dialog box in Windows 98

1. Click Start, and then click Run.

2. In the Run dialog box, type **regedit** in the Open box and click OK.

3. In the left pane of the Registry Editor window, expand the HKEY_CLASSES_ROOT folder by clicking the plus sign next to it.

4. Scroll down the tree, and click exefile. (Don't click .exe.)

5. In the right pane, double-click Edit Flags.

6. In the Edit Binary Value dialog box, carefully edit the Value Data entry to change it from *D8 07 01 00* to *D8 07 00 00*, and click OK. ▶

7. Close the Registry Editor.

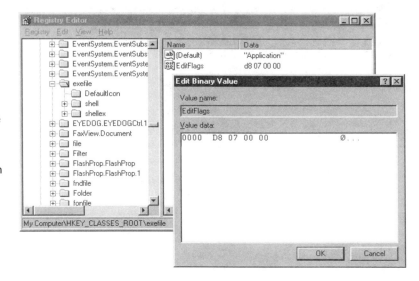

Organizing downloaded files

The whole point of saving the files you download is to have them handy so that you don't have to download them all over again. Sometimes you need to reinstall programs, for example, or run their setup programs again to change options. But what's the point of saving downloaded files in folders if you can't find them or even tell what they are from their cryptic file names?

To organize downloaded files, you should create a download folder and save files in it. You can also easily create subfolders within the download folder for different programs. To do so, in the File Download dialog box, click Save This Program To Disk and then click OK. In the Save As dialog box, browse to and open your download folder, and then click the Create New Folder button. ▶

Type a name for the folder, press Enter, and then be sure to open the new folder you've created before clicking Save in the Save As dialog box. You can also change the file name in the Save As dialog box to something that'll be easier to understand. Choose a name that will make sense when you look at the folder again a year from now. If you're downloading a software upgrade, for example, don't be afraid to use a long and descriptive name for its folder, such as *Upgrade to Version 2*. Don't worry: changing the name of an .exe or a .zip file won't prevent the program from working. But be careful not to change the file extension (.exe or .zip, for example). Changing the extension can keep a program from working.

Downloading stops or shows an error message

Source of the problem

Any number of things might cause downloading to just stop or to display an error message and then give up. But the most common causes are a busy server at the other end of the connection, a technical problem at your Internet service provider (ISP) or an ISP that's overburdened with users, an Internet slowdown, or even a glitch in your phone line. The following steps will solve the problem, regardless of the cause.

How to fix it

- Try a different server. Many sites list several servers you can download a file from. If you have a problem with one server, try another.

- If that didn't work, try a different file download site. In many instances, you'll find the same file at other download sites on the Web. Popular file download sites such as *www.cdrom.com*, *www.tucows.com*, and *www.download.com* often offer the same files.

- Another option is to try one of the site's *mirrors* or *affiliates*. These are sites that duplicate the primary file download site at other geographical locations. Mirrors or affiliates are often listed by location so that you can pick the closest site. But if the closest site doesn't work, try the second closest.

- You might want to try the download at a later time. Sometimes it's just a losing battle—too many other people are vying for the same capacity at your ISP, on the Internet, or at the server. A few hours later, you may have no problem.

- Download a shareware FTP program for downloading files from the Internet, and then look on the Web site for information about using FTP transfers to obtain files. FTP is helpful because it lets you resume a transfer from the point at which the initial transfer failed.

- Disconnect from the Internet, reconnect, and then try the download again. You might establish a better connection the second time.

> **Tip**
>
> After you've been downloading for a while, you'll get an idea of your average download speed, which shows up in the download progress dialog box as the Transfer Rate. If you see an unusually slow transfer rate for a download you've started, don't hesitate to cancel the download and try again at a different file download site or server. Some sites have faster connections than others and fewer people trying to download from them.

I can't start downloading a file by clicking a Web page link

Source of the problem

Web pages that offer files you can download usually have a *Click here to download* link or a Download button that you can click. But depending on how the Web site is designed and which Web browser version you use, you might not be able to download a file just by clicking the link to the file, even when the link is clearly labeled. Fortunately, there's an alternative method you can use to start the download, and it's described here.

How to fix it

1. Right-click the download link on the Web page.

2. On the shortcut menu, click Save Target As. ▶

3. In the Save As dialog box, click the Save In down arrow if you want to change the folder to which the file will be downloaded, and click a folder in the list.

3. If you want, replace the existing file name in the File Name box with a file name that you'll remember more easily.

4. Click Save.

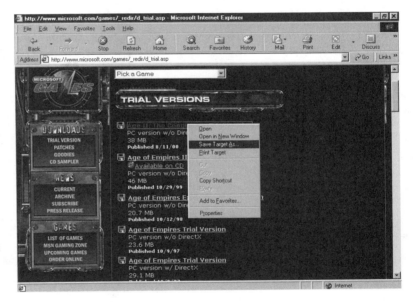

Pulling other items off Web pages

Just as you can right-click and choose Save Target As to pull a file from a Web site, you can also right-click pictures on Web pages to download copies to your hard disk. To download a picture, right-click the picture and click Save Picture As on the shortcut menu. In the Save Picture dialog box, choose a destination folder for the picture and click Save. A copy of the picture will be saved in that folder.

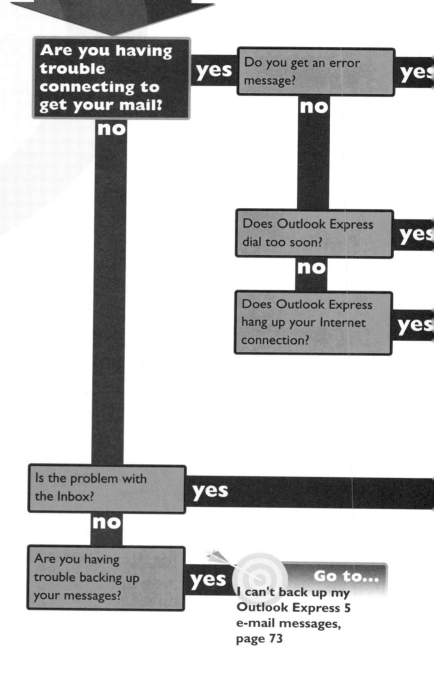

Are you having trouble connecting to get your mail?

yes → Do you get an error message? **yes**

no

Does Outlook Express dial too soon? **yes**

no

Does Outlook Express hang up your Internet connection? **yes**

Is the problem with the Inbox? **yes**

no

Are you having trouble backing up your messages? **yes**

Go to...
I can't back up my Outlook Express 5 e-mail messages, page 73

E-Mail, receiving

Is it about a password problem?

yes

Quick fix

Even though you've typed your correct user name and password, your ISP might require that you type a domain name preceding your user name, in this format: domain name/user name. For example, you might have to enter something like **MSN/username** rather than just **username**. Check your ISP for instructions on properly entering your user name.

no

Go to...

I get a *Host could not be found* error message, page 70

Go to...

Outlook Express automatically dials my ISP, page 68

Quick fix

If Outlook Express hangs up your connection after it sends and receives e-mail, but you want to continue browsing the Web, clear the Hang Up When Finished check box in the message box that opens when Outlook Express dials a connection to the Internet and also follow these steps:

1. On the Tools menu, click Options.
2. On the Connection tab of the Options dialog box, clear the Hang Up After Sending And Receiving check box.

Are messages missing?

yes

Go to...

The Inbox doesn't show all my e-mail messages, page 72

no

Go to...

My e-mail messages are mixed in with everyone else's, page 74

If your solution isn't here
Check these related chapters:
  Dial-Up Networking, page 34
  E-Mail, sending, page 76
  Internet, connecting to, page 164

Or see the general troubleshooting tips on page xiii

Outlook Express automatically dials my ISP

Source of the problem

Even if you have an unlimited use plan with your ISP, you still should be judicious about connecting with your modem. Each call costs something, even if it's only the few cents you must pay your local phone company. But if you have the connection set up wrong, Outlook Express dials each time it starts and dials again whenever it checks for mail, which might be too often for your needs. You should regain control of your Internet connection, dialing when you want, not when Outlook Express sees fit.

How to fix it (in Outlook Express 4)

1. On the Tools menu, click Options, and in the Options dialog box, click the Dial Up tab.

2. In the When Outlook Express Starts section of the Dial Up tab, click Do Not Dial A Connection, and click OK. ▶

    If you instead want to be prompted before Outlook Express dials, click Ask Me If I Would Like To Dial A Connection, and click OK.

3. Click the General tab of the Options dialog box, clear the Check For New Messages Every x Minute(s) check box, and click OK. ▶

4. On the Tools menu, click Accounts, and in the Internet Accounts dialog box, click the Mail tab.

5. Click the mail account you use, and click Properties.

6. On the Connection tab of the Properties dialog box, make sure the Connect Using My Phone Line option is selected, and click OK.

7. Right-click the Internet Explorer icon on the desktop, and click Properties on the shortcut menu.

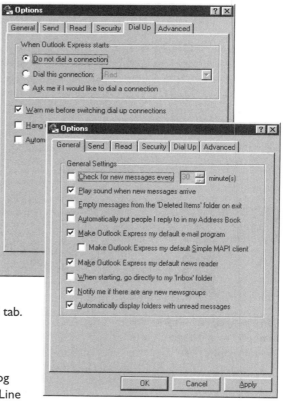

8. On the Connection tab of the Internet Properties dialog box, click Connect To The Internet Using A Modem and click OK.

9. Start Internet Explorer, and click Cancel in the Dialing Progress dialog box.

10. In the Dial-Up Connection dialog box, clear the Connect Automatically check box. ▶

How to fix it
(in Outlook Express 5)

1. On the Tools menu, click Options, and on the Connection tab in the Options dialog box, click Change to open the Internet Properties dialog box.

  The settings in the Internet Properties dialog box are shared by both Internet Explorer and Outlook Express.

2. On the Connections tab of the Internet Properties dialog box, click Never Dial A Connection and click OK. ▶

3. On the General tab of the Options dialog box, clear the Check For New Messages Every x Minute(s) check box and click OK. ▶

4. On the status bar at the bottom of the Outlook Express window, double-click Working Online to change to Working Offline mode so that Outlook Express won't try to connect while you are working on a message. Double-click Working Offline to return to Working Online mode when you are ready to connect to your ISP and check for new e-mail. ▶

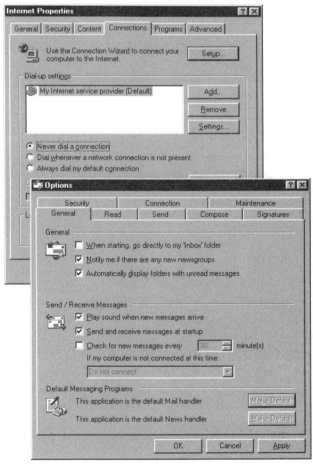

Working Online
button on the
status bar

I get a *Host could not be found* error message

Source of the problem

The *host* is the e-mail server at your ISP that keeps all your e-mail until you retrieve it. If the host can't be found when you try to get e-mail, your connection is not working, the name of the e-mail server is incorrect in your mail account settings, or the e-mail server might have a technical problem and so is not currently available.

How to fix it

1. Start Internet Explorer and see whether your home page opens. If it does not, the problem is your Internet connection. See "I Frequently Lose My Connection to the Internet," on page 174.

2. If you confirmed that your Internet connection is working in step 1, start Outlook Express, and on the Tools menu, click Accounts.

3. On the Mail tab of the Internet Accounts dialog box, click the mail account through which you are unable to get e-mail and click Properties.

4. In the Properties dialog box for the mail account, click the Servers tab, and examine the name in the Incoming Mail (POP3) box. The name you see should exactly match the name of the e-mail server given to you by your ISP. If it does not, delete the incorrect name, type the correct name, and click OK. ▶

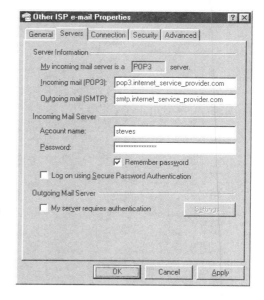

5. If the e-mail server name in the account Properties dialog box is correct, the e-mail server is probably unavailable at the moment. Either wait and try to get your e-mail later or contact your ISP to determine when the e-mail server will again be working.

Getting your e-mail even when your ISP's mail server is down

When having constant access to your e-mail messages is critical, you might be able to forward copies of your incoming e-mail messages to another mail account, such as a free Hotmail account. If your ISP's e-mail server is temporarily unavailable, you can check the account to which you've forwarded mail. You'll find e-mail messages that your server forwarded before it went temporarily kaput. You'll have to get the rest after the server is fixed.

Tip

E-mail servers that deliver e-mail messages to you are called *Post Office Protocol (POP)* servers. Outgoing mail servers are called *Simple Mail Transfer Protocol (SMTP)* servers. The POP server often has a different name from the SMTP server. For example, the incoming mail server at MSN is named *pop3.email.msn.com*, whereas the outgoing server is named *smtp.email.msn.com*.

Outlook Express 4 forgets the password for my mail server

If Outlook Express 4 is unable to remember the password for your mail account, you won't be able to retrieve messages from your e-mail server. To solve this problem, follow these steps:

1. Click Start, point to Programs, and click MS-DOS Prompt.

2. In the MS-DOS Prompt window, type **cd \Windows\ System** and press Enter.

3. Type **pstores –install** and press Enter.

4. Type **exit** and press Enter to close the MS-DOS Prompt window.

   Now, any new passwords you enter will be remembered in Outlook Express mail accounts.

ISPs that offer e-mail forwarding as an option usually let you change preferences or options to turn on forwarding and to enter the e-mail address to which you'd like copies of all your e-mail messages sent. Forwarding e-mail messages to a Web-based e-mail service such as Hotmail or Yahoo! Mail also enables you to read your incoming e-mail from any computer that has an Internet connection. When you travel, you can read your e-mail messages at many hotel business service offices, at Web browsing terminals at airports, and at cybercafés.

Tip

If you're unable to receive an attachment, the attachment may be larger than the size allowed by your ISP or online service. Or the attachment might have been blocked by your corporate e-mail system as a protective measure against viruses, which often arrive hidden within attachments.

The Inbox doesn't show all my e-mail messages

Source of the problem

E-mail messages can disappear if you inadvertently change the view in Outlook Express. If the Inbox hides messages you've already read, your old messages look as good as gone. Messing with the settings that sort messages can also make messages seem to disappear. Sorting the Inbox by the name of the sender, by the subject, or by anything other than the date received can cause new or unread messages to show up in the middle of the Inbox list, which might be quite far down if the list is dozens or even hundreds of messages long.

How to fix it

1. Start Outlook Express, and click Inbox in the Folders list.

2. On the View menu, point to Current View and click Show All Messages (in Outlook Express 5), or click All Messages (in Outlook Express 4). ▶

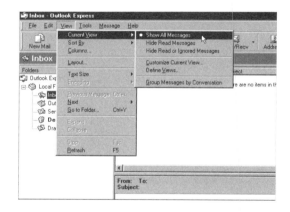

3. If you do not see an arrow on the Received button at the top of the column of dates and times in the Inbox, or if the arrow points up rather than down, click the Received button. An arrow pointing down indicates that the messages are sorted in reverse order by date and time received, meaning that the newest messages are at the top of the list. ▶

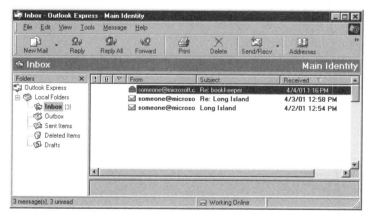

I can't back up my Outlook Express 5 e-mail messages

Source of the problem

Outlook Express 5 doesn't offer an automated solution for backing up e-mail messages, so you need to look after them yourself, copying your e-mail files to a backup disk or removable drive. But the Outlook Express mail files aren't easy to find because they're buried deeply within folders that have cryptic names on your hard disk. Here's how to determine where your mail files are stored so that you can find them and copy them to a backup disk.

How to fix it

1. On the Outlook Express 5 Tools menu, click Options.

2. In the Options dialog box, click the Maintenance tab, and click Store Folder.

3. In the Store Location dialog box, select the entire folder name.
   The best way to do this is to click at the beginning of the entry, hold down the Shift key, and press the End key. ▶

4. Press Ctrl+C to copy the folder name, and click Cancel.

5. Click Cancel to close the Options dialog box.

6. Double-click My Computer on the desktop.

7. Click the Address bar, press Ctrl+V to paste the folder name, and press Enter to open the folder.

8. Copy the .dbx files from the folder you found in step 3 to a backup disk, a removable drive, or an online file storage Web site such as *www.driveway.com*.

My e-mail messages are mixed in with everyone else's

Source of the problem

Outlook Express 5

If other people in your family or office use your computer, you might find that their e-mail messages are mixed in with yours in Outlook Express. Besides the nuisance of locating your e-mail messages among many others, you can read everyone else's e-mail messages and so can they. If you use Outlook Express 5, you can solve this problem by setting up a separate identity for each person who uses the computer. Identities are a new feature added in Outlook Express 5. If you use Outlook Express 4, see "But I Use Outlook Express 4," on the facing page.

How to fix it

1. On the File menu of Outlook Express, point to Identities, and click Add New Identity.

2. In the Identity section in the New Identity dialog box, type your name. ▶

3. If you want your e-mail to be password-protected, select the Ask Me For A Password When I Start check box (in Outlook Express 5.5, select the Require A Password check box), type a password in the Enter Password dialog box, and click OK.

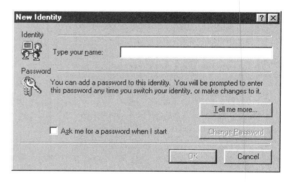

4. Click OK, and then click Yes when you are asked whether you want to switch to the new identity.

5. When the Internet Connection Wizard opens, type your name and click Next.

6. Type your existing e-mail address. In Outlook Express 5.5, click Use An Existing Internet Mail Account and click Next.

7. Type the incoming and outgoing mail server names given to you by your ISP, click OK, and click Finish to proceed. In Outlook Express 5.5, click Accept Settings to use the settings from your existing mail account.

8. Type your ISP account name and password. Click Remember Password to avoid having to type the password each time you check for mail. In Outlook Express 5.5, you can skip this step.

9. Click Next, and then click Finish to close the wizard.

10. If the Outlook Express Import dialog box opens because you have existing Outlook Express messages and an existing address book, click Do Not Import At This Time, and then click Finish.

Switching identities

As long as you switch to your own identity when you start Outlook Express, you'll be working with your own e-mail messages and settings.

1. On the File menu in Outlook Express, click Switch Identity.

2. In the Switch Identities dialog box, click the identity you want to use and click OK. ▶

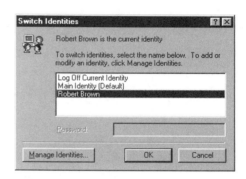

Managing identities

You can add more identities, remove an identity, or change the properties of an identity by following these steps:

1. On the File menu in Outlook Express, point to Identities, and click Manage Identities.

2. In the Manage Identities dialog box, you can do all of the following:
   - Add an identity by clicking New
   - Remove an identity by clicking an identity in the list and clicking Remove
   - Change the name of an identity or give an identity a password by selecting an identity and clicking Properties

Tip
It's your computer, so your identity should be the one Outlook Express uses when it starts. To set your identity as the default, click File, point to Identities, and click Manage Identities. Click the Start Up Using down arrow (in Outlook Express 5.5, click the Use This Identity When Starting A Program down arrow), and click your identity in the list.

But I use Outlook Express 4

If you haven't yet upgraded to Internet Explorer 5, which includes Outlook Express 5, you can still set up multiple mail accounts (one for each user of the computer) and multiple folders, but everyone must be conscientious about dragging their own e-mail messages from the main Inbox to their personal message folders. You can also use message rules (on the Tools menu, click Message Rules) to move messages to different folders based on the addressee.

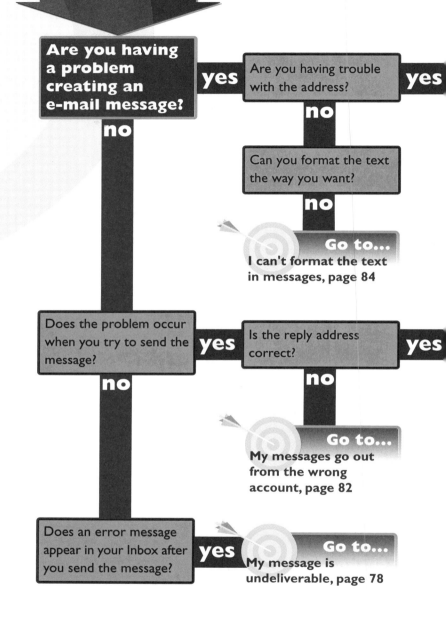

Are you having a problem creating an e-mail message?

yes → Are you having trouble with the address?

yes

no ↓

Can you format the text the way you want?

no ↓

Go to...
I can't format the text in messages, page 84

no ↓

Does the problem occur when you try to send the message?

yes → Is the reply address correct?

yes

no ↓

Go to...
My messages go out from the wrong account, page 82

no ↓

Does an error message appear in your Inbox after you send the message?

yes → **Go to...**
My message is undeliverable, page 78

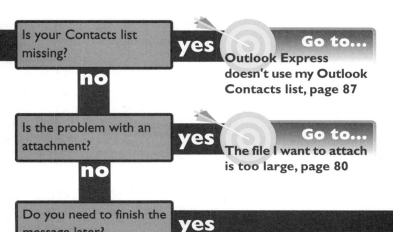

Is your Contacts list missing?

yes → **Go to...** Outlook Express doesn't use my Outlook Contacts list, page 87

no

Is the problem with an attachment?

yes → **Go to...** The file I want to attach is too large, page 80

no

Do you need to finish the message later?

yes →

Quick fix
Click Save on the Outlook Express File menu to save the incomplete message in the Drafts folders. Later you can open the Drafts folder, open and finish the message, and click Send.

Does the message get sent before you can write another?

yes → **Go to...** Outlook Express won't let me send all my messages at one time, page 86

no

Do you get a Relay error when you try to send the message?

yes →

Quick fix
You must connect directly to most ISPs to send messages through their mail servers. This prevents unauthorized users from sending junk mail through your ISP's server. If you need to send mail through another ISP (when you are traveling, for example), set up a separate Outlook Express mail account, but change the Reply Address to your primary e-mail address so that responses go to that account.

If your solution isn't here
Check these related chapters:
Dial-Up Networking, page 34
E-mail, receiving, page 66
Internet, connecting to, page 164
Laptops, page 178
Or see the general troubleshooting tips on page xiii

My message is undeliverable

Source of the problem

When the program that handles outgoing mail at your own Internet service provider (ISP) can't deliver an e-mail message or the incoming mail server at the other end can't find the addressee, one server or the other will send a notice to your Inbox so that you won't wait in vain for an answer from the recipient. This is how you'll know that your message was undeliverable.

Most e-mail that does not arrive at its destination is simply misaddressed. A single typo in the address is all it takes. If the outgoing mail server at your ISP can't find the domain you've put in the e-mail address (the domain is the part after the @ symbol, including the .com, .net, or .org, for example), it can't properly route the message. If the incoming mail server at the destination can't find the addressee you've entered (the name to the left of the @ symbol), it can't deliver the message. Either way, the message won't make it to the recipient, and you'll get an Inbox message telling you so.

How to fix it

1. Start Outlook Express, and click Address Book on the Tools menu.

2. On the toolbar in the Address Book window, click Find (in Outlook Express 4) or Find People (in Outlook Express 5).

3. In the Find People dialog box, click the Look In down arrow, and click one of the directory services in the list. ▶

4. In the Name box, type the name of the person to whom you want to address an e-mail message, and click Find Now.

5. If the directory service does not find the e-mail address you want, click a different directory service in the Look In list, and try the search again.

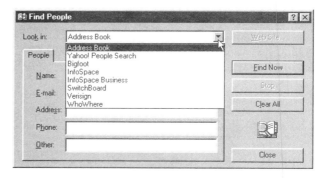

What are directory services?

Directory services are online databases that you can search to find someone's e-mail address, phone number, and other information that's public. The Address Book in Outlook Express is set up to connect to and search several directory services, including Bigfoot, InfoSpace, SwitchBoard, and WhoWhere.

Directory services vary in the breadth of the information they collect and maintain, and they also vary in their conscientiousness about removing obsolete e-mail addresses, so you might need to try a few services to find the most current e-mail address. Directory services are usually unable to give you the e-mail addresses of individuals who reach the Internet through America Online, MSN, EarthLink, AT&T Worldnet, and other large, national ISPs. To protect the privacy of their members, many of these organizations don't release e-mail addresses.

If you work for a large organization, you might have access to a directory service that lists everyone in your organization. Your system administrator can tell you how to reach this directory service.

Looking up e-mail addresses on line

You can also find or verify someone's e-mail address at one of the Web sites that let you search online address books. Sites such as *www.switchboard.com* and *www.infospace.com* have e-mail searches you can use in addition to their standard searches for phone numbers and regular postal addresses. Several Internet portals and search engines—for example, Yahoo!—also provide e-mail address searching. ▶

InfoSpace

When the problem is the attachment

If you receive a return message from a mail server complaining about the size of an attachment you've sent, you might need to remove the attachment, reduce its size, or take other measures to get a file to someone else on the Internet. For information about attachments, see "The File I Want to Attach Is Too Large," on the next page.

The file I want to attach is too large

Source of the problem

Even though your friends and family might welcome every one of your digitized pictures, songs, and video files, their ISPs might not be too happy when those files are huge attachments in your e-mail messages. Some ISPs limit the size of attachments they will handle to reduce the load on their mail servers. They'll bounce a message back to you when the size of an attachment exceeds their restrictions. To get around this problem, you have several options.

How to fix it

- Attach only one file per message. Some ISPs have trouble with multiple attachments in messages anyway, so it's always safer to send multiple messages with one attachment each than multiple attachments in one message. Using WinZip, described next, is another option.

- Use WinZip to compress a file before attaching it. With WinZip, you can also copy multiple files into a single .zip file, so you'll have only one file to send. For more about WinZip, see "I Can't Open .zip Files," on page 58.

- No matter what file type your digital camera or scanner produces, send picture files as .jpg images rather than .bmp or .tif files. Image files in the .jpg format are compressed, so they're a fraction of the size of .bmp or .tif picture files but they look just as good. For information about converting other file types to .jpg, see "The Desktop Won't Show the Picture I Want," on page 16.

> **Tip**
> You can quickly add someone's e-mail address to the Address Book by opening a message that person has sent, right-clicking the name in the From line, and then clicking Add To Address Book on the shortcut menu.

- Use an image editing program to shrink the dimensions of pictures to reduce their file size. Most image editing programs have a Resize command, which reduces pictures to preset, smaller sizes. Even though your digital camera produces pictures that are 1600 by 1200 pixels in size, few people have screens with that many pixels, so most people won't be able to see your entire picture. (Pictures with that many pixels are good for printing, though, because your printer can produce many more dots than your screen.) Your pictures will fit most people's screens better if they are 640 by 480 pixels or 800 by 600 pixels in size. A 1600 by 1200 pixel .jpg image can be nearly 200 KB, while the reduced 800 by 600 pixel version might be just 60 KB.

Using Web-based file sharing services

An alternative to e-mailing large files to friends and family is to post the files at a Web site that provides online file sharing. Web sites like Driveway (*www.driveway.com*) allow you to upload files to a personal storage area and provide others with password-protected access so that they can download the files whenever they want, at their convenience. You don't have to go to the trouble of sending the files, and your family and friends won't be subjected to long mail downloads when they're not expecting them. ▶

Driveway provides 25 MB of file storage and gives you an additional 5 MB when you share your storage area with others. You can earn additional storage capacity by referring other clients. MSN Online File Cabinets offers a similar service (*communities.msn. com/filecabinets*).

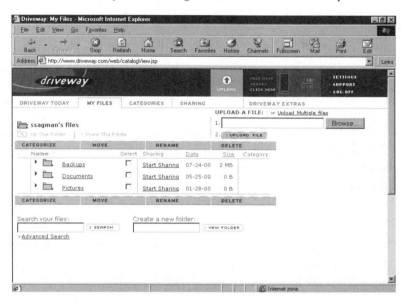

Sharing files in online communities

MSN and other ISPs, such as Yahoo! (*photos.yahoo.com*), allow you to set up communities and photo albums in which you can place files and photos that you want to share with others. You create photo albums, upload your photos into the albums, and then invite others to view the albums. Only the people you've invited are allowed to enter your private, password-protected community.

MSN makes it particularly easy to create photo albums (*communities.msn.com/home*). A special tool helps you choose photos on your hard disk and upload them automatically. If you allow others to upload their photos too, you can have an active community of picture swappers. You can even set up a message board and chat room to turn your space on the service into a real gathering place. ▶

My messages go out from the wrong account

Source of the problem

These days everyone who's anyone has an e-mail address, and many people have several e-mail accounts: a primary account from an ISP, a corporate account for business, and perhaps a free e-mail account from a Web service like Hotmail. A free account is great for checking your messages from airports, hotels, and Web browsers when you travel.

Fortunately, Outlook Express can use as many accounts for e-mail as you set up. But if you write a message that then goes out from the wrong e-mail account—meaning that it has the wrong return address—you might face confusion and even potential embarrassment if, for example, the return address you use for your corporate messages turns out to be the e-mail address you use for your home-based business. Here's how to make sure your e-mail goes out from the account you want.

How to fix it

1. In Outlook Express 4, click Compose Message. In Outlook Express 5, click New Mail.

2. If you're using Internet Explorer 5 or later, in the New Message window, click the From down arrow, click the mail account you want to use, and then click Send. ▶

   If you're using Outlook Express 4, the version that came with Windows 98, point to Send Message Using on the File menu, and then click the proper mail account on the submenu.

Outlook Express 5

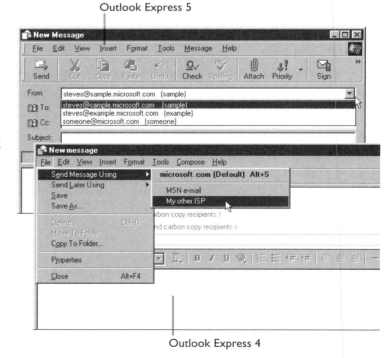

Outlook Express 4

3. Create another e-mail message if you want, using the same mail account or a different one. Outlook Express will connect to your mail servers one by one and send the correct message through the correct server.

What if I don't specify a default mail account?

One of the mail accounts you've set up in Outlook Express is the *default account.* Outlook Express sends your message through this account unless you specify a different account before you click Send.

To determine which account is the default, on the Tools menu in Outlook Express, click Accounts, and then in the Internet Accounts dialog box, click the Mail tab. The default account shows *(default)* next to the account type. ▶

To change the default, click a different account and click the Set As Default button.

Changing the reply address

If you'd like to maintain the appearance that messages are coming from your desk rather than from your hotel in Aruba, you can type your business e-mail address in both the E-Mail Address box and the Reply Address box in each account's Properties dialog box. No matter which account you use to send e-mail, even if it's one of the free e-mail accounts provided on the Web, the recipient of the message will see the return address you've entered. Just remember this while you're lounging in the sun: Despite the commercials, a laptop's screen is hard to see in bright sunlight.

To change the e-mail address and reply address for an account, click Accounts on the Tools menu in Outlook Express, click the Mail tab, click the account you want to change, and click Properties. On the General tab, type your preferred e-mail address in the E-Mail Address and Reply Address boxes, click OK, and then click Close to close the Internet Accounts dialog box.

You can achieve the same results at many Web sites that offer free e-mail, and you might even be able to do the same with your new wireless e-mail device, changing the reply address to hide where you're sending messages from. (On some services, the reply address is called the Reply-To address.) Be aware, though, that anyone determined to pinpoint the source of an e-mail message can examine the message header, which usually reveals the origination point of the message, even after you've changed the reply address.

I can't format the text in messages

Source of the problem

You've received messages that use large text and colorful fonts, but you can't create your own unless you switch the format of the message to Hypertext Markup Language (HTML). HTML is the language of the Web, and it's what enables Web pages to show formatted text and pictures in a designed layout. Outlook Express can interpret and produce the HTML in a message that gives the text its styling, size, color, bullet points, indents, centering, and other formatting attributes.

When you use HTML format to create a message instead of using plain text, the formatting toolbar appears in the New Message window. To apply formatting, you select the text you want to modify and click the buttons on the toolbar. Here are the steps for using HTML in a message.

How to fix it

1. On the Outlook Express toolbar, click the Compose Mail (Outlook Express 4) or New Mail (Outlook Express 5) button.

2. In the New Message window, on the Format menu, click Rich Text (HTML).

3. Type the message. To format the text, select the word or words you want to change and click a button on the formatting toolbar. ▶

4. Click Send to send the message.

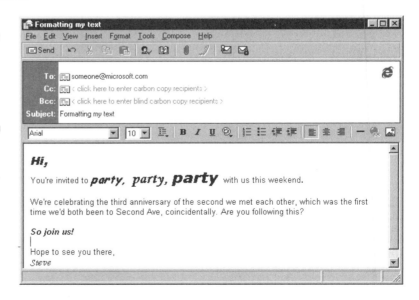

The recipient doesn't see my formatting

All the latest e-mail programs can interpret the HTML coding in messages and display your message with all the formatting you've applied, but some older e-mail programs don't understand HTML, so they show the coding itself rather than use it to format the text. The first time someone with such a mail program gets an HTML message from you, they'll write to complain about all the computerese in your message. In the future, you can turn off HTML and return to plain text for these people by clicking Plain Text on the Format menu in the New Message window.

When you know someone will have a problem with HTML messages, you might as well go one step further and change that recipient's entry in the Address Book so that Outlook Express will always use plain text for that person. To do so, click Address Book (Outlook Express 4) or Addresses (Outlook Express 5) on the toolbar, click the person's name in the list of addresses, and click Properties. On the Personal tab of the Properties dialog box, select the Send E-Mail Using Plain Text Only check box, click OK, and then close the Address Book window. ▶

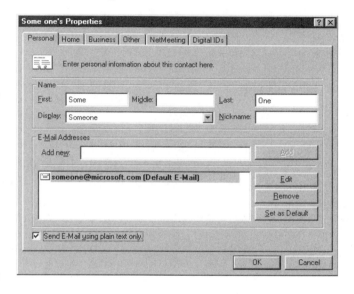

People who have mail programs that are more current but still incapable of understanding HTML will see the message you've written in plain text accompanied by an attachment in the message that contains the HTML version. To see the attachment, they can double-click it to open it in their browser.

Switching to HTML for the long haul

If you don't see the formatting toolbar when you create a new message, HTML is not the default mail sending format. To set HTML as the default, on the Tools menu, click Options. On the Send tab in the Options dialog box, click HTML in the Mail Sending Format section.

Decorating the background

In addition to formatting text, HTML can change the background color of a message and display a background picture. Be sparing when you include pictures, as pictures makes messages larger and therefore more time-consuming to send and receive.

To change the background color in a message or add a picture, open a new message, point to Background on the Format menu, and either choose a color from the Color submenu or click Picture and then choose a picture file from a folder on your hard disk. If you know that the recipient will appreciate your originality, you can also include a sound file by clicking Sound on the submenu.

Outlook Express won't let me send all my messages at one time

Source of the problem

If you've set the Outlook Express option to send messages immediately, Outlook Express jumps into action and dispatches each message as soon as you finish it, dialing your Dial-Up Networking connection if necessary. But if you plan to write more messages, you should have Outlook Express wait until you've composed all the messages you want to send.

If you're already connected to the Internet or you've got a full-time Internet connection such as a cable modem or a Digital Subscriber Line (DSL), Outlook Express dispatches the messages quietly and efficiently in the background, so you won't experience this problem.

Here's how to make Outlook Express wait until you're ready to send all the messages you've written.

> **Tip**
> If you find that the messages you send do not appear in the Sent Items folder, click Tools on the Options menu of Outlook Express, click the Send tab in the Options dialog box, and select the Save Copy Of Sent Messages In The 'Sent Items' Folder check box.

How to fix it

1. In Outlook Express, click Options on the Tools menu.

2. On the Send tab of the Options dialog box, clear the Send Messages Immediately check box. ▶

3. Click OK to close the dialog box.

Sending a message later

If you've selected the Send Messages Immediately option, you can override it by clicking Send Later on the File menu of the New Message dialog box. The message goes to the Outbox, but it won't be sent until you specifically click Send And Receive (or Send/Recv, depending on your version of Outlook Express).

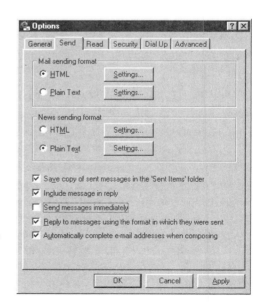

Outlook Express doesn't use my Outlook Contacts list

Source of the problem

If you use Microsoft Outlook, which is part of Microsoft Office, you've probably spent lots of time carefully entering information for everyone you know into the Outlook Contacts list. But even though your Outlook Contacts list contains all the e-mail addresses you need, it won't show up in Outlook Express, because Outlook Express uses the separate Windows Address Book unless you tell it to do otherwise. You can copy names and e-mail addresses from Outlook to the Windows Address Book, but that's an extra step, and you'll need to keep both lists current whenever you have a change to make. A better solution is to instruct Outlook Express to use the Outlook Contacts list rather than the Windows Address Book.

Tip
If you'd prefer to use an existing address book from another mail program, such as Eudora, don't use the Outlook Contacts list. Instead, use the Address Book: On the File menu in the Address Book, point to Import and click Other Address Book. In the Address Book Import Tool dialog box, click the program or file type and click Import.

How to fix it

1. On the Outlook Express toolbar, click Address Book (Outlook Express 4) or Addresses (Outlook Express 5).

2. In the Address Book window, click Tools, and then click Options on the Tools menu.
   Options appears on the Tools menu only if you are using Microsoft Outlook in addition to Outlook Express.

3. In the Options dialog box, click the first option to share address data between the applications. ▶

4. Click OK, and close the Address Book window.

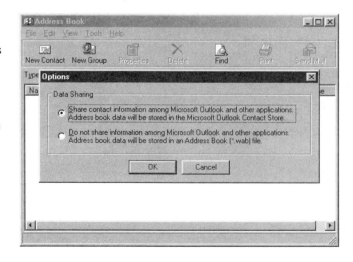

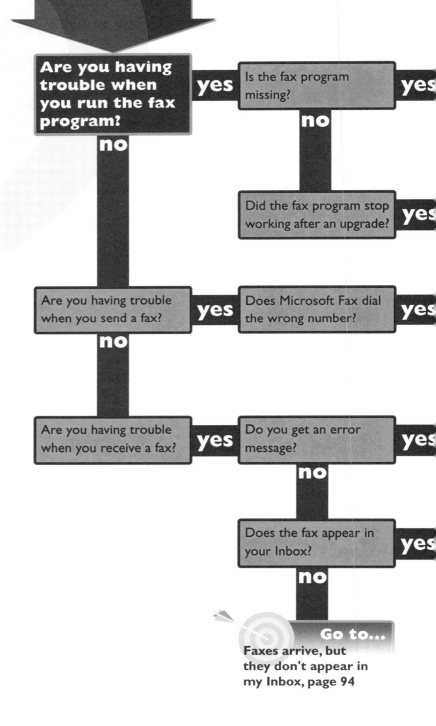

Are you having trouble when you run the fax program?

yes → Is the fax program missing? **yes**

no

Did the fax program stop working after an upgrade? **yes**

Are you having trouble when you send a fax? **yes** → Does Microsoft Fax dial the wrong number? **yes**

no

Are you having trouble when you receive a fax? **yes** → Do you get an error message? **yes**

no

Does the fax appear in your Inbox? **yes**

no

Go to...
Faxes arrive, but they don't appear in my Inbox, page 94

Faxing

Go to...

My fax program disappeared when I upgraded to Windows 98, page 90

Go to...

Faxing stopped working when I upgraded to Windows 98 Second Edition or Microsoft Office 2000, page 92

Quick fix

If Microsoft Fax tries to dial an "h" rather than the number you want, you've installed a program that uses a newer version of TAPI, the Windows component that handles modems. The solution is to install Microsoft Fax by running the awfax.exe program, which is located in the Tools\Oldwin95\Message\Us folder on the Windows 98 CD.

Go to...

An error message tells me I can't receive a fax from a certain phone number, page 96

Go to...

The faxes I receive are garbled, page 97

If your solution isn't here

Check these related chapters:

Files, page 98

Hardware, page 138

Programs, page 252

Setting up Windows, page 272

Or see the general troubleshooting tips on page xiii

My fax program disappeared when I upgraded to Windows 98

Source of the problem

Windows 98 If you sent and received faxes and kept a list of fax numbers in Windows 95 without installing a separate fax program, you were using Microsoft Exchange and Microsoft Fax, two programs that came with Windows 95. But Windows 98 Setup doesn't install these two programs, so you need to install them yourself to get the same faxing service you used in Windows 95. The two programs you need are on the Windows 98 CD.

If you plan to install Microsoft Office 98 or Microsoft Office 2000, don't follow this procedure, as you'll get much better faxing capability in Microsoft Outlook 98 or Microsoft Outlook 2000.

How to fix it

1. Insert the Windows 98 CD.

2. If a welcome screen appears, click Browse This CD and skip to step 3. If a welcome screen doesn't appear, double-click My Computer, right-click the icon for your CD-ROM drive, and click Explore on the shortcut menu.

3. Double-click these folders in sequence: Tools, Oldwin95, Message, and US (or Intl if you're using an international version). ▶

4. Double-click Wms, and install Windows Messaging. Restart Windows after Windows Messaging is installed.

5. Return to the same folder, and double-click Awfax to install Microsoft Fax. Restart Windows after Microsoft Fax is installed.

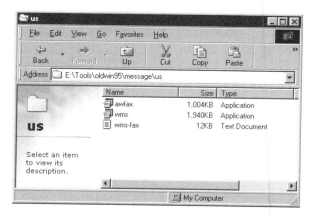

Creating a profile

After you install Windows Messaging, you'll need to set up a Microsoft Mail post office and a profile for faxing.

1. Create a folder on your hard disk, and name it Postoffice.

2. Click Start, point to Settings, click Control Panel, and double-click the Microsoft Mail Postoffice icon.

3. On the Microsoft Workgroup Postoffice Admin page, click Create A New Workgroup Postoffice, and click Next.

4. On the next page of the wizard, click Browse, navigate to the Postoffice folder you created in step 1, click OK, and then click Next. Click Next again to confirm the creation of the new post office.

5. On the Enter Your Administrator Account Details page, type your name and a password, click OK, and click OK again to close the message box. Leave the other options on this page at their default settings.

6. In Control Panel, double-click the Mail icon.

7. In the Mail dialog box, click Add.

8. On the first page of the Inbox Setup Wizard, make sure both Microsoft Mail and Microsoft Fax are selected and click Next. ▶

9. When the Inbox Setup Wizard asks you to provide a path to the location of the post office, check to see whether the default path is correct. If it isn't, click Browse, navigate to the Wgpo000 subfolder of the Postoffice folder you created in step 1, click OK, and click Next.

10. Select the name you entered in step 5 in the list, and click Next. In the Password box, type your password, and click Next.

11. On the next few pages of the wizard, specify your area code, select your fax modem, specify whether you want Microsoft Fax to answer incoming calls, type your name and fax number, and type the path to your existing personal address book, clicking Next after each step and clicking Finish after the last step.

Tip
If you are using User Profiles in Windows 98, logging on with your user name and password loads your user profile and also your Windows Messaging profile. If you log on and don't see Microsoft Fax listed as a service, make sure you've logged on with your correct user name and password.

Faxing stopped working when I upgraded to Windows 98 Second Edition or Microsoft Office 2000

Source of the problem

Windows 98 Installing Windows 98 Second Edition or Microsoft Office 2000 replaces a critical file that Microsoft Fax needs with a version that leaves Microsoft Fax disabled. You can reinstall the older file to continue using Microsoft Fax by following the procedure below, but if you've installed Microsoft Office 2000 and you're not on an office network, be sure to see "I'm Using Outlook 2000," on the facing page.

How to fix it

1. Click Start, point to Find, and click Files Or Folders.

2. In the Find All Files dialog box, type **mapi32*.dll** in the Named box.

3. Click the Look In down arrow, click My Computer in the list, and click Find Now.

4. In the list of found files that appears at the bottom of the dialog box, right-click the Mapi32.dll file contained in your \Windows\System folder, and click Rename on the shortcut menu.

5. Type **mapi32.old** and press Enter. ▶
   If you find a file named Mapi32x.dll, and if the file is either 708 KB or 709 KB in size, rename the file Mapi32.dll.

6. If you are using Windows 98 or Windows 98 Second Edition, skip to "Reinstalling Microsoft Fax in Windows 98" on the facing page. If you are using Windows 95, insert the Windows 95 CD.

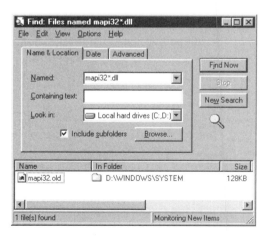

7. Click Start, point to Settings, click Control Panel, and then double-click Add/Remove Programs.

8. Click Windows Setup, click Microsoft Fax, and then follow the prompts to reinstall Microsoft Fax.

Reinstalling Microsoft Fax in Windows 98

If you're using Windows 98 or Windows 98 Second Edition, follow these steps to reinstall Microsoft Fax.

1. Insert the Windows 98 or Windows 98 Second Edition CD.

2. On the desktop, double-click My Computer.

3. If a welcome screen appears, click Browse This CD and skip to step 4. If a welcome screen doesn't appear, double-click My Computer, right-click the icon for your CD-ROM drive, and click Explore on the shortcut menu.

4. Double-click these folders, in sequence: Tools, Oldwin95, Message, US (or Intl if you're using an international version). ▶

5. Double-click Awfax to reinstall Microsoft Fax.

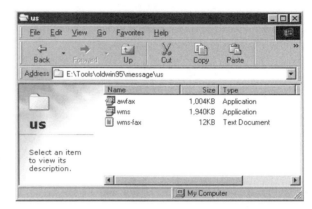

I'm using Outlook 2000

If you use Microsoft Office 2000, there's a good chance you use Microsoft Outlook 2000 to handle your Internet e-mail messages. If you don't connect to a corporate or office network and don't use Outlook 2000 to handle e-mail on an office e-mail system, you probably use Outlook 2000 in its Internet Only configuration. In this configuration, you can use the Symantec WinFax Starter Edition program, which is an optional component that you can install from the Office 2000 CD using the Office 2000 setup program, to handle all your faxing. ▶

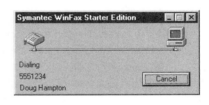

Symantec WinFax Starter Edition is easy to use and it works with Outlook 2000. When faxes arrive, they appear in the Outlook Inbox so you can easily organize them along with your incoming e-mail messages.

You won't be able to use Symantec WinFax Starter Edition if you use Outlook 2000 in its Corporate or Workgroup configuration to handle office e-mail because it's compatible only with the Internet Only configuration.

Faxes arrive, but they don't appear in my Inbox

Source of the problem

If Microsoft Fax goes through all the motions of receiving a fax but then never moves the fax to your Inbox, a few problems could be occurring. There may have been transmission errors or noise on the phone line while the fax was coming in, or the fax message might be so many pages that it required a file size of more than 1 MB, which can stop Microsoft Fax in its tracks. Any of these problems can cause the message to get stuck in a file in the folder that's created by Microsoft Fax to store incoming faxes. You need to force the Inbox to grab the fax from the incoming faxes folder and display it in the list of incoming messages, where you can open and read it.

How to fix it

1. Exit the Inbox.

2. Double-click My Computer on the desktop.

3. On the View menu, click Folder Options.

4. In My Computer, double-click the drive that contains the Windows folder, and then double-click the Windows folder. Click Show All Files, and then double-click the Spool and Fax folders.

5. On the View tab of the Folder Options dialog box, click Show All Files under Hidden Files in the Advanced Settings list, clear the Hide File Extensions For Known File Types check box, and click OK.

6. Write down the names of the two files you find in the Fax folder. One is an RCV*xxxxx*.mg3 file, and the other is an RCV*xxxxx*.efx file. (The *xxxxx* represents a hexadecimal number consisting of five numbers and letters.) ▶

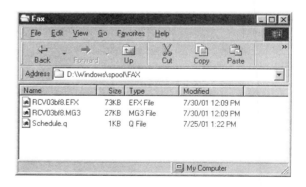

7. Create a folder on your hard disk, and then copy these two files to that folder for safekeeping.

8. Click Start, click Run, type **regedit** in the Open box, and press Enter.

9. In the left pane of the Registry Editor window, click the plus sign next to these folders, in sequence: HKEY_LOCAL_ MACHINE, Software, Microsoft, At Work Fax, and Local Modems. Then click the Received folder. ▶

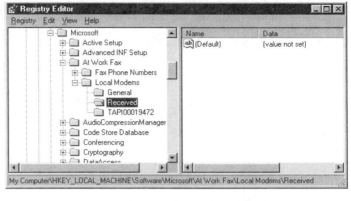

10. Right-click the right pane of the Registry Editor, point to New on the shortcut menu, and click String Value. In the Value Name box, type **F00** and press Enter. Double-click this new value, type the exact name of the .mg3 file from step 6 (for example, RCV03bf8.mg3) in the Value Data box, and click OK. ▶

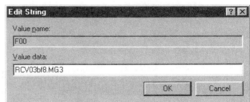

11. Right-click the right pane again, point to New on the shortcut menu, and again click String Value. Name this string value **R00**, double-click the value, and then type **001** in the Value Data box.

12. Repeat step 10, but create the string value *F01*, and type the name of the .efx file as its value data.

13. Repeat step 11, but create the string value *R01*, and enter **001** as its value data.

14. Close the Registry Editor, and reopen the Inbox. The fax messages should now appear in the Inbox.

My fax modem answers the phone but can't establish a link with the fax machine at the other end

If your fax modem answers the phone when an incoming fax call arrives but never establishes a successful connection with the fax machine that is calling, some other program may be rushing to handle the call before Microsoft Fax can get to it.

The quickest you can set Microsoft Fax to answer the phone is after two rings. That may be one ring too many, though. Dial-Up Networking and other programs can pick up the phone after a single ring, so another program might be intercepting the call and preventing Microsoft Fax from doing its job.

If you are able to, disable the automatic answering capabilities of the program that's beating out Microsoft Fax. If the other program is a Dial-Up Networking server, you'll have to decide which service you want to use—either Dial-Up Networking or Microsoft Fax—because only one program at a time can control a fax modem.

An error message tells me I can't receive a fax from a certain phone number

Source of the problem

Windows 98

In Windows 98, an error message that reads *Error receiving fax from <xxx-xxx-xxxx>* indicates that Imaging for Windows is not installed. Imaging for Windows is a Windows accessory that allows you to view and print images (incoming faxes are image files), rotate images (useful when someone faxes a document to you upside down), and add text notes, highlights, and simple drawn shapes, such as lines and rectangles.

When Microsoft Fax tries to open a fax file when Imaging for Windows is not installed, it doesn't know which program to use because no program is associated with the Microsoft Fax file type (.awd). To resolve this problem, install Windows Imaging by following the procedure below.

How to fix it

1. Click Start, point to Settings, click Control Panel, and double-click the Add/Remove Programs icon.

2. On the Windows Setup tab of the Add/Remove Programs Properties dialog box, click Accessories, and then click Details.

3. Select the Imaging check box and click OK. ▶

4. Click OK to close the Add/Remove Programs Properties dialog box.

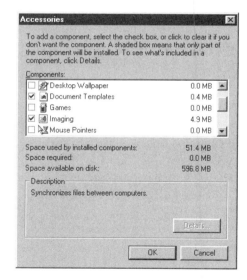

Tip

For more information about file associations, see "The Wrong Program Opens When I Double-Click a File," on page 260.

The faxes I receive are garbled

Source of the problem

Certain modems can cause incoming faxes to look like the bar code on your breakfast cereal box. Even worse, if that's possible, the faxes you receive when you use these modems can appear to be completely blank when you try viewing them in Microsoft Fax Viewer.

You end up with blank faxes when fax modems in the Class 2 category reverse the bit order of incoming faxes. That may not mean much to you or me, but it's enough to make a mess out of a faxed document.

How to fix it

1. Click Start, click Run, and in the Open box, type **regedit** and press Enter.

2. In the left pane of the Registry Editor window, click the plus sign next to these folders, in sequence: HKEY_LOCAL_MACHINE, Software, Microsoft, At Work Fax, and Local Modems.

3. Click the TAPI*xxxxxxxx* folder. (*xxxxxxxx* is a number that corresponds to your fax modem.)

4. In the right pane, look for a CL2SWBOR setting. If you see it, double-click it, and in the Edit String dialog box, type 1 in the Value Data box. ▶

   If you do not see CL2SWBOR, right-click anywhere in the right pane, point to New, and then click String Value. Type the name **CL2SWBOR** and press Enter. Then double-click the name, and in the Value Data box, type 1. Be sure to restart your computer.

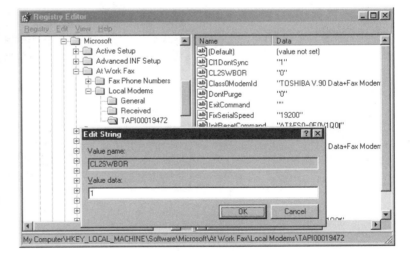

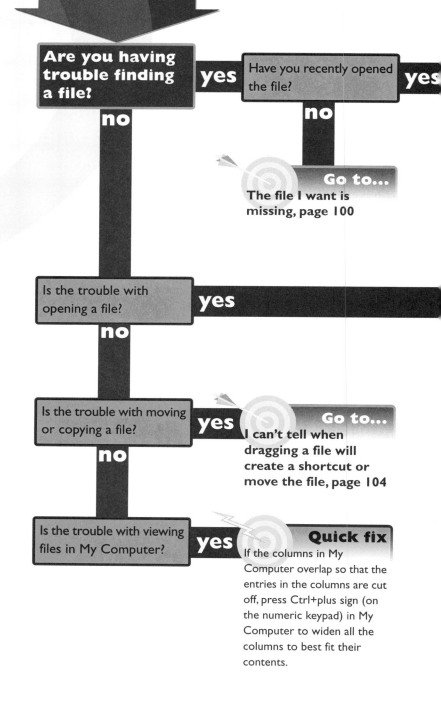

Are you having trouble finding a file?

yes → **Have you recently opened the file?** **yes**

no

no

Go to...
The file I want is missing, page 100

Is the trouble with opening a file? **yes**

no

Is the trouble with moving or copying a file? **yes** → **Go to...**
I can't tell when dragging a file will create a shortcut or move the file, page 104

no

Is the trouble with viewing files in My Computer? **yes** → **Quick fix**
If the columns in My Computer overlap so that the entries in the columns are cut off, press Ctrl+plus sign (on the numeric keypad) in My Computer to widen all the columns to best fit their contents.

Go to...
I can't find a document I've saved, page 102

Have you been able to open the file in the past?

yes

no

Go to...
A file I've double-clicked won't open, page 103

Quick fix

If you rename a file and then find that the Open With dialog box opens when you double-click the file, you've inadvertently changed the file extension. When the file extension changes, Windows can no longer tell which program to use to open the file. Here's how to restore the file and prevent the same problem in the future.

1. Right-click the file, and click Rename on the shortcut menu.

2. Edit the file extension to restore the original, and press Enter.

3. Click View, and then click Folder Options.

4. On the View tab of the Folder Options dialog box, select the Hide File Extensions For Known File Types check box.

If your solution isn't here
Check these related chapters:
   The desktop, page 14
   Downloading files, page 56
   Folders, page 106
   Hard disks, page 128
Or see the general troubleshooting tips on page xiii

The file I want is missing

Source of the problem

It's easy to lose files in the layers of subfolders on your hard disk, so you must be meticulous to a fault about assigning a place to every file you save. Or you can hire an efficiency expert to come in and reorganize your folders and files. But if neither of these options is practical, rely on the Find or Search command in Windows to dig up files that you'd given up for lost. These commands scour your disks for folders and files by name. If you can't remember the exact file name, they can even search the text within files for a match.

Tip

In Windows Me, the Search command replaces the Find command, the Search Results dialog box replaces the Find All Files dialog box, and the Search Now button replaces the Find Now button.

How to fix it

1. Click Start, point to Find, and click Files Or Folders. (In Windows Me, point to Search and click For Files Or Folders.)

2. In the Find All Files dialog box, type any part of the file name you know. The more of the file name you enter, the better. ▶

3. Click the Look In down arrow, and click your hard disk or, if you have multiple hard disks, click Local Hard Drives.

4. In Windows 98 only, make sure the Include Subfolders check box is selected to search through every folder.

5. Click Find Now.

6. In the search results list, double-click a file to open it, or drag the file to a program window to open it in the program, or drag the file to a folder in My Computer to put it somewhere you'll remember. ▶

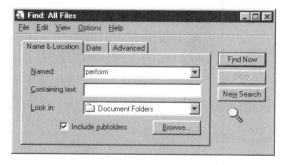

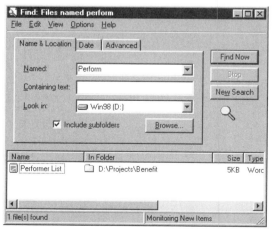

Digging deeper

When you can't remember the name of a file and the names you've tried with the Find or Search command haven't turned up anything, it's not time to give up. It's time to dig deeper.

On the Date and Advanced tabs of the Find All Files dialog box (or in the Search Options section in Windows Me), you can limit your search to a particular time interval and a particular file type. For example, to look for a Microsoft Excel worksheet that you created last week, click Between on the Date tab (in Windows Me, expand Search Options and select Date), and choose the starting and ending dates of the week. On the Advanced tab, click the Of Type down arrow (in Windows Me, select Type in the Search Options section), click the file type you want in the list, and click Find Now (or Search Now in Windows Me). ▶

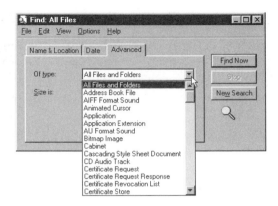

Looking inside files

If you still haven't turned up the file you want, another option is to search through the text within files. If you're looking for a file pertaining to a certain project, for example, you can enter the project name and Find or Search will open each file and search for that name within the text. The Find or Search command opens and checks each file, so a search can take a long time.

In the Find dialog box (or the Search Results dialog box in Windows Me), type the text you want to find in the Containing Text box. Click Browse (in Windows Me, click the Look In down arrow and click Browse in the list), and click the folder that's most likely to contain the file, or if you're not sure, click the hard disk. ▶

Tip

If you haven't been exactly scrupulous about organizing your files, use Find or Search to collect related files from various folders into a single folder. After you search for files of a particular type or with a particular set of characters in their names (that might connote a particular project, for example), drag all the files you've found from the search results list to a new folder you've created just for those files.

If you use Microsoft Office, searching for text within files is much faster if you use the File Open dialog box in any application. Open the File Open dialog box by clicking Find on the Tools menu. Microsoft Office provides its own file indexer, called Find Fast, which tracks the text in all your documents. When you use the File Open dialog box, Office searches its index of the text in documents, so it doesn't need to open and search each document.

I can't find a document I've saved

Source of the problem

Unless you're very conscientious about specifying a folder when you save a document, the file is saved in a folder that's determined by the program you're using. Because each program has its own default folder, documents can become scattered around your hard disk in various default folders.

To help you reopen a document you've recently used, Windows tracks the last 15 documents you've opened and lists them on the Documents submenu of the Start menu. Many applications also list the last few documents you've used on their File menus. A new feature added in Windows 98 and slighted enhanced in Windows Me is the My Documents folder on the desktop. This folder serves as a default filing location that many applications use, so it's the first place to look for a missing document. Here's the easiest way to find a document.

How to fix it

1. Click Start, and point to Documents. ▶

2. On the Documents submenu, click the document you want to reopen.

Looking on the File menu

You might find a list of recently used documents on the File menu in the program you used to create the file. Sometimes these files appear at the bottom of the File menu, and sometimes they're on a submenu named Recent or Recent Files.

Checking My Documents

Beginning in Windows 98, you'll find a My Documents folder on the desktop. Many programs use this folder as their default storage folder for files. You can also set the My Documents folder as the default folder for saved files in all your programs. To organize files within the My Documents folder, create subfolders in the My Documents folder to segregate files by type.

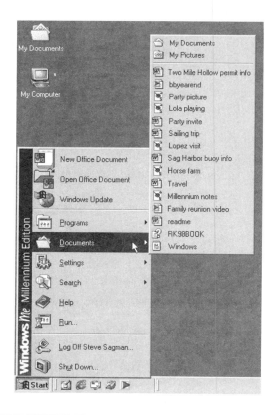

A file I've double-clicked won't open

Source of the problem

Although you might have gotten the hang of double-clicking files to start programs or to open documents (or to do both simultaneously), you can't open every file on your hard disk by double-clicking it. Some files in folders are program components that you can't open independently, or they are holders for configuration settings. Other files are system files that are used by Windows. To help determine which files you can open and which you can't, follow the procedure below.

How to fix it

1. In My Computer or Windows Explorer, click Details on the View menu.

2. Click the View menu again (the Tools menu in Windows Me), and click Folder Options.

3. On the View tab of the Folder Options dialog box, click the Like Current Folder button. ▶

4. Click Yes when you are asked whether you want to set all folders to match the current folder's view settings.

5. In the Advanced Settings list, click Do Not Show Hidden Files Or System Files (in Windows Me, click Do Not Show Hidden Files And Folders), and then click OK.

6. Double-click any folder in My Computer or Windows Explorer, and examine the description of the file in the Type column to find applications and documents, both of which you can double-click to open. ▶

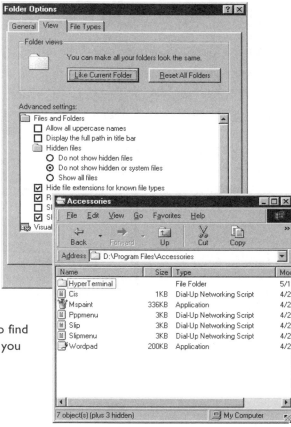

I can't tell when dragging a file will create a shortcut or move the file

Source of the problem

Windows follows a set of rules to determine whether it will move or copy a file or folder you are dragging or whether it will create a shortcut instead. If you don't know the rules, you won't know what to expect, and if Murphy's Law holds true, whatever happens will probably be exactly the opposite of the outcome you anticipated. Here's a foolproof method for moving or copying files.

How to fix it

1. Double-click My Computer on the desktop, and open the folder containing the file.

2. Double-click My Computer again, and open the folder to which you want to move or copy the file.

3. Point to the file or folder you want to move or copy, and then press and hold down the right mouse button.

4. Drag the file to the destination folder, and then release the mouse button.

5. On the shortcut menu, click Move Here, Copy Here, or Create Short-cut(s) Here. ▶

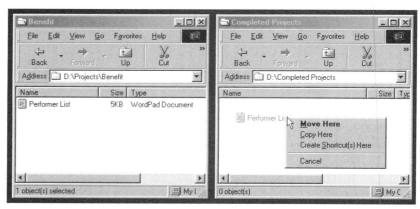

Knowing the rules

Using the right-click and drag technique described above is a surefire solution, but it requires an extra step—clicking an option on a shortcut menu. If every click matters to you, take a minute to memorize these simple rules so that you'll know what to expect when you drag a file or folder by holding down the left mouse button:

● Dragging *moves* a file or folder to a folder on the *same* drive.

- Dragging *copies* a file or folder to a folder on a *different* drive.

- Dragging *creates a shortcut* when the file is an *application*. In Windows Me, dragging an application file moves it.

Watching the signs

As you drag a file or folder, the mouse pointer changes appearance to show exactly what will happen when you release the mouse button. Keep an eye on the pointer to determine the result of a drag operation. ▶

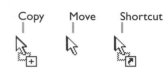

When releasing the mouse button will cause the file to be copied, a small plus sign appears next to the pointer. If no plus sign appears, the file will be moved. If the file is an application and releasing the mouse button will create a shortcut, a shortcut arrow appears next to the pointer.

Forcing the issue

No matter what Windows thinks it should do when you drag a file or folder, you can override the rules by pressing either the Ctrl key or the Shift key as you drag:

- If dragging will *move* a file or folder, press *Ctrl* to force the file or folder to be copied.

- If dragging will *copy* a file or folder, press *Shift* to force the file or folder to be moved.

- If dragging will create a *shortcut* to an application, press *Ctrl* to copy the application file or press *Shift* to move the application file.

Sending a link on a network

When you right-click and drag files between folders on your own computer and click Create Shortcut(s) Here on the shortcut menu, you create shortcuts that point to the files or folders you dragged. Shortcuts are helpful because you can have one copy of a file but point to it from several folders. For example, you can refer to a master schedule file for a project from within each of the project's folders. You don't accumulate multiple copies of the file, so you don't have to worry about discrepancies between the duplicates, and you can update the single file to which all the shortcuts point. Similarly, when you're on a network, you can right-click and drag a file or folder on your computer into an e-mail message as a shortcut and send the shortcut to another person on the network. A recipient who has access to your disk or folder can double-click the shortcut to open the file or folder. This saves not only having to duplicate files, but also having to e-mail the files to someone else in your office and accumulate them in your e-mail program.

To send a shortcut, open a new e-mail message in Outlook Express, and right-click and drag a file into the message. Then click Create Shortcut(s) Here on the shortcut menu.

> **TIP**
> The desktop is just another folder, so if you're dragging a file or folder to the desktop, all the rules given here apply. The desktop folder is usually on the same drive as the Windows files.

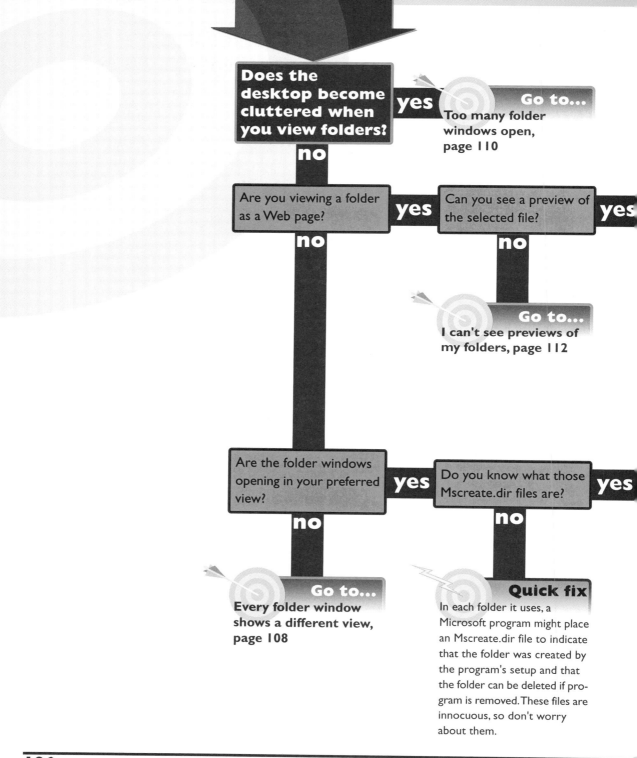

Does the desktop become cluttered when you view folders?

yes → **Go to...** Too many folder windows open, page 110

no

Are you viewing a folder as a Web page?

yes → Can you see a preview of the selected file?

yes

no

no → **Go to...** I can't see previews of my folders, page 112

Are the folder windows opening in your preferred view?

yes → Do you know what those Mscreate.dir files are?

yes

no

no → **Go to...** Every folder window shows a different view, page 108

Quick fix
In each folder it uses, a Microsoft program might place an Mscreate.dir file to indicate that the folder was created by the program's setup and that the folder can be deleted if program is removed. These files are innocuous, so don't worry about them.

Folders

Are you having trouble viewing the folder in Windows Explorer?

yes

Quick fix

If you use View As Web Page in Windows Explorer but the windows in Windows Explorer are blank, you need to enable style sheets in Internet Explorer.

1. Start the Registry Editor by clicking Run on the Start menu, typing **regedit** in the Run dialog box, and clicking OK.

2. Click the plus sign next to these folders, in sequence: HKEY_CURRENT_USER, Software, Microsoft, Internet Explorer. Then click Main.

3. Double-click Use Stylesheets in the right pane and type **yes** in the Value Data box. If you do not see Use Stylesheets, right-click the right pane, point to New on the shortcut menu, click String Value, type **Use Stylesheets**, and press Enter. Press Enter again, type **yes** in the Value Data box.

4. Click OK, and quit the Registry Editor.

Do you need to enter a path?

yes

Go to...

I need to enter a path for a file or folder, page 114

If your solution isn't here
Check these related chapters:
The desktop, page 14
Files, page 98
Hard disks, page 128
Programs, page 252
Or see the general troubleshooting tips on page xiii

Every folder window shows a different view

Source of the problem

For every folder it displays, My Computer can remember the view you chose last—a convenience if you always prefer to view a folder of program files as icons and to view a folder of picture files as thumbnails. But if you prefer the consistency of maintaining the same view in every folder over the excitement of giving each folder its own view, you can set all folders to be displayed in the same way. Of course, that doesn't mean that you have to be rigid about it. You can choose a different view of any folder at any time you want.

How to fix it

1. Double-click My Computer on the desktop.

2. Open any folder in My Computer.

3. On the View menu, click one of the four views in (Large Icons, Small Icons, List, or Details) or five views in Windows Me (Large Icons, Small Icons, List, Details, or Thumbnails). ▶

4. Set the position and size of the My Computer window by dragging its title bar and borders.
   Other windows will open at the same location and the same size.

5. On the View menu or on the Tools menu in Windows Me, click Folder Options.

6. On the View tab of the Folder Options dialog box, click Like Current Folder and click OK. ▶
   Like Current Folder sets all future folder windows to look like the folder you have selected.

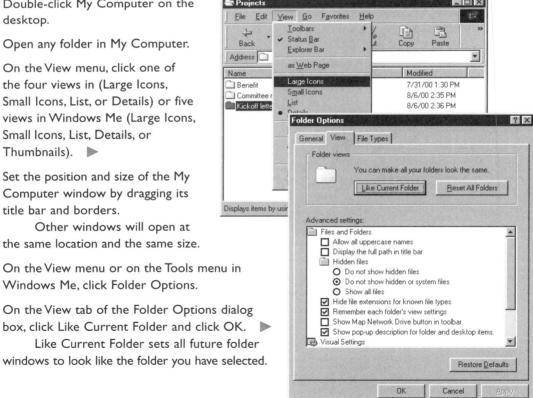

There's more to do in Details view

In Details view, you can set a few additional defaults. Drag the right edge of any heading button at the top of a column to widen or narrow the column. Click a heading button at the top of a column to sort the information according to the information in that column. For example, click the Total Size button (the Size button in Windows Me) to sort the listings by size from smallest to largest. Click the same button again to reverse the sort of the listings, from largest to smallest.

Turning off the View memory

If you'd like to return to the good old days when every folder had its own view, follow these steps:

1. On the View menu or the Tools menu (in Windows Me), click Folder Options.

2. On the View tab of the Folder Options dialog box, click Reset All Folders to return the folders to the way they were displayed when you first installed Windows.

3. In the Advanced Settings list on the same tab, select the Remember Each Folder's View Settings check box, and then click OK.

Advanced View settings you can save

In addition to the basic settings you can choose on the View menu or in the Details view window, you can store many more settings by selecting them in the Advanced Settings list on the View tab in the Folder Options dialog box.

- **Display The Full Path In Title Bar** Shows the hard disk and all the folders that contain the current folder in the title bar of the folder window.

- **Display The Full Path In The Address Bar (Windows Me only)** Shows the same information in the Address bar of folder windows.

- **Hidden Files** Lets you show or hide files that you designate as hidden. (To hide a file, right-click the file name, click Properties, and select the Hidden check box.) In Windows Me, this option is named Hidden Files And Folders.

- **Hide File Extensions For Known File Types** Prevents the file extensions of file types that are associated with programs from being displayed. Hiding them makes the file list cleaner and prevents you from changing the file extension inadvertently when you rename a file.

- **Hide Protected Operating System Files (Windows Me only)** Hides files you shouldn't modify because they're part of Windows.

- **Show My Documents On The Desktop (Windows Me only)** Reveals the My Documents icon.

- **Show Pop-Up Description For Folder And Desktop Items** Displays a small box containing a description of any desktop or folder item you point to and pause the mouse pointer on.

Too many folder windows open

Source of the problem

If Windows open a new folder window whenever you open a folder by double-clicking it, your screen can soon become clogged with windows. With a separate window for each folder, you can drag files and folders from one window to another. But every window you open is another window you have to close, and having multiple folder windows open can clutter your desktop. The solution is to have every folder you double-click open in the same window. The display of the current folder's contents will replace the display of the previous folder's files.

How to fix it

1. Double-click My Computer on the desktop.

2. On the View menu or the Tools menu (in Windows Me), click Folder Options.

3. Click Settings on the General tab of the Folder Options dialog box. Skip this step if you use Windows Me.

4. Click Open Each Folder In The Same Window, and click OK. ▶

5. In Windows 98, click Close.

Avoiding desktop clutter with Windows Explorer

Windows Explorer presents the same information as a My Computer window but adds a second pane to the left of the folder and file listing. This pane shows the tree structure of disks and folders on your computer and, if you're connected to a network,

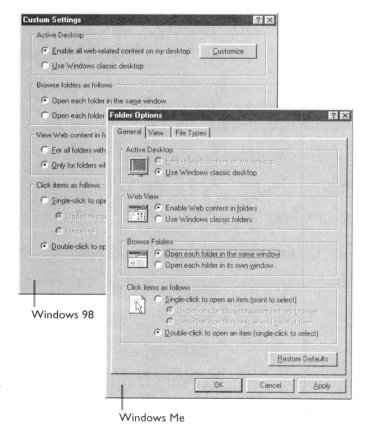

Windows 98

Windows Me

the computers, disks, and folders that you have access to on the network. ▶

To start Windows Explorer rather than My Computer, right-click My Computer and click Explore on the shortcut menu. You can also right-click any folder in My Computer and click Explore on the shortcut menu to open a Windows Explorer window that shows the folder.

Opening one Windows Explorer window can provide the same benefits as opening several My Computer windows. In a Windows Explorer window, you can open a folder by clicking it in the left pane. The contents of the folder

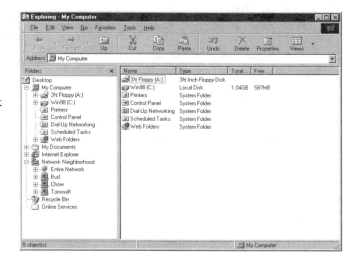

are displayed in the right pane. You can then drag a file or folder from the right pane to any other folder that you can see in the left pane.

Transforming My Computer into Windows Explorer

Rather than open a second My Computer or Windows Explorer window to drag a file to another folder, you can add a left pane containing the folder list to the My Computer window, converting My Computer to Windows Explorer. ▶

To add a folders list, on the View menu in My Computer, point to Explorer Bar and click Folders.

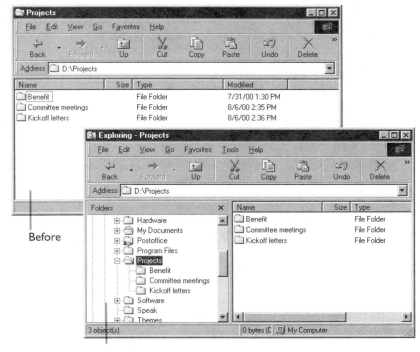

Before

After

I can't see previews of my folders

Source of the problem

In Windows 98 and Windows Me, you can peek inside some of the files in your folders by viewing them in small squares called *thumbnails* that show their content. Windows can show you thumbnails of .gif, .bmp, .jpg, .html, and PowerPoint .ppt files, plus a few other graphics file types. To see thumbnails is to love them, so if you've lost them or if you never had them in the first place, here's how to make them appear.

How to fix it

Windows Me shows thumbnails by default, but in Windows 98, you must turn them on by following these steps:

1. On the View menu in My Computer or Windows Explorer, click As Web Page.

2. A new information area containing details about the currently selected disk, folder, or file should open to the left of the folders and files icon. If it doesn't, widen the My Computer or Windows Explorer window by dragging its right edge farther to the right.

3. Click a picture file or saved HTML file to see a thumbnail preview in the information area on the left. ▶

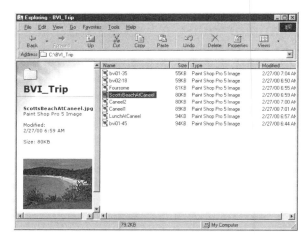

Viewing all folders as Web pages

You can turn this new information area on for all folders by following these steps:

1. In My Computer or Windows Explorer, click Folder Options on the View menu. In Windows Me, click Folder Options on the Tools menu.

2. On the General tab of the Folder Options dialog box in Windows 98, click Custom, Based On Settings You Choose and click the Settings button. In Windows Me, click Enable Web Content In Folders, click OK, and you're done.

3. In the Custom Settings dialog box in Windows 98, click For All Folders With HTML Content and click OK. Click Close to close the Folder Options dialog box.

Viewing all files in a folder as thumbnails

Windows 98   If you have folders that contain mostly pictures, such as folders in which you store the pictures from your digital camera, you can use Thumbnail view to display all the files in the folder as thumbnails. In Windows 98, you need to enable Thumbnail view for a folder before you can use it. Windows Me enables Thumbnail view by default.

1. In Windows 98, right-click a folder in Windows Explorer that contains mostly picture files, and click Properties on the shortcut menu.

2. In the Properties dialog box, select the Enable Thumbnail View check box and click OK.

3. In either Windows 98 or Windows Me, open the folder and click Thumbnails on the View menu. ▶

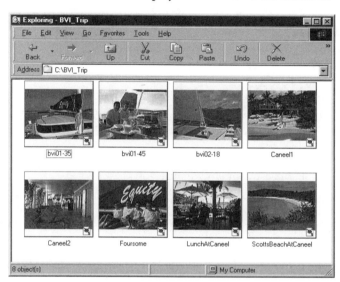

Previewing multimedia files in Windows Explorer

Windows Explorer in Windows 98 lets you preview multimedia files, such as .avi video files, in addition to pictures, but only if you enable the multimedia preview feature.

1. In the left pane of Windows Explorer, click the plus sign next to the Windows folder and then click the Web folder.

2. On the View menu, click Customize This Folder, click Next, and click Next again.

3. On the Search menu in Notepad, click Find, type **wantMedia** in the Find What box, click Find Next, and click Cancel.

4. Change the word *false* on that line in Notepad to *true* so that the line reads *var wantMedia = true; // cool, but may hinder media file manipulation.*

5. On the File menu, click Save, and then quit Notepad, click Finish, and quit Windows Explorer.

6. Restart Windows Explorer, click a folder that contains a media file, and click the file in the right pane to see the preview in the left pane.

I need to enter a path for a file or folder

Source of the problem

MS-DOS programs and even some older Windows programs don't use the Windows method of visually depicting files in folders on your hard disk. Instead, they ask you to spell out the location of a file or folder by using a line of text called a *path*, which looks something like this: *c:\program files\accessories\wordpad.exe*. When a program asks you for a path to specify the location of a file or folder, you need to translate the information in a folder window into a path.

How to fix it

1. Double-click My Computer on the desktop.

2. On the View menu or the Tools menu (in Windows Me), click Folder Options.

3. On the View tab of the Folder Options dialog box, clear the Hide File Extensions For Known File Types check box.

4. If you are using Windows Me, select the Display The Full Path In The Address Bar check box.

5. Click OK.

6. In My Computer, open the folder that contains the file you want to specify, and make a note of the file name.

If you'll be using the file name in an MS-DOS program, right-click the file name and make a note of the MS-DOS name shown in the Properties dialog box.

7. If the program that wants a path is an MS-DOS program, make a note of the text in the Address bar. If the program is a Windows program, click the box in the Address bar and press Ctrl+C to copy the text. ▶

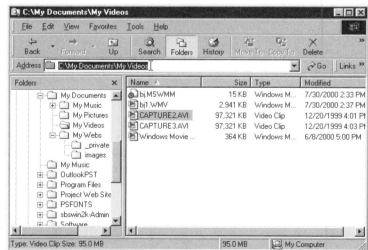

8. Start the program, and perform the task or choose the command that asks for the path.

9. If the program is an MS-DOS program, type the path that you noted in step 7. If the program is a Windows program, press Ctrl+V to paste the path.

10. If you need to specify a file in a folder, type a backslash (\) immediately following the last folder name in the path and then type the file name from step 6, including the file extension.

More about paths

You can almost always get around in Windows without entering a path, but you still see paths in the Address bar in My Computer and in dialog boxes, so you might want to understand just a little bit about them.

The files on your hard disk are organized in folders and some of these folders are located within other folders. Windows represents this organizational scheme visually. You see folders within folders in Windows Explorer and in the Save In and Look In lists in the dialog boxes that you use to save and open files. ▶

But you might not know that this scheme of folders within folders pre-dated Windows. MS-DOS, the operating system before Windows, gave users a way to type a line of text to describe a path to any folder on a hard disk. That path still shows up in Windows today in the Address bar. ▶

The first entry in a path is the disk name, such as *C:*, followed by a backslash (\). After that comes the first folder you must look in, again followed by a backslash. Each subfolder you must open is added to the path and followed by a backslash. The last entry on the line is the file name, if you want to be that specific.

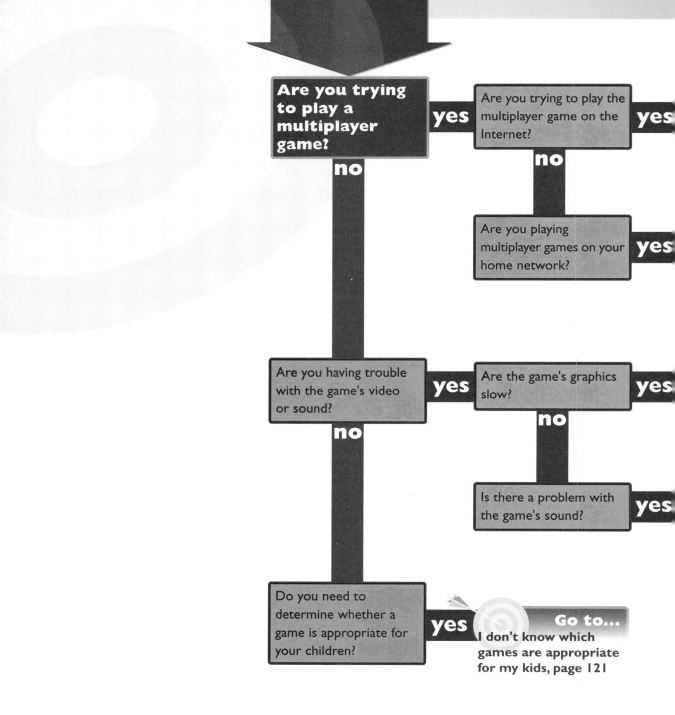

Are you trying to play a multiplayer game?

yes → Are you trying to play the multiplayer game on the Internet? **yes** →

no ↓

Are you trying to play the multiplayer game on the Internet?
no ↓

Are you playing multiplayer games on your home network? **yes** →

Are you having trouble with the game's video or sound? **yes** → Are the game's graphics slow? **yes** →

no ↓

Are the game's graphics slow?
no ↓

Is there a problem with the game's sound? **yes** →

Do you need to determine whether a game is appropriate for your children? **yes** →

Go to...
I don't know which games are appropriate for my kids, page 121

Does your network use Internet Connection Sharing?

yes

no

Quick fix

If your computer is connected to the Internet through someone else's computer using Internet Connection Sharing, you can't play multiplayer games on the Internet. You must disable Internet Connection Sharing and connect your computer directly to the Internet through a regular modem, cable modem, or DSL line. For more information about Internet Connection Sharing, see "I Can't Set Up Internet Connection Sharing," on page 202.

Go to...
I can't connect to other players on my home network, page 124

Go to...
Multiplayer Internet games run too slowly, page 126

Go to...
The graphics in my game are slow or jerky, page 118

Go to...
My game doesn't sound right, page 122

> **If your solution isn't here**
> Check these related chapters:
> Hardware, page 138
> Networks, home, page 196
> Programs, page 252
> Sound, page 280
> Or see the general troubleshooting tips on page xiii

The graphics in my game are slow or jerky

Source of the problem

The hottest action games for the PC demand a lightning-fast graphics card along with a powerful processor, such as a fast Intel Pentium III or Celeron. If either the card or the processor is feeble, the animation in your games will be slow, and movements will look jerky rather than smooth. Simulations, high-speed action games, and first-person shooters such as Quake are particularly demanding. If you plan to play against the machine, you might be fine, but if you want to play against other players on line, you won't have much of a chance. They're just too good. So if you hope to stand any chance of keeping up, follow these steps.

How to fix it

- Upgrade your computer to a newer model if you hope to survive alien wars, the Grand Prix, or a shootout in a dark hallway of a secret underground lab.

    If you have a Pentium or Pentium II, upgrade to a fast Celeron, or even better to a Pentium III. Get the fastest processor you can afford; speed is indicated by the MHz number (600 MHz is better than 500 MHz, and so on). In addition to getting more raw performance, which will also help in your other guise (mild-mannered business application user), your new computer is likely to come with faster components on its main circuit board (the *motherboard*), a faster and larger hard disk, and a speedier graphics card, which is powered by a newer and more advanced graphics chip.

- Replace your graphics card with a newer model.

    Next to updating to a faster processor, updating the graphics card in your computer will have the greatest effect on the speed of most games. New graphics cards based on the latest graphics chips are produced almost monthly, offering vast increases in their power to create smooth movement and realistic scenery.

    Replacing the graphics card is a fraction of the cost of replacing the entire computer. But keep in mind that the graphics card and the main processor (the CPU, such as the Pentium chip) in a computer interact, so putting the very latest graphics card in an early-model PC won't let the card run at its full speed. You'll see an improvement, but not as much as if you'd upgraded the CPU too.

    For information about the latest graphics chips, visit Web sites devoted to gaming graphics, such as *www.Tweak3D.net*.

● Upgrade DirectX, the gaming component in Windows.

DirectX has gone through a succession of revisions. To learn which version of DirectX is the latest, go to *www.microsoft.com/directx*.

To determine which version you're using, click Run on the Start menu, type **dxdiag** in the Open box, and press Enter. The System tab in the DirectX Diagnostic Tool dialog box shows the current DirectX version. ▶

To download for free the latest version of DirectX, use Windows Update in Windows 98 and Windows Me.

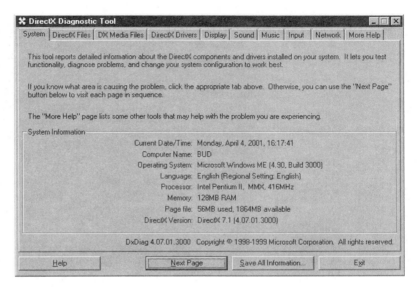

● Download the latest update patch for your games.

Popular games are frequently updated to fix problems and provide greater speed. To find these patches, go to the manufacturer's Web site or visit a site devoted to gaming, such as *www.gamespot.com*, *www.gamecenter.com*, or *www.bluesnews.com*.

● Download the latest driver for your graphics card.

Graphics card manufacturers frequently release new drivers for their cards that wring every last bit of performance from the graphics chip and often provide noticeable improvements in game speed. Visit the manufacturer's Web site to download the latest driver.

Follow the driver's installation instructions carefully, but even if the instructions don't say so, it's a good idea to set your display adapter to Standard Display Adapter (VGA) and restart your computer before installing a new driver. To do so, follow these steps:

1. Right-click My Computer on the desktop, and click Properties on the shortcut menu.
2. On the Device Manager tab in the System Properties dialog box, click the plus sign next to Display Adapters.
3. Click your display adapter, and click Properties.

To continue with this solution, go to the next page.

The graphics in my game are slow or jerky

(continued from page 119)

4. On the Driver tab in the Properties dialog box, click Update Driver to start the Update Device Driver Wizard. ▶

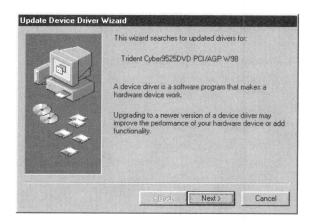

5. Click Next on the first page of the wizard, and click Display A List. In Windows Me, click Specify The Location of the Driver, click Next, and click Display A List Of All The Drivers In A Specific Locations, So You Can Select The Driver You Want.

6. Click Next, and then click Show All Hardware.

7. In the Manufacturers list, click Standard Display Types, and in the Models list, click Standard Display Adapter (VGA). ▶

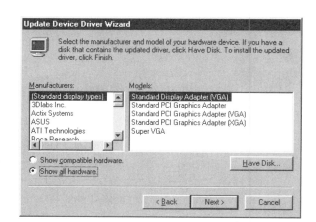

8. Click Next, and then click Yes if you're asked whether you want to use this driver.

9. Click Yes if you're asked whether you want to restart your computer.

● Tune up your computer.

Follow the procedures in "My Hard Disk Seems Slower," on page 234, and "Windows Has Become Sluggish," on page 236, to optimize the performance of your hard disk and the speed of Windows.

● Check out Web sites devoted to gaming and gaming hardware.

Legions of game fans depend on Web sites designed for and by gaming enthusiasts to find the latest ideas for getting the most out of their current computers or upgrading to the latest and greatest hardware.

I don't know which games are appropriate for my kids

Source of the problem

Before you let your kids buy a computer game, you can check its Entertainment Software Rating Board (ESRB) rating to determine whether the game is suitable for them. The ESRB has developed a standardized rating system that gives parents information about the content of computer games. (It also rates video games for popular gaming consoles.) Games are rated by three independent, trained raters drawn from a pool that includes, among others, retired school principals and parents.

How to fix it

Look on the game box for the ESRB rating before you purchase a game. If you can't accompany your kids to the store and check the box yourself, visit *www.esrb.org*, where you can look up game titles and check their ESRB rating. You can search for a particular game at *www.esrb.org/search/index.html*.

Rating categories provided by the ESRB include the following:

- **Early Childhood (EC)** Appropriate for ages 3 and older. No inappropriate content.

- **Everyone (E)** Appropriate for ages 6 and older. Titles may contain minimal violence, some comic mischief, or crude language.

- **Teen (T)** Appropriate for ages 13 and older. Titles may contain violent content, mild or strong language, and suggestive themes.

- **Mature (M)** Appropriate for ages 17 and older. Titles may contain intense violence and language and mature sexual themes.

- **Adults Only (AO)** Appropriate for ages over 18. Titles may include graphic depictions of sex and violence.

The ESRB rating is often accompanied by a *content descriptor*, which gives additional information about the title's content, such as "Contains scenes involving characters/animated/pixelated characters in the depiction of unsafe or hazardous acts or violent situations."

My game doesn't sound right

Source of the problem

Any good gamer will tell you that sound is an integral part of the gaming experience, especially when it's three-dimensional, surround sound that helps you identify the direction of an impending danger. Sophisticated sound cards can create three-dimensional sound with only two speakers, but serious gamers use four speakers for true surround sound. If your sound isn't working the way you expect, or if it doesn't sound three-dimensional, here are a few things to try.

How to fix it

1. Double-click the Volume icon on the taskbar, near the clock.

2. Make sure the Volume sliders for Volume Control, Wave, and MIDI (or Synth, Synthesizer, or SW Synth) are not at the bottom of the scale and the corresponding Mute check boxes are not selected. ▶

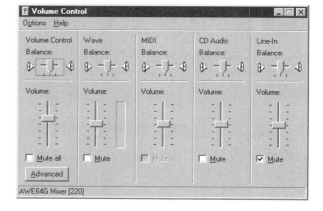

3. If your sound card has its own icon on the taskbar, double-click the icon to open the controls for the card. Look for an option with which you can enable three-dimensional sound and other features.

   If the sound card doesn't have its own icon, click Start, point to Programs, and look for a controlling program for the card.

If the sound still isn't right, you should reinstall the sound card's drivers and accompanying programs (you'll need the disk that came with the sound card) by following these steps:

1. Click Start, point to Settings, click Control Panel, and double-click Add/Remove Programs. (In Windows Me, you might be able to single-click Add/Remove Programs if it's an underlined link.)

2. On the Install/Uninstall tab in the Add/Remove Programs dialog box, select the sound card's software in the list, and click Add/Remove.

3. If you are asked whether you want to restart the computer, click No. (You still have things to do.)

4. Right-click My Computer on the desktop, and click Properties on the shortcut menu.

5. On the Device Manager tab in the System Properties dialog box, click the plus sign next to Sound, Video, And Game Controllers. ▶

6. Click your sound card in the list, and click Remove.

   Be sure to click all other entries related to your sound card, such as the joystick controller or MIDI support, and remove them too.

7. Click OK to close the System Properties dialog box.

8. Restart the computer and let it redetect the sound card and reinstall its drivers.

9. Reinstall the software for the sound card using the disk or CD that accompanied the sound card or that came with your computer.

10. Restart the computer, if necessary.

Disabling onboard sound

Some computers come with built-in sound capabilities—in the form of a chip inside the computer that can produce music and sound effects. But if you've just purchased the latest three-dimensional sound card for the ultimate gaming experience, you might need to turn off the sound capabilities in the computer so that they don't conflict with your new sound card.

Your computer's documentation should tell you whether the sound in your computer comes from an add-in board that you can easily replace or from circuitry built into the computer's main circuit board (the *motherboard*).

If you don't have the computer's documentation, shut down the computer and unplug it from the wall, and then carefully open the computer's case and look inside the computer for connections that lead from the jacks into which you plug the speakers and microphone. If these connections lead to an add-in board, you can replace the board. If they lead to plugs on the motherboard instead, you'll need to disable the sound circuitry by using the configuration program that's built into the computer. To start this program, you usually press a particular key, such as the Ctrl key, while starting the computer. Watch the screen carefully as you start the computer for a message that tells you to press a key to start the setup program.

Tip
In some computers, you disable the onboard sound controller by flipping a switch on the motherboard. If you don't have the documentation for the computer, which provides appropriate instructions, go to the Web site for the computer's manufacturer and try to obtain documentation or assistance there.

Tip
Be sure to check the sound card manufacturer's Web site for updated drivers for the sound card installed in your computer. These drivers may fix an incompatibility problem that's preventing your sound from working.

I can't connect to other players on my home network

Source of the problem

What's the point of having multiple PCs connected in a home network if you can't invite people over to play multi-player games? With a home network, you and your friends can cooperate to defeat a common enemy or engage in all-out, room-to-room warfare. Windows Me's Home Networking Wizard and the setup programs that come with home networking kits, such as home phone-line networking devices, ease the process of setting up a home network, but if you're not using Windows Me or if you can't see other players on the network, you should configure Windows for home networking manually.

How to fix it

1. If the computers on the network are sharing one of the computers' Internet connection, go to any computer other than the computer that is connected directly to the Internet. Or, if you are not sharing an Internet connection, go to any computer on the network.

2. Right-click Network Neighborhood or My Network Places (in Windows Me) on the desktop, and click Properties on the shortcut menu.

3. In the Network dialog box, click TCP/IP → [the network adapter] in the network components list, and click Properties. ▶

4. On the IP Address tab in the TCP/IP Properties dialog box, click Specify An IP Address.

5. Press Tab, and type **192.168.0.2**.

6. Press Tab again, and type **255.255.255.0**. ▶

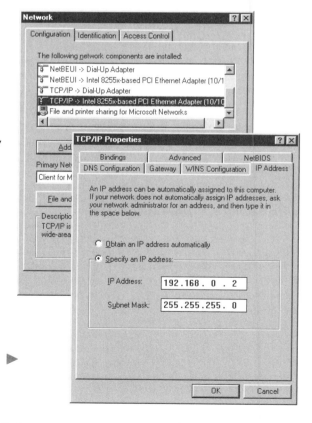

7. Click the Advanced tab, and select the Set This Protocol To Be The Default Protocol check box.

8. If you are not sharing an Internet connection provided by one of the computers on the network, click the WINS Configuration tab, click Disable WINS Resolution, and click OK. If you are sharing an Internet connection, skip this step and simply click OK.

In the Network dialog box, add the IPX/SPX-compatible protocol, if necessary, by following these steps:

1. In the Network dialog box, look for IPX/SPX-Compatible Protocol in the list of network components. If it's there, skip these two steps. If it's not there, click Add, and double-click Protocol in the Select Network Component Type dialog box.

2. In the Select Network Protocol dialog box, click Microsoft in the Manufacturers list, click IPX/SPX-Compatible Protocol in the Network Protocols list, and click OK.

Verify the computer and workgroup names and finish up by following these steps:

1. In the Network dialog box, click the Identification tab, and in the Computer Name box, type a name for the computer that's unique on the network.

2. In the Workgroup box, type an identifying name such as *MSHOME*. (MSHOME is the default workgroup name in Windows Me.) You can use any name as long as you type the same name in the Workgroup box on all the computers in your network.

3. Click OK to close the Network dialog box, and click Yes when asked whether you want to restart your computer.

4. After the computer restarts, right-click Network Neighborhood or My Network Places (in Windows Me), and click Properties on the shortcut menu.

5. In the network components list, click IPX/SPX-Compatible Protocol → Dial-Up Adapter, click Remove so that the game doesn't try to dial the modem, click OK to close the Network dialog box, and click Yes if you are asked whether you want to restart the computer.

6. Repeat the steps above on each computer in your home network, but in step 5 in the first set of steps, type **192.168.0.3** as the IP address on the next computer, type **192.168.0.4** as the IP address on the following computer, and so on.

7. Double-click Network Neighborhood or My Network Places (in Windows Me) on the desktop, and look for the other computers on your network. If you see no other computers, check the settings in the Network dialog box again.

8. Start the game on each computer, and go to the networking settings in the game. If you can, choose TCP/IP for the network protocol. Otherwise, choose IPX/SPX.

Multiplayer Internet games run too slowly

Source of the problem

Some of the games you can play across the Internet don't require blisteringly fast connections. Online chess and strategy games work just fine at any speed. Action games, on the other hand, require not only lightning reflexes but also ultrafast Internet connections; otherwise, you'll experience dreaded *lag*—that interminable pause between the moment you move the mouse and the instant your racecar begins to turn. Here are a number of steps you can take to reduce your *ping*—the time it takes for commands to get to the Internet game.

How to fix it

● Make sure no other programs that use the modem connection are running.

Remove unnecessary network protocols by following these steps:

1. Right-click Network Neighborhood or My Network Places (in Windows Me), and click Properties on the shortcut menu.

2. In the Network dialog box, click each NetBEUI entry in the network components list in turn and click Remove. Do the same for each IPX/SPX-Compatible Protocol entry. After you finish playing on line, you might need to add these protocols again to reenable your home network.

3. Click OK, and click Yes when you are asked whether you want to restart the computer.

Follow these steps to check your modem and dialing settings:

1. Download and install the latest driver for your modem.

2. Disable call waiting by pressing the number sequence on the phone's keypad that disables that service in your area.

    If you use Dial-Up Networking to establish an Internet connection, double-click Modems in Control Panel, select the modem you use for your Internet connection, click Dialing Properties, select the To Disable Call Waiting, Dial option, type the disable call-waiting sequence for your area in the box, and click OK twice to close the dialog boxes.

3. If you hear noises on the line (hisses, crackles, or static), contact your phone company and request a service visit to clear the line.

4. If you have a Winmodem, replace it with a modem that does not require Windows to operate. Winmodems are a brand of modem that rely on the computer's processor to do some of their work. They can slow your computer just when you need it running at peak performance.

Two advanced configuration changes can make a minor performance improvement:

1. Right-click Network Neighborhood or My Network Places (in Windows Me), and click Properties on the shortcut menu. In the Network dialog box, click Dial-Up Adapter and then click Properties.

2. On the Advanced tab in the Dial-Up Adapter Properties dialog box, click IP Packet Size in the Property list, click the Value down arrow, and then click Small in the list. ▶

3. Click OK, and then click OK again to close the Network dialog box. Click Yes if you are asked whether you want to restart the computer.

4. Click Start, click Run, type **regedit** in the Open box, and click OK.

5. In the left pane of the Registry Editor window, click the plus signs next to these folders in sequence: HKEY_LOCAL_MACHINE, System, CurrentControlSet, Services, Class, Net.

6. Click each of the numbered folders under Net, and look in the right pane to find the folder whose Data setting for DriverDesc is *Dial-Up Adapter*. ▶

7. Look for the SLOWNET entry in the list in the right pane, and if its Data setting is *01*, double-click SLOWNET and change the last two digits in the Value Data box from *01* to *00*.

Look for *Dial-Up Adapter*

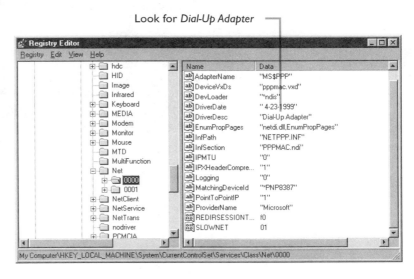

8. Close the Registry Editor, and then restart the computer.

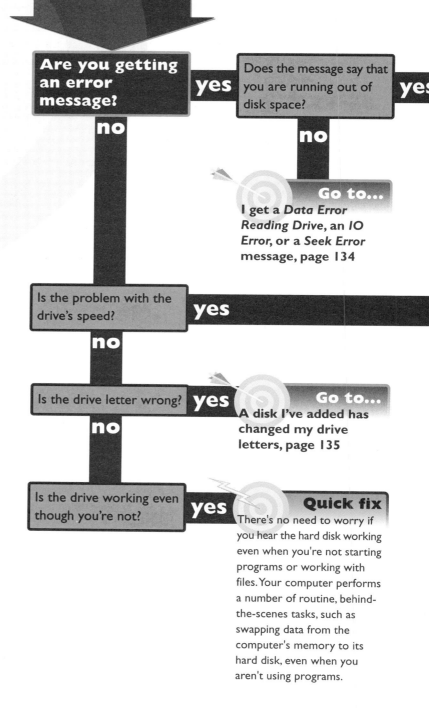

Are you getting an error message?

yes → Does the message say that you are running out of disk space?

yes →

no ↓

no →

Go to...
I get a *Data Error Reading Drive,* an *IO Error,* or a *Seek Error* message, page 134

Is the problem with the drive's speed?

yes →

no ↓

Is the drive letter wrong?

yes

Go to...
A disk I've added has changed my drive letters, page 135

no ↓

Is the drive working even though you're not?

yes

Quick fix
There's no need to worry if you hear the hard disk working even when you're not starting programs or working with files. Your computer performs a number of routine, behind-the-scenes tasks, such as swapping data from the computer's memory to its hard disk, even when you aren't using programs.

Go to...
I've run out of space on my hard disk, page 130

Are you trying to defragment the hard disk?

yes **Go to...**
The Disk Defragmenter keeps starting over, page 136

no

Go to...
My hard disk seems slower, page 234

If your solution isn't here
Check these related chapters:
  Files, page 98
  Folders, page 106
  Hardware, page 138
  Optimizing, page 226
Or see the general troubleshooting tips on page xiii

I've run out of space on my hard disk

Source of the problem

Just as clothes stuff your closets, files fill your hard disk—almost as if your files multiply when you turn your back. Eventually, your hard disk just can't store any more, but before then, inexplicable Windows problems can crop up. Hang-ups and error messages can signal a space crunch on your hard disk even before the Disk Cleanup program in Windows pops up with a message that you are running out of hard disk space. To free up space, either take the measures described here—such as emptying the Recycle Bin, removing unused programs, and converting a disk from the FAT file system to FAT32, which stores files more efficiently—or handle them through Disk Cleanup, as described in "Using Disk Cleanup," on page 133.

How to fix it

1. Double-click My Computer on the desktop, right-click the hard disk that's nearly full, and click Properties on the shortcut menu to see a pie chart showing the disk's used and free space. ▶

2. Note the name of the file system (FAT or FAT32) for later.

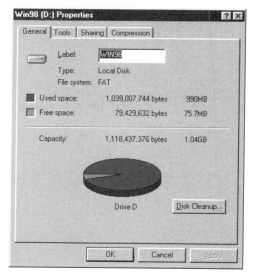

Now that you have the specifics of your disk's free space and file system, begin by running ScanDisk, which fixes errors and removes extraneous chunks of files that were left on the hard disk by programs. For more about ScanDisk, see "I Get a *Data Error Reading Drive*, an *IO Error*, or a *Seek Error* Message," on page 134.

1. Click the Tools tab in the Properties dialog box, click Check Now, and then click Start.

2. Quit ScanDisk, and click OK to close the Properties dialog box for the disk.

Next, empty the Recycle Bin by following these steps:

1. Right-click the Recycle Bin icon on the desktop, and click Empty Recycle Bin on the shortcut menu.

2. Click Yes to confirm the file deletion.

That helps your immediate disk space problem, but for a more permanent fix, remove programs and components you don't need.

1. Click Start, point to Settings, and click Control Panel.

2. In Control Panel, double-click Add/Remove Programs.

3. In the list of installed programs on the Install/Uninstall tab in the Add/Remove Programs Properties dialog box, select a program that you rarely or never use, and click Add/Remove. ▶

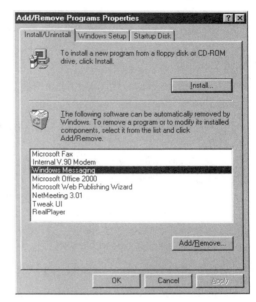

4. Follow the procedure for uninstalling the program. If you are prompted to do so, restart your computer after the removal is complete.

5. Repeat steps 1 through 4 above to remove all other programs that you use rarely or never.

6. Click Start, point to Settings, and click Control Panel. In Control Panel, double-click Add/Remove Programs again, and in the Add/Remove Programs dialog box, click the Windows Setup tab.

7. Clear the check boxes for all Windows components that you rarely or never use, and click OK to remove these components.

If you have a disk with a FAT file system, you should convert it to FAT32 by following these steps:

1. If the name of the file system you noted at the beginning of this section is FAT, click Start, point to Programs, point to Accessories, point to System Tools, and click Drive Converter (FAT32).

2. Follow the Drive Converter Wizard, clicking Next after each step, to convert the file system on the hard disk to FAT32. ▶

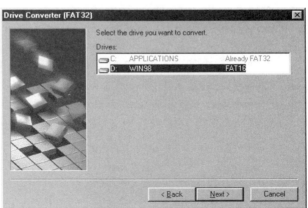

If this solution didn't solve your problem, go to the next page.

I've run out of space on my hard disk

(continued from page 131)

Another method that works well, no matter what file system you have on your hard disk, is to back up and remove files you don't need: If you have a tape backup drive or a removable disk, copy to it old or rarely needed files, and then delete those files from the hard disk. To delete other files that you might not need, follow these steps:

1. Double-click My Computer on the desktop, double-click the hard disk, and double-click the Windows folder. If you don't see a list of folders and files, click Show Files or click View The Entire Contents Of This Folder (in Windows Me). In the Windows folder, double-click the Temp folder, and delete all the files in the folder. If you get an *Access Denied* message for a file, indicating that the file is in use, delete the rest of the files.

2. Click Start, point to Settings, and click Control Panel.

3. In Control Panel, double-click Internet Options.

4. On the General tab of the Internet Properties dialog box, click Delete Files to delete temporary Internet files.

> **Windows Me**
>
> Unlike Double Space in Windows 95 and DriveSpace in Windows 98, which compress an entire hard disk, Compressed Folders in Windows Me lets you selectively compress files. You can create multiple compressed folders arranged by project, file type, or another scheme of your choosing.

Windows 98   Finally, if you're using Windows 98, you should compress your hard disk. This provides more space by shrinking files and folders when they're stored and then expanding them again when they're retrieved from the hard disk.

1. Click Start, point to Programs, point to Accessories, point to System Tools, and click DriveSpace. Click the disk you want to compress, and on the Drive menu, click Compress. ▶

2. Click Start, click Compress Now, and when the compression is complete, click Yes when you are asked whether you want to restart your computer.

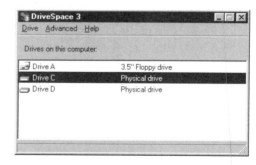

Windows Me   If you're using Windows Me, you can use the Compressed Folders system tool, which enables you to set up folders that are compressed. Any files you move to these folders will be compressed, so they're a good place to store large files such as images.

1. If you have installed Compressed Folders on the Windows Setup tab of Add/Remove Programs, double-click My Computer on the desktop and double-click the hard disk that needs more space.

2. On the File menu, point to New, and click Compressed Folder. Type a name for the folder and press Enter. Move files or other folders into the compressed folder to compress them and free up disk space. ▶

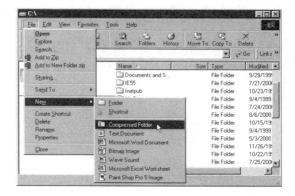

Using Disk Cleanup

In Windows 98 and Windows Me, you can perform many of the tasks listed in the steps above by using Disk Cleanup. A message box offering Disk Cleanup as an option appears when you have nearly run out of disk space on a hard disk, but you can start Disk Cleanup at any time.

Disk Cleanup scours your hard disk for files that it can remove and then reports how much hard disk space you'll gain. Before Disk Cleanup removes files, you can approve of the categories of files it will delete, and you can even view the actual files that will be removed before making the commitment.

1. Double-click My Computer on the desktop, right-click the hard disk, and click Properties on the shortcut menu.

2. In the Properties dialog box, click Disk Cleanup.

3. On the Disk Cleanup tab of the Disk Cleanup dialog box, select the check boxes for the categories of files you want to delete, clear the check boxes for the categories of files you want to keep, and then click OK. ▶

    If you want to view the files you are about to delete or delete files selectively within a category, click the View Files button. In the folder window that opens, you can delete individual files. Then close the folder window and clear the check box for the category. If the View Files button is not available, you've selected a category of files that Disk Cleanup can't show you.

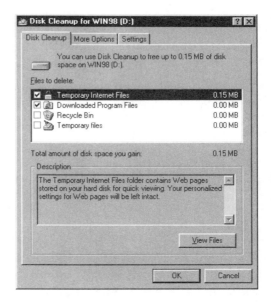

To free more space, you can click the More Options tab in the Disk Cleanup dialog box and use the additional options to remove Windows components and installed programs that you do not use.

I get a *Data Error* *Reading Drive,* an *IO Error,* or a *Seek Error* message

Source of the problem

All of these messages indicate that the hard disk either has physical damage or contains damaged files. A dropped laptop is the most common cause of a disk problem, but all mechanical components fail eventually, even well-made ones that last for years. ScanDisk, the disk error-checking program in Windows, can repair most files, and it can even attempt to repair files in areas of the hard disk that have been physically damaged.

How to fix it

1. Double-click My Computer on the desktop.

2. Right-click the hard disk, and click Properties on the shortcut menu.

3. On the Tools tab of the Properties dialog box, click Check Now.

4. In the ScanDisk dialog box, click the hard disk, and in the Type Of Test section, click Thorough. ▶

5. Select the Automatically Fix Errors check box.

6. Click Start.

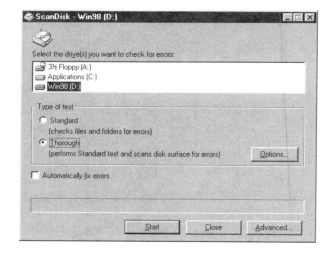

ScanDisk checks the files and folders on the disk for errors and then scans the disk surface for errors. It fixes all errors it can. If it finds damaged data, ScanDisk gives you the option of saving the data to a file or discarding the data.

If ScanDisk is unable to fix a disk, or if you continue to get error messages after using ScanDisk, contact the computer or disk manufacturer. The disk needs to be checked by a service professional.

A disk I've added has changed my drive letters

Source of the problem

Your computer assigns drive letters, such as *A:*, *C:*, and *E:*, to the floppy disks and hard disks you install, but Windows assigns drive letters to CD-ROM drives, Zip drives, USB drives, and other removable drives. If you install a program that requires a CD, for example, and then add a removable drive, the drive letter of the CD-ROM drive might change. The program will then be unable to find the CD unless you restore the original drive letter to the CD-ROM, as described here.

How to fix it

1. Right-click My Computer, and click Properties on the shortcut menu.

2. On the Device Manager tab of the System Properties dialog box, click the plus sign next to CDROM in the list of devices. If you want to change the drive letter of a Zip drive or other removable drive, click the plus sign next to Disk Drives.

3. Click the CD-ROM drive or removable drive in the list, and click Properties. ▶

4. On the Settings tab of the Properties dialog box for the drive, click the Start Drive Letter down arrow, click a drive letter in the list, and click OK. If End Drive Letter is different from Start Drive Letter, make them the same, and click OK. ▶

5. Click Yes when asked whether you want to restart your computer.

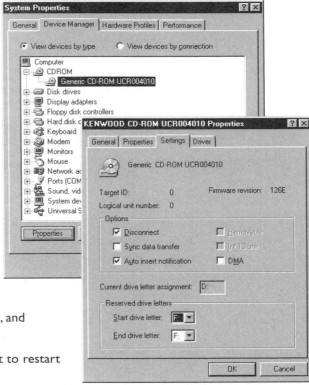

The Disk Defragmenter keeps starting over

Source of the problem

You probably know the importance of defragmenting your hard disk regularly to keep it running well. Defragmenting reassembles the chunks of files that Windows scatters across empty spots on the hard disk into complete files so that the hard disk can read them faster. But sometimes the Disk Defragmenter gets only partway through defragmenting the disk before it stops and starts over from the beginning. Defragmenting a disk isn't exactly a speedy process, so a defragmenter that keeps restarting from the beginning can make you crazy.

The solution is to stop other programs from writing to the hard disk while the Disk Defragmenter is working and to turn off the screen saver, which also makes the Disk Defragmenter loop back to the beginning.

How to fix it

1. Quit all programs that are running.

2. Press Ctrl+Alt+Delete.

3. In the Close Program dialog box, click any program in the list other than Explorer and Systray, and click End Task.

4. Repeat step 3 until you've closed all the programs except Explorer and Systray. ▶

5. In the system tray, next to the clock, right-click each icon, and click Close or Exit on the program's shortcut menu. If the shortcut menu for the program doesn't have a Close or Exit command, you can leave the program as is and go on to the next icon. ▶

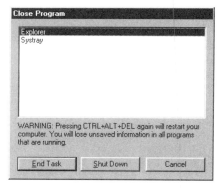

System tray icons

Now that you've closed the programs that are running, you should also disable your screen saver by following these steps:

1. Right-click the desktop, and click Properties on the shortcut menu.

2. On the Screen Saver tab of the Display Properties dialog box, click None in the Screen Saver list, and click Settings.

3. Click the Power Schemes tab in the Power Management Properties dialog box, and write yourself a note showing the settings. Click the down arrows and click Never in both the two System Standby lists and the two Turn Off Hard Disks lists, and then click OK twice to close the dialog boxes. ▶

In Windows Me, click the Power Schemes tab in the Power Options Properties dialog box, make a note of the settings, and click Never in both the Turn Off Hard Disks list and the System Stand By list. Click OK twice to close the dialog boxes. ▶

4. If you are using Microsoft Office, double-click the Find Fast icon in Control Panel (in Windows Me, click View All Control Panel Options to see the Find Fast icon), and on the Index menu in the Find Fast window, click Pause Indexing if the command is available.

5. Double-click My Computer on the desktop, right-click the hard disk you want to defragment, click Properties on the shortcut menu, and on the Tools tab of the Properties dialog box, click Defragment Now. When the Disk Defragmenter finishes, click OK to close the Properties dialog box.

6. Repeat steps 1 and 2, but select the screen saver you want in the Screen Saver list.

7. Repeat step 3, but restore the previous settings in the Power Management Properties or Power Options Properties dialog box.

8. Click Start, click Shut Down, click Restart in the Shut Down Windows dialog box, and click OK to restart the computer and restart the programs that start when Windows starts.

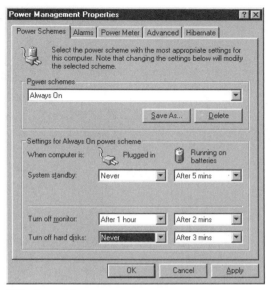

Windows 98

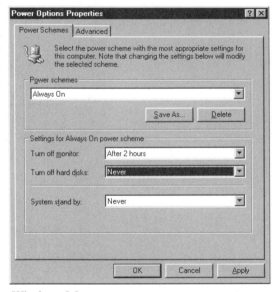

Windows Me

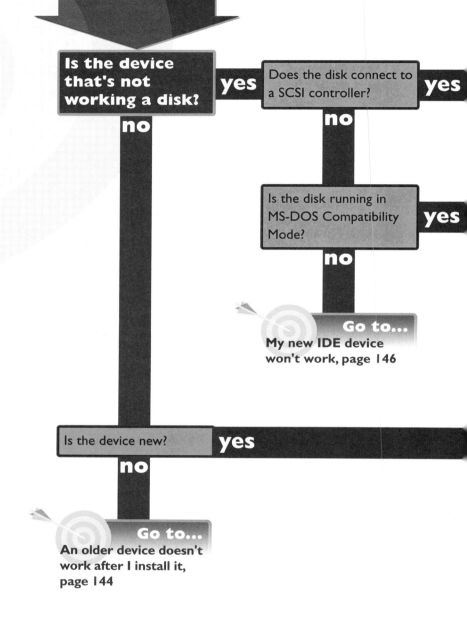

Is the device that's not working a disk?

yes — Does the disk connect to a SCSI controller? **yes**

no

Is the disk running in MS-DOS Compatibility Mode? **yes**

no

Go to...
My new IDE device won't work, page 146

Is the device new? **yes**

no

Go to...
An older device doesn't work after I install it, page 144

Go to...
My SCSI device won't
work, page 147

Quick fix

Right-click My Computer on the desktop, click Properties on the
shortcut menu, and click the Performance tab (it's good form to check
the Performance tab to make sure your system is configured for optimal
performance). If you see a message reporting that your hard disk is
running in MS-DOS Compatibility mode, you should go to the Microsoft
Knowledge Base on the Microsoft Web site (*search.support.microsoft.com/
kb/c.asp*) and follow the troubleshooting steps in article Q130179
("Troubleshooting MS-DOS Compatibility Mode on Hard Disks"),
because MS-DOS Compatibility mode slows the hard disk considerably.

Go to...
A new device I've
installed doesn't work,
page 140

If your solution isn't here
Check these related chapters:
  Hard disks, page 128
  Laptops, page 178
  Optimizing, page 226
  The screen, page 264
Or see the general troubleshooting tips on page xiii

A new device I've installed doesn't work

Source of the problem

Eight out of ten times, the solution to fixing a display adapter that won't display, a scanner that won't scan, a digital camera that won't transfer pictures, or any other device that just won't work is to remove and then reinstall the software that controls the device, called the *device driver*, or just the *driver* for short. The ninth time, the solution is to install an updated driver from the manufacturer that fixes the problem you (and others) are having. The tenth time requires more effort because it involves configuring an older device that Windows can't detect and set up automatically. That tenth time's solution is covered in "An Older Device Doesn't Work After I Install It," on page 144. Here's how to handle those first nine instances.

How to fix it

1. Right-click My Computer on the desktop, and click Properties on the shortcut menu.

2. On the Device Manager tab of the System Properties dialog box, see whether the device is visible in the list of devices. If the device isn't visible, click the plus sign next to the category of the device. ▶

    If you still do not see the device, go to "My Device Isn't Listed," on page 142.

3. Click the device in the list, and click Remove. If the Confirm Device Removal dialog box opens, click OK.

4. Click Close in the System Properties dialog box.

5. Click Start, click Shut Down, click Restart in the Shut Down Windows dialog box, and click OK.

6. If Windows can't find and reinstall the driver for the device when it restarts, it opens the Add New Hardware Wizard. Click Next on the first page of the wizard.

7. If you have a disk or CD that contains the driver for the device, insert it into the drive, click Next, and then select the Removable Media check box. ▶

In Windows 98 only, you must select the Floppy Disk Drives or CD-ROM Drive check box rather than the Removable Media check box, depending on whether you've inserted a disk or a CD, and click Next.

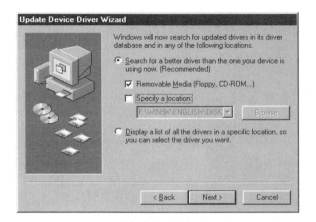

8. If you have downloaded the driver for the device from the manufacturer's Web site, select the Specify A Location check box and type the location of the driver, or click Browse to browse the folder containing the driver.

9. If the Add New Hardware Wizard reports that it has found new hardware, click Next to install the driver, and click Finish when the wizard reports that the driver is installed. Restart the computer if you are prompted to do so. ▶

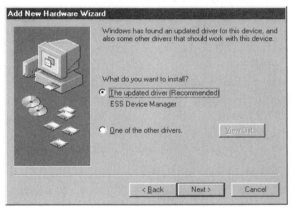

Downloading an updated driver

Most hardware manufacturers put updated device drivers on their Web sites to fix problems they've discovered or that have been reported by other users. If you can't get a device to work as expected, check the manufacturer's Web site for an updated driver for the device. Download the driver, making a note of the folder in which you've placed it, and follow these steps:

1. Right-click My Computer, click Properties on the shortcut menu, click the Device Manager tab, and in the list of devices, click the device. (Click the plus sign next to the device category if the device isn't visible.)

2. Click Properties, and on the Driver tab of the Properties dialog box, click Update Driver to open the Update Device Driver Wizard. Click Next. In Windows Me, click Specify The Location Of The Driver and then click Next.

3. Click Display A List Of All The Drivers In A Specific Location, So You Can Select The Driver You Want, and then click Next.

To continue with this solution, go to the next page.

A new device I've installed doesn't work

(continued from page 141)

4. Click Have Disk, click Browse in the Install From Disk dialog box, and select the folder to which you downloaded the driver.

5. Click OK, click your device in the list in the Select Device dialog box, click OK, click Next, and click Finish.

6. Follow the remaining steps of the wizard, and restart the computer if you are prompted to do so.

My device isn't listed

If you don't see your device listed under the proper category in the Device Manager, the driver for the device isn't installed. If the device is fairly new and it's Plug and Play compatible (the specifications on the box or in the user manual specifically include the words *Plug and Play*), you can have Windows detect the device and install the driver. If the device is somewhat older, you might need to follow the manufacturer's step-by-step instructions for installing the device. These devices usually require configuration by hand as opposed to automatic detection and configuration by Windows. For information about installing non–Plug and Play devices, see "An Older Device Doesn't Work After I Install It," on page 144.

To install a Plug and Play device, follow these steps:

1. Make sure the device is properly plugged into or attached to your computer. Unless the device is a PC card, shut down Windows and turn off the computer, and then make sure the device is inserted into a slot or plugged tightly into a port. Then restart the computer.

2. Click Start, point to Settings, and click Control Panel. (In Windows Me, click View All Control Panel Options if you see only six options in Control Panel.)

3. Double-click Add New Hardware, and click Next on the first page of the Add New Hardware Wizard. Click Next again to start the search.

4. If the wizard asks whether you want Windows to search for your new hardware, click Yes.

5. When the wizard lists the new devices it found, see whether your device is listed. If it is, make sure that the Yes, The Device Is In The List option is selected, click the device in the list, and click Next. ▶

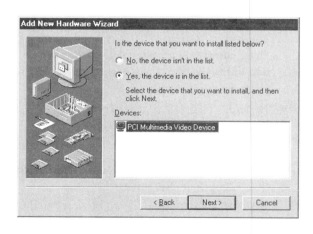

If your device is not in the list, you can still install the device, but it's not Plug and Play capable. See "An Older Device Doesn't Work After I Install It," on page 144.

6. When the Add New Hardware Wizard asks whether you want to search for the best driver or display a list of drivers, leave the Search option selected and click Next.

7. If you have an installation disk or CD that contains the driver for the device, insert it into the drive, and then click either Floppy Disk Drives or CD-ROM Drive. If you've downloaded the driver for the device, click Specify A Location and then type the location of the driver, or click Browse to browse the folder that contains the driver and click OK.

8. Click Next, and click Finish to install the driver.

Is the device disabled?

Even if a device is listed, its driver is installed, and it reports no conflicts or problems, the device won't work if it's disabled in the current hardware profile. Hardware profiles let you record different hardware configurations when you use a computer with different devices at different times. For a laptop, for example, you can have one hardware profile to use when the laptop is plugged into a docking station and a second hardware profile to use when it's independent. To make sure a device isn't disabled, in the Device Manager tab, click the device and click Properties. In the Properties dialog box, make sure the Disable In This Hardware Profile check box is cleared.

Tip
You can download many updated drivers for devices from the Microsoft Windows Update Web site. (Click Windows Update on the Start menu.) When you are asked whether you want to search for a new driver or display a list of drivers in the Add New Hardware Wizard, click Search and click Next. On the next page of the wizard, select the Microsoft Windows Update check box and click Next.

Tip
For Plug and Play to work, both your computer and the devices you install must be Plug and Play capable. Nearly all computers made within the last five years are Plug and Play capable, but if you're not sure about yours, check the computer's user guide. If the computer is not Plug and Play capable, check the manufacturer's Web site to see whether you can download and run a program that will upgrade the computer (the computer's BIOS) to Plug and Play capability.

Installing USB devices

Installing a USB device generally requires a different procedure than most other devices. Usually, before you plug in a USB device, you must install a driver by running an installation program from a disk or CD that accompanies the new device. Only after you install the driver can Windows recognize and install the USB device when it's plugged into the USB port on your computer. Before you install a USB device, carefully read the installation instructions for the device to determine how it must be installed.

An older device doesn't work after I install it

Source of the problem

The Plug and Play features in Windows assign an add-in device, such as an internal modem or a network adapter, to any available address (computers have two kinds of addresses, IRQ and I/O, both of which are limited resources in every computer), but an older device (Microsoft calls these *legacy devices*) requires a fixed address. As a result, the device may squabble with another device that wants the same address, producing a resource conflict. Resource conflicts generate error messages, or the devices involved in the battle just plain grind to a halt.

If you must use an older device (your aging, but still fully functional high-speed printer, which requires its own add-in card, for example), you have a few options. You can identify a free address and set the older device to use the address, as described below, or you can rearrange the addresses used by other devices to free them up for the older device. You can also remove or disable the older device. That's not a good solution, of course, but you may prefer it when you find out how many steps might be required to find a free resource and set a device to use it.

How to fix it

1. Make sure you have the user manual, which tells you how to set jumpers or switches on the device to change settings like the IRQ, DMA, and I/O address.

     If you do not have this information, you won't be able to complete this procedure. Try the manufacturer's Web site to obtain the information, or look on the device itself. Sometimes the information is printed right on the device.

2. Right-click My Computer on the desktop, and click Properties on the shortcut menu.

3. On the Device Manager tab of the System Properties dialog box, look in the list of devices to see whether the icon for the older device shows a yellow exclamation point or a red check mark. These symbols can indicate that the device has a problem such as a resource conflict. ▶

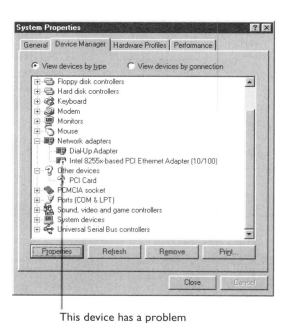

This device has a problem

4. Click the older device, and click Properties. The Conflicting Device List in the Properties dialog box identifies the resource conflict. ▶

5. In the Properties dialog box, click the Resources tab, and clear the Use Automatic Settings check box.
If the Properties dialog box doesn't have a Resources tab, you can't change its resources, so you must change other, conflicting devices instead.

6. Click the Setting Based On down arrow, and click a different basic configuration in the list.

7. Examine the Conflicting Device List to see whether the list reports No Conflicts. If so, make a note of the setting, click OK to try the new setting, and then click Yes when the Creating A Forced Configuration message box appears.

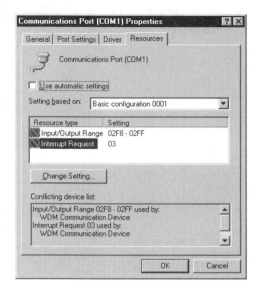

8. Shut down the computer, remove the device from the computer, and change the jumper or switch on the device to match the setting you've changed.

9. Restart the computer and try using the older device again. If it still doesn't work, repeat steps 2 through 8, choosing different basic configurations in step 6 until the device works. If you exhaust basic configuration options without getting the device to work, continue to step 10.

> **Tip**
> Some devices come with installation programs that you can run to change the settings on the device. Check the user manual for the device to determine the procedure you need to follow.

10. In the Resource Type column on the Resources tab in the device's Properties dialog box, click a resource type and click Change Setting. If the error message *This resource setting cannot be modified* appears, click a different resource type.

11. In the Edit dialog box, scroll through the settings in the Value box, and click a different setting when the Conflicting Device List box reports No Conflicts.

12. Click OK, click OK again, click Yes when the Creating A Forced Configuration message box appears, and restart the computer. If the device still doesn't work, continue trying other available settings for the resource until you find one that works.

When to give up

Finding resources that don't conflict and getting a device to work with those resources can be a laborious task. Before you waste all that time, see whether you can buy a new, Plug and Play version of the device. Check the manufacturer's Web site for information or go to a computer mail-order company's Web site. You might be surprised to find that the new device is much less expensive than you'd anticipated and that it offers new features that will be well worth the cost.

My new IDE device won't work

Source of the problem

The hard disk in most popular computer models connects to an IDE (Integrated Drive Electronics) connection within the computer, the most popular type of connection for disk drives. Some CD-ROM drives and tape backup drives also connect to an IDE connection.

When you buy a computer, its hard disk is usually configured properly (in fact, Windows is usually installed so you can turn on the computer and get right to work or play), but when you need to add or replace a hard disk, you must be careful to use the correct IDE settings when you configure the computer or the IDE device won't work.

How to fix it

1. Make sure to set one hard disk as the *master* and the other hard disk as the *slave* if you connect two hard disks to the same IDE cable in your computer. Usually, you choose the master or slave designation for a hard disk by changing the position of a small electrical connector on the disk called a jumper. Check the hard disk's manual for information about changing the jumper.

2. Make sure that the secondary IDE connection has not been disabled if you've added the hard disk to the second IDE connection in the computer. You can enable the secondary IDE connection by using the computer's BIOS configuration program. Check your computer's user manual to determine how to start the BIOS configuration or setup program. (In many computers, you start the BIOS configuration program by pressing the Delete key while the computer is starting.)

3. Check the user manual for the hard disk to determine the *mode* in which your hard disk operates, and then use the computer's BIOS configuration or setup program to choose the correct mode. IDE hard disks operate in one of several modes; these modes determine the speed of the connection.

4. Make sure that the cable connecting the IDE connection and the hard disk is not connected upside down. Both the IDE connection and the hard disk should have an end labeled *1* or *Pin 1*, which corresponds to the side of the cable that's marked with a stripe.

My SCSI device won't work

Source of the problem

Although most popular computers use IDE hard disks, in which the controlling electronics for the disk are embedded right in the disk drive, computers designed for sophisticated applications such as video editing and computer graphics often use Small Computer System Interface (SCSI, pronounced "scuzzy") hard disks, which connect to a SCSI controller in the computer.

You can trace most glitches with SCSI devices to two problems: an incorrect SCSI ID number assigned to the device (each device requires a unique number), and lack of termination of the SCSI cables (every SCSI circuit needs to be capped off at both ends by a terminator). But you should also ensure that the SCSI controller is properly configured in Windows. Here's how to fix all these problems.

How to fix it

1. Start the configuration program for the SCSI controller card using the instructions in the SCSI controller card's documentation. Usually you start the configuration program by pressing a combination of keys while the computer is starting.

2. In the configuration program, select the option that lists the SCSI ID numbers and the devices that are assigned to numbers to find an available SCSI ID number.

3. Change the device's SCSI ID number to an available SCSI ID number. Consult the device's user manual to learn how. No two devices may be assigned to the same ID number.

   Make sure the hard disk is set to SCSI ID 0 if the hard disk is the primary hard disk in your computer and the one that the computer uses when it boots.

4. Make sure that the connection between the SCSI controller and the hard disk is properly terminated at both ends. To terminate a SCSI cable, you attach a plug called a SCSI terminator. Most SCSI controller cards terminate themselves automatically. Check the controller's user manual for instructions about terminating the controller.

5. Right-click My Computer, and click Properties on the shortcut menu. On the Device Manager tab of the System Properties dialog box, click the plus sign next to SCSI Controllers, click the SCSI controller card, and click Properties. On the General tab of the Properties dialog box for the card, make sure you see This Device Is Working Properly in the Device Status section. If this does not appear, follow the procedure in "A New Device I've Installed Doesn't Work," on page 140.

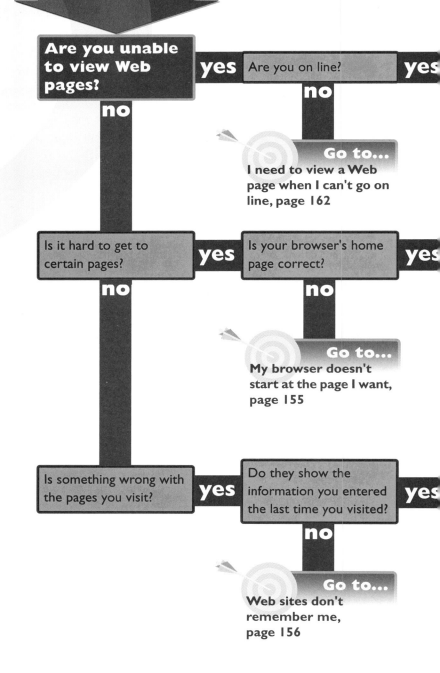

Are you unable to view Web pages?

yes → Are you on line? **yes**

no ↓

Go to...
I need to view a Web page when I can't go on line, page 162

Is it hard to get to certain pages?

yes → Is your browser's home page correct? **yes**

no ↓

Go to...
My browser doesn't start at the page I want, page 155

Is something wrong with the pages you visit?

yes → Do they show the information you entered the last time you visited? **yes**

no ↓

Go to...
Web sites don't remember me, page 156

Do you see an error message?

yes

Go to...
I get a message saying *The page cannot be displayed*, page 150

no

Go to...
Internet Explorer crashes, page 158

Are you getting a message about authorization?

yes

Go to...
I get a message saying *You are not authorized to view this page,* page 161

no

Quick fix

Windows Me hides favorites you haven't used for a while. To show all favorites, follow these steps:

1. On the Tools menu in Internet Explorer, click Internet Options.

2. On the Advanced tab of the Internet Options dialog box, clear the Enable Personalized Favorites check box, and click OK.

Are they missing pictures and sound?

yes

Go to...
Web pages don't show pictures or play sound, page 154

If your solution isn't here
Check these related chapters:
Dial-Up Networking, page 34
Downloading files, page 56
E-mail, receiving page 66
Internet, connecting to, page 164
Or see the general troubleshooting tips on page xiii

I get a message saying
The page cannot be displayed

Source of the problem

Whenever Internet Explorer can't display a Web page, it shows instead a page that reads *The page cannot be displayed*. Either Internet Explorer can't reach the Web page you've requested, or it found the Web site but the browser's configuration is keeping it from showing the page. To find the culprit and fix the problem, you need to first rule out a number of possible causes, such as the connection, the Web page address, and proxy settings.

How to fix it

1. Connect to the Internet. If your computer dials an Internet connection when you start Internet Explorer or your e-mail program, go ahead and start Internet Explorer.

2. Click Start, click Run, and in the Run dialog box, type **winipcfg** in the Open box and click OK.

3. In the IP Configuration dialog box, click More Info, make a note of the address (the four numbers separated by periods—such as 192.168.0.1) shown in the DNS Servers box, and click OK. ▶

4. Click Start, point to Programs (in Windows Me, also point to Accessories), and click MS-DOS Prompt.

5. At the prompt, type **ping** followed by a space and then the exact address you recorded in step 3, and then press Enter. ▶

   The Ping command tells you how many packets of information it sent to the address you specified and how many were received back. If you received four packets, your Internet connection is fine. If all four packets were lost, your Internet connection is not working. If you received only two or three of the four packets, your Internet connection is working, but not

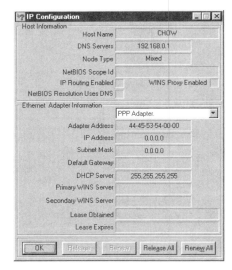

reliably. To learn how to troubleshoot your Internet connection, see "I Can't Connect to My Internet Service Provider," on page 168.

6. Close the MS-DOS Prompt window.

If your computer connects to the Internet through a network, you may need to enter *proxy settings* because your computer must communicate with the Internet through a *proxy server.* Proxy servers protect your computer from being exposed on the Internet. If your ISP or your network administrator has not told you to use proxy settings, skip to "More Sleuthing," on the next page.

1. Click Start, point to Settings, and click Control Panel.

2. Double-click Internet if you use Internet Explorer 4 or Internet Options if you use Internet Explorer 5. In Windows Me, double-click Internet Options.

3. In the Internet Properties dialog box, click the Connection tab (Internet Explorer 4) or the Connections tab (Internet Explorer 5).

4. If you use Internet Explorer 4, select the Access The Internet Using A Proxy Service check box, and in the Address and Port boxes, type the information given to you by your ISP or network administrator. Click OK. ▶

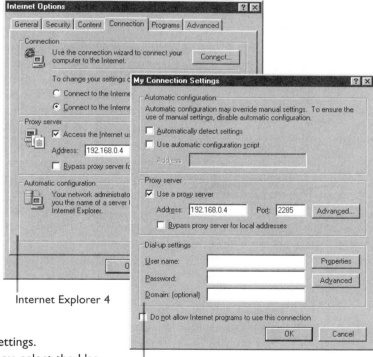

Internet Explorer 4

Internet Explorer 5 and Dial-Up Networking

If you use Internet Explorer 5 and a Dial-Up Networking connection to connect to an ISP, click the connection in the Dial-Up Settings list in the Internet Options dialog box, and click Settings. If you are connected to a network that provides Internet access, click LAN Settings.

In the Settings dialog box, select the Use A Proxy Server check box, and in the Address and Port boxes, enter the information given to you by your ISP or network administrator. Then click OK. ▶

If this solution didn't solve your problem, go to the next page.

I get a message saying *The page cannot be displayed*

(continued from page 151)

More sleuthing

If your connection isn't the problem, perhaps it's the Web page address, the temporary Internet files, or the version of the Winsock file you're using. Here's how to check these possibilities:

1. Carefully check the address you typed in Internet Explorer's Address bar for typos. An extra space, an incorrect letter, or an extra or missing period might be the problem. ▶

   If you clicked a link rather than typed an address, the link could be wrong. Click another link to jump to another Web page. If that works, you might be able to reach your destination by going to the home page of the Web site (type only the address portion, ending in .com, .net, or .org, without anything following) and then navigating to the page from there.

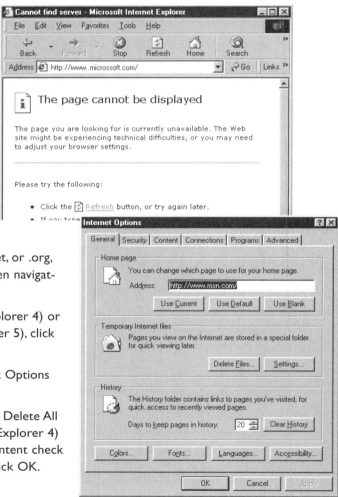

2. On the View menu (in Internet Explorer 4) or the Tools menu (in Internet Explorer 5), click Internet Options.

3. On the General tab of the Internet Options dialog box, click Delete Files. ▶

4. In the Delete Files dialog box, click Delete All Subscription Content (in Internet Explorer 4) or select the Delete All Offline Content check box (in Internet Explorer 5), and click OK. Click OK again.

If this step fixes the problem, click Internet Options on the Tools or View menu again, and on the General tab of the Internet Options dialog box, click Settings. Under Amount Of Disk Space To Use, drag the slider slightly to the right so that Internet Explorer won't run short of temporary file space again, click OK, and click OK again.

5. Click Start, point to Find or Search (in Windows Me), and click Files Or Folders or For Files Or Folders (in Windows Me).

6. In the Find All Files dialog box, type **Winsock.dll** in the Named box, click the Look In down arrow, click Local Hard Drives in the list, and click Find Now. Or in the Search Results dialog box (in Windows Me), type **Winsock.dll** in the Search For Files Or Folders Named box, click the Look In down arrow, click Local Hard Drives in the list, and click Search Now. ▶

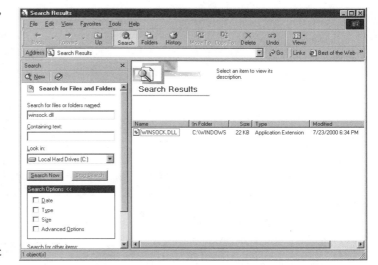

7. In the list of found files, right-click each Winsock.dll file that is *not* located in the Windows or Windows\System folder, click Rename, and rename the file Winsock.tmp to make sure it will not be used by Windows.

8. Repeat steps 6 and 7, but search for copies of Winsock32.dll, Wsock.vxd, and Wsock32.vxd that are not located in the Windows or Windows\System folder. Rename each of these using .tmp as the new file extension.

If deleting duplicate Winsock files fixes the problem but one of your Internet programs no longer functions properly, check the manufacturer of the malfunctioning program's Web site for assistance.

If all else fails, try again a little while later. The Web site might be overloaded with other users or temporarily unable to send the Web page.

Web pages don't show pictures or play sound

Source of the problem

To speed up Web browsing, particularly when you're using a slow modem line, you can turn off graphics, multimedia, videos, and sounds and view only the text on Web pages. Text comes in across a slow modem line quickly; everything else takes much longer. But if you don't see pictures when you want them and you can't hear sounds or play multimedia files, you need to reenable multimedia and graphics.

How to fix it

1. Double-click the Internet Explorer icon on the desktop.

2. On the View menu (in Internet Explorer 4) or the Tools menu (in Internet Explorer 5), click Internet Options.

3. In the Internet Options dialog box, click the Advanced tab, and select the Play Animations, Play Sound, Play Videos, and Show Pictures check boxes under Multimedia in the list. ▶

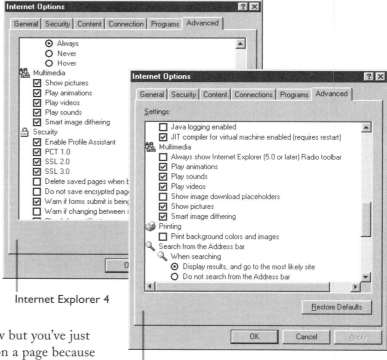

Internet Explorer 4

Internet Explorer 5

Showing one picture

If you've intentionally turned off graphics because your modem connection is slow but you've just got to see a particular picture on a page because the text that appears in its place is so tantalizing, right-click the placeholder text, and click Show Picture on the shortcut menu.

My browser doesn't start at the page I want

Source of the problem

Unless you specify a different home page, each time you start your Web browser you'll see the default home page. In Internet Explorer, the initial default home page is *www.msn.com*, but other browsers have their own initial default home pages that can be changed.

MSN is a great starting place for your exploration of the Web, but you might want to change your home page to another Internet portal that offers similarly helpful information like news, stock market updates, movie reviews, and television schedules, or you might want to start at a Web page devoted to your hobby or special interest. Of course, if you've created your own Web site, you can make it your home page.

How to fix it

1. Double-click the Internet Explorer icon on the desktop.

2. In the Address bar, type the address of the Web page that you'd like to make your new home page, and press Enter.

3. On the View menu (in Internet Explorer 4) or the Tools menu (in Internet Explorer 5), click Internet Options.

4. On the General tab in the Internet Options dialog box, click Use Current in the Home Page section, and click OK. ▶

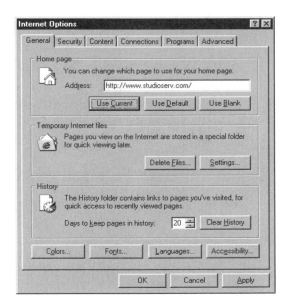

Going home

Clicking the Home button on the Internet Explorer toolbar always takes you back to your home page.

Web sites don't remember me

Source of the problem

Many Web sites send your computer very small files called *cookies* so that they can identify you the next time you visit. When you return to a site that has sent a cookie, the site retrieves the cookie, identifies you, and personalizes the Web pages you see. But if you have Internet Explorer set to refuse cookies because you're worried about privacy, Web sites can't tell that you're a returnee, so they can't display your personalized information. An online shopping site, for example, can't greet you by name and display products that fit the interests you identified on an earlier visit. If you mind that Web sites that greeted you warmly in the past have now forgotten who you are, you need to restore Internet Explorer's ability to accept cookies.

How to fix it (in Internet Explorer 4)

1. Double-click the Internet Explorer icon on the desktop.

2. On the View menu, click Internet Options.

3. In the Internet Options dialog box, click the Advanced tab, click Always Accept Cookies under Cookies in the list, and click OK. ▶

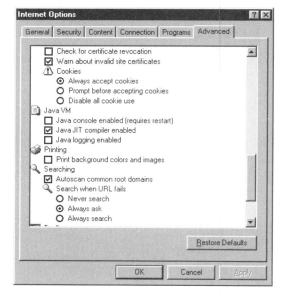

How to fix it (in Internet Explorer 5)

1. Double-click the Internet Explorer icon on the desktop.

2. On the Tools menu, click Internet Options.

3. In the Internet Options dialog box, click the Security tab, drag the Security Level For This Zone slider from High to Medium, and click OK. (In Windows Me, you'll need to click Default Level to see the Security Level For This Zone slider.) ▶ facing page

If the Security Level is already at Medium or lower, click Custom Level, click Enable under Allow Cookies That Are Stored On Your Computer in the Settings list, and click OK. ▶ below

4. Click OK again to close the Internet Options dialog box.

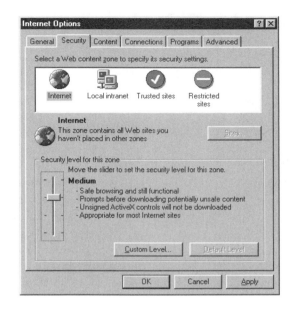

Choosing your cookies

Rather than reject all cookies outright or accept every cookie a Web site sends your way, you can review each cookie when it arrives and decide whether you want to accept or reject it. This gives you the ultimate in control, but it can also make browsing annoying, as endless messages about incoming cookies pop up. To try this option, follow the steps for enabling cookies above, but instead of choosing Enable, choose Prompt Before Accepting Cookies (in Internet Explorer 4) or Prompt (in Internet Explorer 5). When you see how many cookies arrive, you'll almost certainly want to avoid being prompted about each one.

Worried about your privacy?

Cookies give Web site operators the ability to store information on your hard disk about you and your visit. The cookies record your personal preferences, selections you've made, or any other personal information that you've entered in forms. Cookies were established as a convenience, enabling you to return to a Web site, receive a personalized greeting, and find all your preferences instituted. The Web site reads your cookie and puts all your customized settings in place. But cookies can also be used to track you on line, and they allow those who create Web sites to create a profile about you without your realizing it.

Whether you choose to accept cookies or universally reject them is up to you. But if you reject cookies, you'll be trading convenience for privacy on the odd chance that a Web site has malicious intent. Remember, cookies can store only the information that you've entered about yourself at a Web site, so you might want to focus your efforts on being cautious about the information you choose to reveal.

Internet Explorer crashes

Source of the problem

If you get an error message when you try to open a Web page, if Internet Explorer stops responding as you scroll through a page, or if Internet Explorer won't display a full page, you should systematically eliminate a number of possible causes, including clearing the Internet Explorer cache and history folders, which might contain a bad file; giving Internet Explorer more Windows resources; updating the display drivers for your video adapter; updating the DirectX software that helps display graphics; and removing old cookies, which keep a record of visits to each Web site. Any one of these items could cause Internet Explorer to crash. In addition, there could be a problem with the TCP/IP protocol that your computer uses to communicate with Web pages. If all else fails, you should delete and reinstall TCP/IP, as described in "Reinstalling TCP/IP," on page 160.

How to fix it

1. Start Internet Explorer, and on the View menu (in Internet Explorer 4) or the Tools menu (in Internet Explorer 5), click Internet Options.

2. On the General tab of the Internet Options dialog box, click Delete Files, click OK, click Clear History, and click Yes. ▶

3. In Internet Explorer 4, click the Advanced tab, and under Browsing in the Settings list, select the Browser In A New Process check box.

   In Internet Explorer 5, select the Launch Browser Windows In A Separate Process check box. (Internet Explorer 5.5 does not have this option.) ▶ facing page

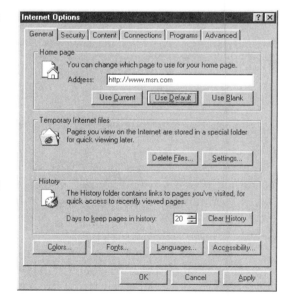

In addition to these changes, you should make sure you've installed the latest driver for your display adapter as Internet Explorer uses the drivers to display Web page graphics.

1. Check the manufacturer's Web site for an updated driver, and if a new driver is available, see "Downloading an Updated Driver," on page 141.

If an updated driver is not available, click Internet Options on the View menu (in Internet Explorer 4) or the Tools menu (in Internet Explorer 5). In the Internet Options dialog box, click the Advanced tab, and clear the Use Smooth Scrolling check box.

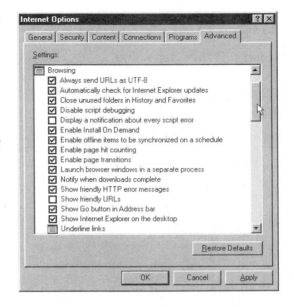

2. Install the latest version of DirectX after downloading it from *www.microsoft.com/directx/homeuser/downloads/default.asp.*

Check to make sure TCP/IP is working by following these steps:

1. Click Start, point to Programs (in Windows Me, also point to Accessories), and click MS-DOS Prompt.

2. In the MS-DOS Prompt window, type **ping 127.0.0.1** at the prompt, and press Enter.

If you see a *Request timed out* or *Transmit failed* error message, go to "Reinstalling TCP/IP," on page 160.

Finally, if Internet Explorer still crashes, check to see whether a cookie is causing a problem by following these steps:

1. Double-click My Computer on the desktop, and in the My Computer window, double-click your hard disk.

2. Double-click the Windows folder to open it, click Show Files (in Windows 98) or View The Entire Contents Of This Folder (in Windows Me), and double-click the Cookies folder.

3. Select all the files in the Cookies window except index.dat, press Ctrl+X to cut them, and close the Cookies window.

4. Right-click the desktop, point to New, and click Folder. Type **Cookies**, press Enter, and press Ctrl+V to paste the cookies in the new folder.

If Internet Explorer now works without crashing, copy a few of the cookies back to the Cookies folder in the Windows folder and try browsing again. Continue to copy cookies back to the original Cookies folder until you get an error message. When this happens, cut the last few cookies you copied and copy them back one by one until you get an error message. Delete the last cookie you copied—it's the one causing the problem.

5. Delete the Cookies folder on the desktop.

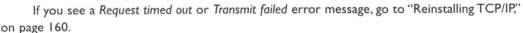

If this solution didn't solve your problem, go to the next page.

Internet Explorer crashes

(continued from page 159)

Reinstalling TCP/IP

If none of the other solutions has prevented Internet Explorer from continuing to crash, it's possible that one of the files for the TCP/IP protocol that your computer uses to communicate with the Internet has been damaged. Because you can't repair or replace individual files, you should remove TCP/IP and reinstall it by following these steps:

1. Right-click Network Neighborhood or My Network Places (in Windows Me) on the desktop, and click Properties on the shortcut menu.

2. On the Configuration tab in the Network dialog box, click one of the network components that is labeled TCP/IP, and click Remove. ▶

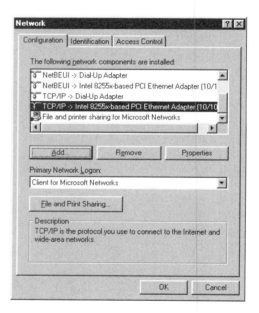

3. Repeat step 2, clicking other TCP/IP-related network components and clicking Remove until all are removed.

4. Click OK, and click Yes when you are asked whether you want to restart the computer.

5. Click Start, point to Settings, and click Control Panel.

6. In Control Panel, double-click Network. (In Windows Me, you might need to click View All Control Panel Options to see the Network option.)

7. On the Configuration tab in the Network dialog box, click Add.

8. In the Select Network Component Type dialog box, click Protocol and click Add.

9. In the Select Network Protocol dialog box, click Microsoft in the Manufacturers list, click TCP/IP in the Network Protocols list, and click OK.

10. Click OK to close the Network dialog box.

11. If you are asked whether you want to keep the newer version of each file, click No. Click Yes when you are asked whether you want to restart the computer.

I get a message saying *You are not authorized to view this page*

Source of the problem

Most public Web sites are open to everyone—in fact, the more, the merrier. Companies work hard to attract people to their Web sites. But some sites are reserved for private use. They provide information for the customers of the company, or they provide services to employees. You're most likely to encounter a private site if you work in a company that lets departments set up internal Web sites. If you're not a member of the department, you're politely rebuffed with a *You are not authorized to view this page* message.

Webmasters, the people who create and control Web sites, can selectively provide permission to access their sites on the Internet by requiring a user name and password. In a corporate network, Webmasters have more control and can grant admission to people based on their network logon names or the departments to which they belong.

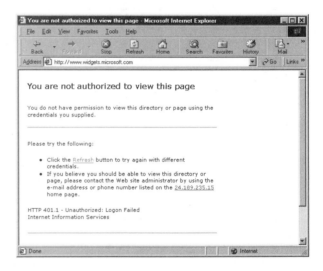

How to fix it

● Contact the Webmaster for the site or your network administrator to obtain a user name and password for the site.

● If you're on a company network, make sure you log on to Windows with your proper user name and password. Don't press Esc or click Cancel in the Windows logon dialog box.

I need to view a Web page when I can't go on line

Source of the problem

Internet Explorer 5 has perfected the fine art of making Web pages available even when you can't connect to the Internet. Of course, when you're not connected, you can't visit new Web sites or update the information on a page, but you can save a page for viewing later by making it available offline. Then when you need to refer to the information on a page, you can view it in Internet Explorer almost as if you were still connected to the Internet.

Internet Explorer 4 gave you the ability to view Web pages off line too, but it was extremely complicated. It's so much easier in Internet Explorer 5 that the improved offline viewing feature alone makes it worthwhile to download the free upgrade to Internet Explorer 5.

How to fix it (in Internet Explorer 5)

Internet Explorer 5

1. Connect to the Internet and, in Internet Explorer, open the Web page you want to view when you're off line.

2. On the Favorites menu, click Add To Favorites.

3. In the Add Favorite dialog box, select the Make Available Offline check box. ▶

4. Enter a more memorable name in the Name box if you want.

5. Click Customize.

6. On the first page of the Offline Favorite Wizard, click Next.

7. On the next page of the wizard, click No if the current Web page is the only page you want to view off line or click Yes if you'll also want to view the pages that are linked to the current page. ▶

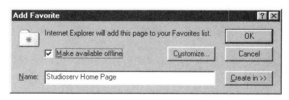

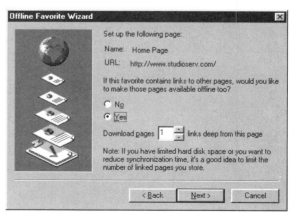

If you click Yes, you can then change the number in the Download Pages box to download additional pages that are linked to the page you're making available off line.

8. Click Next.

9. If you want the page updated (synchronized) on a regular schedule, click Next, and on the next page of the wizard, click I Would Like To Create A New Schedule and click Next. If you'd rather update the page only when you want (by clicking Synchronize on the Tools menu), just click Next and skip to step 10.

10. On the next page of the wizard, type an interval and a time for the page to be synchronized, type a more recognizable name for the schedule if you want, and click Next. ▶

You can also select the check box on this page of the wizard if you want Windows to connect to the Internet at the designated times.

11. If the site requires a password, click the Yes option on the next page of the wizard, enter your user name, and enter the password twice.

12. Click Finish, and click OK.

Tip

Before you save a page for offline viewing, it's best to navigate to the main Web page on the Web site, which contains links to this and other pages you might be interested in viewing off line.

Offline Favorite Wizard

When would you like to synchronize this page?

Every 1 days at 12:54 PM

Name: My Scheduled Update

☐ If my computer is not connected when this scheduled synchronization begins, automatically connect for me

< Back   Next >   Cancel

Viewing an offline page

Later you can view the offline page that you have synchronized.

1. Double-click the Internet Explorer icon on the desktop, and on the File menu in Internet Explorer, click Work Offline.

2. On the Standard Buttons toolbar, click the Favorites button.

3. In the Favorites list, click the link for the Web page.

Tip

To remove a page you've downloaded for viewing off line, right-click the link in the Favorites list, and clear the Make Available Offline check box. Then, in the Confirm Offline Item Delete dialog box, click Yes.

Changing the synchronization schedule

To modify the schedule of links you download, right-click the link to the synchronized Web page in the Favorites list, and click Properties on the shortcut menu. The options on the Schedule and Download tabs of the Properties dialog box let you define how much information you'll download at each synchronization and modify when the synchronizations will occur.

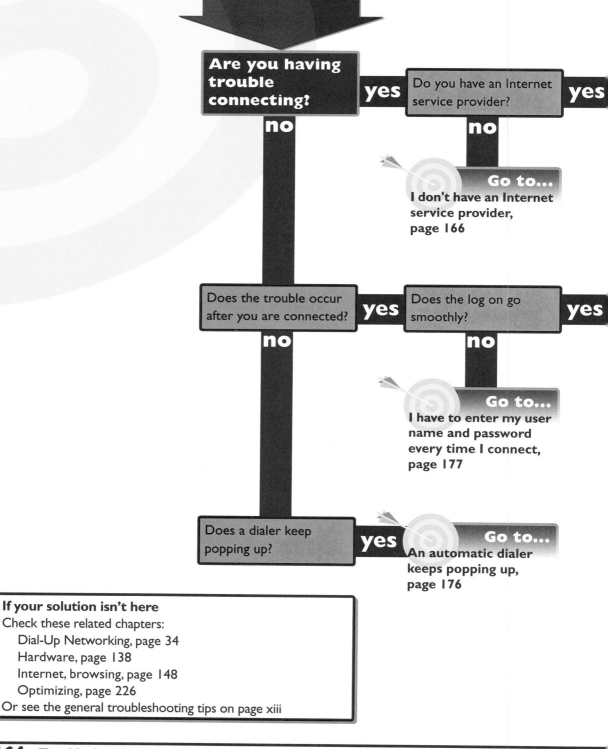

Are you having trouble connecting?

yes → **Do you have an Internet service provider?** **yes**

no ↓

no ↓

Go to...
I don't have an Internet service provider, page 166

Does the trouble occur after you are connected?

yes → **Does the log on go smoothly?** **yes**

no ↓

no ↓

Go to...
I have to enter my user name and password every time I connect, page 177

Does a dialer keep popping up?

yes →

Go to...
An automatic dialer keeps popping up, page 176

If your solution isn't here
Check these related chapters:
Dial-Up Networking, page 34
Hardware, page 138
Internet, browsing, page 148
Optimizing, page 226
Or see the general troubleshooting tips on page xiii

Can Windows make the connection? **yes** Does it take forever to connect? **yes**

Go to...
Connecting takes a long time, page 172

no

no

Go to...
I can't connect to my Internet service provider, page 168

Does it take forever to dial? **yes**

Quick fix
To save a little time whenever your modem dials, follow these steps, which will make the modem dial faster:

1. Click Start, point to Settings, and click Control Panel.

2. Double-click Modems. (In Windows Me, you might have to click View All Control Panel Options first.)

3. Click the modem you use and click Properties.

4. In the Properties dialog box, click the Connection tab, and click Advanced,

5. In the Advanced Connection Settings dialog box, type s11=50 in the Extra Settings box, and click OK.

6. Click OK, click Close, and close Control Panel.

Do you lose the connection? **yes**

Go to...
I frequently lose my connection to the Internet, page 174

I don't have an Internet service provider

Source of the problem

You can't browse the Web without signing up with an Internet service provider (ISP). An ISP provides phone numbers your modem can dial to connect your computer to the Internet. Once you're connected, you can visit Web sites, send and receive e-mail messages, download files, participate in online communities, and take advantage of other services, like videoconferencing and chatting.

Online services, such as America Online, also act as ISPs. They provide Internet connections as well as offering services exclusively for their members, including online news and information, chat rooms, message boards, and e-mail addresses.

Finding an ISP is not hard. Lots of ISPs are looking for your business, and a local ISP probably advertises in your hometown newspaper. But if you don't know where to start or how to get connected, you can take advantage of the Internet Connection Wizard in Windows 98 and Windows Me, which helps you choose an ISP and set up a membership.

How to fix it

1. Double-click the Connect To The Internet icon on the desktop. If the icon is not available, click Start, point to Programs, and point to Accessories. In Windows 98, point to Internet Tools, and click Internet Connection Wizard. In Windows Me, point to Communications, and click Internet Connection Wizard.

2. On the first page of the Internet Connection Wizard, make sure the I Want To Sign Up For A New Internet Account option is selected, and click Next. ▶

3. If the wizard displays multiple phone numbers, click a number and click Next.

4. The wizard connects to the Microsoft Internet Referral Service and downloads information about ISPs in your area. In the Internet Service Providers list, click each

ISP to read about its services and rates. ▶

5. Click the ISP you want to use, and click Next.

6. Follow the remaining steps of the wizard, clicking Next after each step.

The wizard will set up an icon on the desktop that you can double-click to sign up for membership, or it will request the information it needs to set up your account at the ISP and then set up an icon that you can double-click to connect to the ISP.

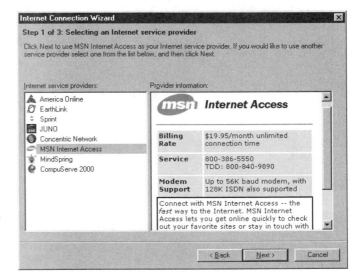

Signing up independently

The Internet Connection Wizard can sign you up with a large, national ISP that offers phone numbers in your area code, but you might prefer to sign up with a local ISP, one that offers a phone number that's a local call. A local ISP also might provide news and services specific to your community and might host your personal or business Web site (although some national ISPs also let you set up home pages).

You can probably find a local ISP by asking friends or by checking in the yellow pages or in the ads in your local newspaper. Another option is to visit a school, library, or cybercafe that offers Internet access and go to a Web site that lists ISPs, such as *www.thelist.com* or *www.isp.com*.

Tip
Before you sign up with any ISP, make sure their phone number is a local call from your home. Also look for unlimited usage for your monthly fee, and be sure to inquire about a setup or activation fee. If you'd like to create your own home page, find out whether the ISP offers Web space that's either free or available for a small monthly fee.

When you don't need to find an ISP

Companies that offer cable modem or Digital Subscriber Line (DSL) service (see "The wonder of a full-time Internet connection," on page 173) can act as your ISP. For a monthly fee, they provide unlimited Internet access, and they usually provide an e-mail address too. But if you want to take advantage of the extra benefits of an online service such as America Online or MSN, you can still sign up for a membership and connect to the online service through your high-speed cable modem or DSL line.

Tip
Free ISPs offer free Web access, but you may have to look at advertising in your browser window.

I can't connect to my Internet service provider

Source of the problem

After you sign up for an account with an Internet service provider (ISP), the ISP you've chosen should provide you with all the information you need to set up a connection. Some ISPs even send disks or CDs with programs you can run to create and configure a connection in Dial-Up Networking. But if you've had a connection running in the past and you can no longer connect, you should check for an incorrect password or phone number, a modem problem, or a corrupt password list by following these steps.

How to fix it

1. Double-click My Computer, and double-click Dial-Up Networking. In Windows Me, click Start, point to Settings, click Dial-Up Networking, and skip to step 3.

2. Click Settings on the Connections menu of the Dial-Up Networking window, select the Prompt For Information Before Dialing check box, and click OK. ▶

3. In Dial-Up Networking, double-click the connection you use to connect to your ISP.
   If your connection is not listed, see "My Dial-Up Networking Connection Is Missing," on page 170.

4. In the Connect To dialog box, verify that the entries in the User Name and Password boxes exactly match those you chose when you set up the ISP account or that were given to you by your ISP, including the capitalization of the letters in your user name. Also, retype your password. ▶

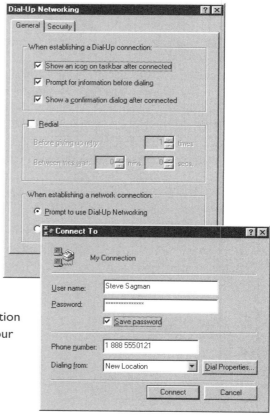

Some ISPs require you to enter a prefix and slash before your user name, such as *MSN/*. If your ISP does, make sure the appropriate prefix precedes your user name in the User Name box.

5. In the Phone Number box, verify the phone number given to you by the ISP, and click Dial Properties.

6. In the Dialing Properties dialog box, verify the information in the I Am In This Country/Region and Area Code boxes. If you need to dial a number to access an outside line using your phone system, type the number in the When Dialing From Here section. Then click OK, and close the Connect To dialog box.

Next check the modem's settings by following these steps:

1. Click Start, point to Settings, and click Control Panel.

2. In Control Panel, double-click Modems. (In Windows Me, you might need to click View All Control Panel Options to see the Modems icon.)

3. In the Modems Properties dialog box, click the Diagnostics tab, click your modem, and click More Info to see the results. ▶

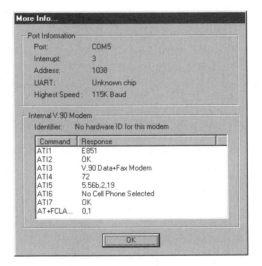

If an error message reports that the modem failed to respond, verify that the modem is turned on and properly plugged into the computer. If the modem is on and connected properly, or if the modem is internal, right-click My Computer on the desktop, click Properties on the shortcut menu, click the Device Manager tab in the System Properties dialog box, and verify that the Device Manager is not reporting a problem with the modem driver (indicated by a yellow exclamation point on the modem's icon). If Device Manager reports a problem, see "A New Device I've Installed Doesn't Work," on page 140, for information about reinstalling or updating the driver.

4. Click OK to close the More Info dialog box.

5. On the General tab in the Modems Properties dialog box, select your modem and click Properties.

6. In the Properties dialog box for the modem, click the Connection tab, click Advanced, and in the Advanced Connection Settings dialog box, make sure the Use Error Control, Compress Data, and Use Flow Control check boxes are selected and that Modulation Type is set to Standard.

To continue with this solution, go to the next page.

I can't connect to my Internet service provider

(continued from page 169)

7. Click OK, click OK again, and click Close to close the Modems Properties dialog box. Also close Control Panel and the Dial-Up Networking window.

If you still can't connect to your ISP, delete your passwords file, which may have become corrupted, by following these steps:

1. Click Start, point to Find, and click Files Or Folders. In Windows Me, click Start, point to Search, and click For Files Or Folders.

2. Type ***.pwl** in the Named box in the Find dialog box. In Windows Me, type ***.pwl** in the Search For Files Or Folders Named box in the Search Results window. ▶

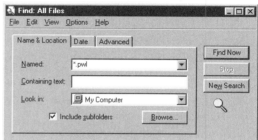

3. Click the Look In down arrow, click the disk that contains the Windows folder, and click Find Now or Search Now (in Windows Me). ▶

4. In the search results list, right-click the *.pwl file, and click Delete on the shortcut menu.

5. Click Start, click Shut Down, and click Restart or click the down arrow and click Restart in the list (in Windows Me). Then click OK.

My Dial-Up Networking connection is missing

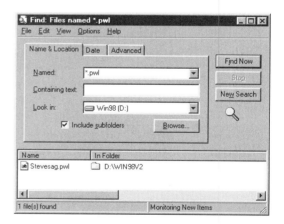

If you discover that the connection you've always clicked in Dial-Up Networking to connect to your ISP is missing, you'll need to create a new connection. If your ISP provided a disk with a program that creates a connection, you should run that program again. Otherwise, you can use the Internet Connection Wizard to create a new ISP connection.

The Internet Connection Wizard can automatically configure some of the larger, national ISPs. But if you use a local ISP, you can also use the wizard to set up your connection.

1. Double-click the Connect To The Internet icon on the desktop, or if the icon is not present, click Start, point to Programs, and point to Accessories. Point to Internet Tools, and click Internet Connection Wizard. In Windows Me, point to Communications, and click Internet Connection Wizard.

2. On the first page of the Internet Connection Wizard, click I Want To Transfer My Existing Account To This Computer and click Next.

3. On the next page of the wizard, click a phone number in the Phone Numbers list and click Next. ▶

4. On the next page of the wizard, click your ISP if it's in the list. Otherwise, click My Internet Service Provider Is Not Listed and click Next. ▶

5. Click Next. If your ISP was listed, the wizard asks you for your account logon information and creates a connection you can double-click. If your ISP was not listed, the wizard asks for your phone number, account logon information, and a name for the connection, and then it creates the connection. You can also set up your mail account using the wizard, but if you've connected to an ISP in the past, you probably have a mail account already set up in your mail program.

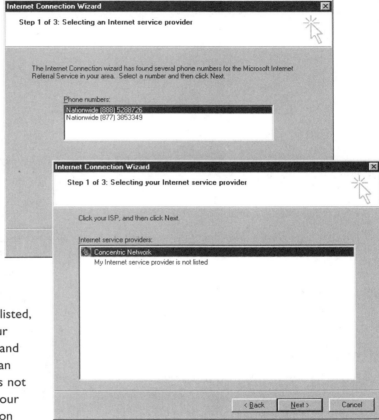

Connecting takes a long time

Source of the problem

Waiting for your modem to dial and connect takes long enough—you don't have to suffer through an even longer delay while Windows and your ISP negotiate a working Internet connection. By changing a few settings for the connection, you can disable features that are intended only for a network connection and not for the Internet connection you want to make. Since you don't need the network connection features if you're not connected to a network, disabling them reduces the time it takes to connect to the Internet.

How to fix it

1. Double-click My Computer, and double-click Dial-Up Networking.
   In Windows Me, click Start, point to Settings, and click Dial-Up Networking.

2. In the Dial-Up Networking window, right-click your ISP connection, and click Properties on the shortcut menu.

3. In the properties dialog box for the connection, click the Server Types tab or the Security tab (in Windows Me).

4. Clear the Log On To Network check box. ▶

5. On the Server Types tab or the Networking tab (in Windows Me), clear the Enable Software Compression, NetBEUI, and IPX/SPX Compatible check boxes, and click TCP/IP Settings. ▶

6. In the TCP/IP Settings dialog box, clear the Use IP Header Compression check box and click OK.

7. Click OK to close the dialog box, and close the Dial-Up Networking window.

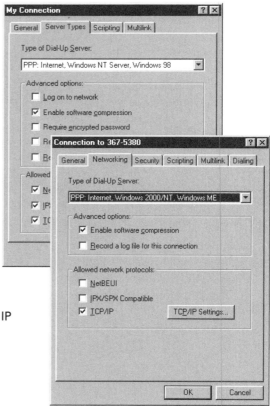

After you change networking settings, you should also change a few modem settings by following these steps:

1. Click Start, point to Settings, and click Control Panel.

2. In Control Panel, double-click Modems. (In Windows Me, you might need to click View All Control Panel Options to see the Modems option.)

3. In the Modems Properties dialog box, select the modem you use to dial your ISP and click Properties.

4. Click the Connection tab, and click Advanced.

5. In the Advanced Connection Settings dialog box, make sure the Use Flow Control check box is selected.

6. In the Use Flow Control section of the Advanced Connection Settings dialog box, make sure the Hardware (RTS/CTS) option is selected. ▶

7. Click OK.

8. Click OK again, and click Close to close the dialog box.

9. Close Control Panel, and then try establishing a new Internet connection with your modem.

The wonder of a full-time Internet connection

If you're lucky enough to have cable modem or DSL service (two types of high-speed, full-time Internet connection) in your area, sign up and sign up quick—especially if you're plagued by poor-quality phone connections. Full-time Internet connections cost a bit more per month than regular dial-up connections, but you might be able to disconnect that second phone line that you use only for a modem.

A full-time, high-speed Internet connection will totally transform the way you use the Internet. Not only will it eliminate the twin problems of getting an Internet connection (no more busy signals) and staying connected, but you'll also be able to click through Web sites at high speed, download files quickly, watch videos on the Web, listen to music and other broadcasts, make phone calls over the Internet, and take advantage of every new technology geared toward people with *broadband access* (a fancy term for a high-speed Internet connection).

I frequently lose my connection to the Internet

Source of the problem

From time to time, everyone gets disconnected from the Internet without warning. Imperfect phone line connections are just part of the challenge of going on line. But if you find that you're disconnected frequently, you can take a number of steps to make your connections more stable and reliable, such as checking your phone line, checking your time-out period at your Internet service provider (ISP), disabling call waiting, and others. You should try all of these procedures.

How to fix it

1. Make sure the connection between your modem and the computer is tight. Also check the line from the modem to the wall jack.

2. Report the problem to your local phone company and request a repair to clean up your phone line and remove static and other noises that can interfere with connections.

   You can do a quick check of your phone line by picking up the handset, listening to the line, and pressing any number other than 0. Listen for snaps, crackles, or pops on the line—not to mention buzzes, clicks, or hisses.

If everything seems OK with your phone line and connection, see whether an ISP time-out or call waiting is disconnecting you by following these steps:

1. Check with your ISP to see whether you are automatically disconnected after a period of inactivity.

   Your ISP might offer unlimited time each month, but it can still disconnect you after a predetermined interval if you don't use the connection for a while. If you find this *time-out* period is too short and your ISP won't increase the interval for your account, you can download utilities from many file download sites on the Web, such as *www.download.com*, that will periodically use the connection to keep it active.

2. Click Start, point to Settings, and click Control Panel.

3. In Control Panel, double-click Modems. (In Windows Me, you might have to click View All Control Panel Options to see the Modems option.)

4. If you do not have call waiting installed on your phone line, skip to step 6. Otherwise, in the Modems Properties dialog box, click Dialing Properties. ▶

5. In the Dialing Properties dialog box, select the To Disable Call Waiting, Dial check box, click the down arrow, click the sequence of keypad presses that will disable call waiting on your line (such as *70), and click OK.

　　You might have to check with your phone company to determine which key sequence will temporarily disable call waiting.

6. In the Modems Properties dialog box, click the modem you use to dial in to your ISP, and click Properties.

7. On the General tab in the Properties dialog box, click the Maximum Speed down arrow, and click a speed value that is half the current speed. For example, if the current speed is 115200, click 57600. ▶

8. Click the Connection tab, and clear the Disconnect A Call If Idle For More Than check box.

9. Click Advanced, and in the Advanced Connection Settings dialog box, clear the Compress Data check box. ▶

10. Check your modem's user manual to see whether it has a setting that forces the modem to stay connected for a short period even without a carrier. If you find such a setting, type it in the Extra Settings box in the Advanced Connection Settings dialog box, and click OK.

11. Click OK again, click Close to close the Modems Properties dialog box, and close Control Panel.

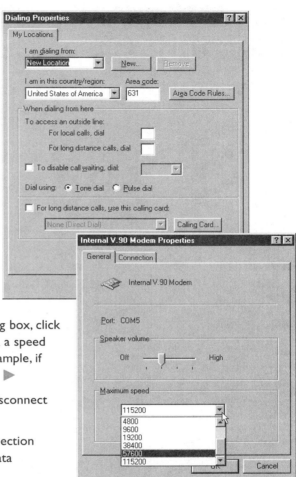

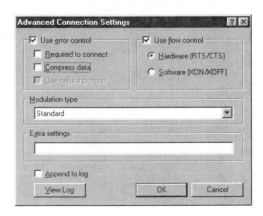

An automatic dialer keeps popping up

Source of the problem

It can be great to have Windows dial your Internet service provider (ISP) whenever an Internet program, such as your e-mail software, needs to go on line, but you'd never know it with all the people who curse this feature every time the Internet dialer pops up unexpectedly. Fortunately, you can stop the dialer in its tracks and prevent it from trying to make an Internet connection when you're not ready. Here's how to take control back from the dialer.

How to fix it

1. Double-click the Internet Explorer icon on the desktop.

2. On the View menu (in Internet Explorer 4) or the Tools menu (in Internet Explorer 5), click Internet Options.

3. In Internet Explorer 4, click the Connection tab in the Internet Options dialog box, and click Connect To The Internet Using A Local Area Network. ▶
     In Internet Explorer 5, click the Connections tab in the Internet Options dialog box, and click Never Dial A Connection. ▶

4. Click OK.

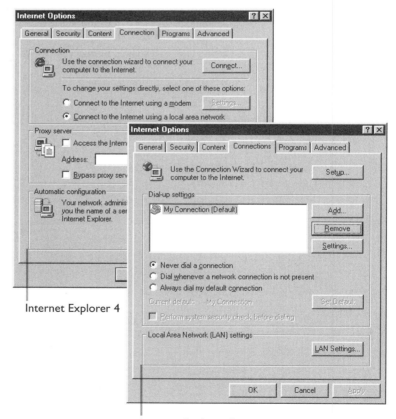

Internet Explorer 4

Internet Explorer 5

I have to enter my user name and password every time I connect

Source of the problem

If your Internet service provider (ISP) supports either Password Authentication Protocol (PAP) or Challenge Handshake Authentication Protocol (CHAP), two methods that Windows can use to establish and verify a connection with an ISP, Windows can enter your user name and password automatically whenever you connect. If your ISP supports neither protocol, you'll need to type in your user name and password each time.

How to fix it

1. Contact your ISP to determine whether it supports either the PAP or CHAP protocol.

2. If your ISP supports neither protocol, consider switching to a different ISP.

Saving your password

Even if your ISP supports PAP or CHAP, Windows will not automatically log you on if you've cleared the Save Password check box in the Dial-Up Networking Connect To dialog box. ▶

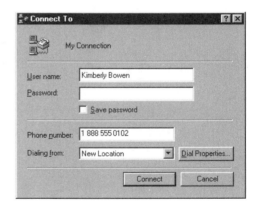

1. Double-click My Computer on the desktop, and double-click Dial-Up Networking. In Windows Me, click Start, point to Settings, and click Dial-Up Networking.

2. In the Dial-Up Networking window, double-click the connection that doesn't have a saved password, and in the Connect To dialog box, select the Save Password check box.

3. Close the Connect To dialog box and the Dial-Up Networking window.

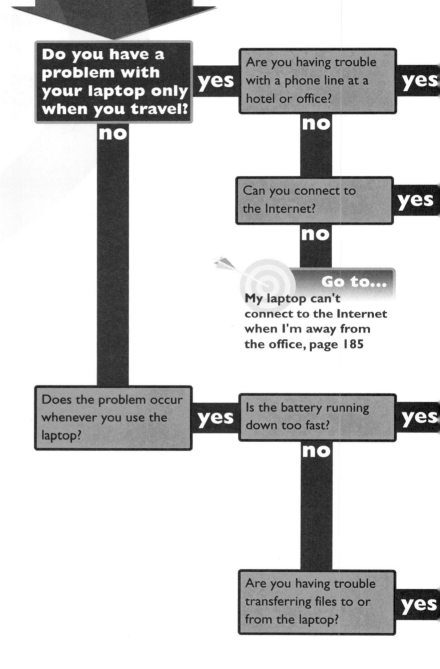

Do you have a problem with your laptop only when you travel?

yes → Are you having trouble with a phone line at a hotel or office? **yes**

no ↓

Can you connect to the Internet? **yes**

no ↓

Go to...
My laptop can't connect to the Internet when I'm away from the office, page 185

no ↓

Does the problem occur whenever you use the laptop? **yes** → Is the battery running down too fast? **yes**

no ↓

Are you having trouble transferring files to or from the laptop? **yes**

Laptops

Go to...
A hotel room phone line or an office phone line won't work with my laptop, page 184

Do you need to print a document? **yes**

Quick fix

You can send a document to a printer even if you're traveling with a laptop and not connected to the printer. When you reconnect to the printer, back at your office or at home, the document will be printed.

1. Click Start, point to Settings, and click Printers.

2. Right-click the printer you want to use, and click Use Printer Offline on the shortcut menu.

   When you return home or to the office and reconnect to the printer, click Use Printer Offline again to clear the check mark on the shortcut menu and begin printing. Right-click the file, and click Rename on the shortcut menu.

Can you use standby mode to conserve power? **yes**

Go to...
The battery runs down too fast, page 180

no

Go to...
My laptop won't come out of standby, page 182

Go to...
I can't transfer files between my desktop and my laptop, page 186

If your solution isn't here
Check these related chapters:
  Dial-Up Networking, page 34
  E-mail, receiving, page 66
  E-mail, sending, page 76
  Hardware, page 138
Or see the general troubleshooting tips on page xiii

The battery runs down too fast

Source of the problem

It's the law of laptops. Laptop batteries always run out before you can finish your work or your game. To squeeze every ounce of juice from your battery, you need to employ power management in Windows, which works with the power management features that are built into your laptop to extend the length of time your battery lasts.

The Advanced Configuration and Power Interface (ACPI) power management system in newer laptops gives you greater control over power management than Advanced Power Management (APM) in older laptops, but Windows works with both power management systems. To determine whether your laptop uses APM or ACPI, see "Checking Your Laptop's Power Management Support," on the facing page. If your laptop provides only APM power management, be sure to also refer to "Turning Off the Laptop's Built-In Power Management," on the facing page.

How to fix it

1. Click Start, point to Settings, and click Control Panel.

2. In Control Panel, double-click Power Management. (In Windows Me, you might have to click View All Control Panel Options and then double-click Power Options.)

3. On the Power Schemes tab in the Power Management Properties dialog box (the Power Options Properties dialog box in Windows Me), click the Power Schemes down arrow and click Portable/Laptop in the list. ▶

4. In the Running On Batteries column, click the System Standby, Turn Off Monitor, and Turn Off Hard Disks down arrows, and reduce the number of minutes after which each power-saving action will occur.

5. Click the Advanced tab, and select the Always Show Icon On The Taskbar check box so that you can right-click the power management icon on the taskbar to change power management properties. Then click OK.

Turning off the laptop's built-in power management

If your laptop provides APM rather than ACPI, the power management built into your laptop and the power management in Windows might vie for control. If the laptop uses APM, you should change how power management works in your laptop and let Windows win this particular battle. Leave power management running in your laptop so that Windows can use it to control your laptop's devices, but you should disable the laptop's ability to turn off or dim its screen, slow the processor, stop the hard disk from spinning, and take other power-saving actions. Windows will take care of those.

Each laptop provides a different way to control its built-in power management. You should check the laptop's documentation or check with the laptop's manufacturer, but the usual method involves restarting the laptop and pressing a key while the laptop is starting up. This starts a configuration program that you can use to disable timings and power management actions, such as putting the computer on standby, turning off the screen, and turning off the hard disk. After you save the configuration settings and restart Windows, you can use power management in Windows instead to control the laptop's systems.

Checking your laptop's power management support

The specifications in your laptop's user manual can tell you the level of power management provided in the laptop, but if you don't have the manual, you can still check by following these steps:

1. Right-click My Computer on the desktop, and click Properties on the shortcut menu.

2. In the System Properties dialog box, click the Device Manager tab.

3. Click the plus sign next to System Devices.
   If you see Advanced Configuration And Power Interface (ACPI) BIOS in the list, your computer supports ACPI. If you see Advanced Power Management Support, click it and click Properties to check the APM version, which is listed on the Settings tab in the Advanced Power Management Support Properties dialog box. ▶

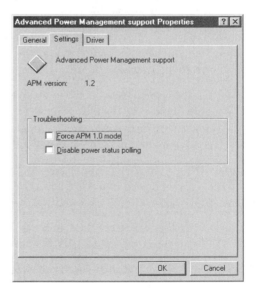

4. Click OK to close any dialog boxes that are open.

APM 1.1 can put your laptop on standby and turn off the screen. APM 1.2 can also stop the hard disk. If your laptop has APM support rather than ACPI, these are the only power-saving features you can control with Windows power management.

My laptop won't come out of standby

Source of the problem

Putting your laptop on standby turns off the screen, stops the hard disk, and puts the laptop in a power-saving mode from which it can emerge quickly—or at least that's the plan. But if Windows is unable to resume operation successfully after entering standby mode twice in a row, it assumes that your computer is incompatible with standby mode and disables standby. You can probably fix standby mode and thereby restore it by following these steps.

How to fix it

● Go to the laptop manufacturer's Web site and check the support area to determine whether you can download and run a file that will update the laptop's BIOS, the program inside the laptop that controls many of the computer's basic functions. Updating the BIOS is the most likely solution for fixing the computer's incompatibility with standby mode.

If that didn't solve the problem, your next action is to determine whether a device driver is interfering with standby mode.

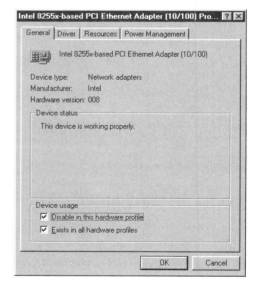

1. Right-click My Computer, and click Properties on the shortcut menu.

2. On the Device Manager tab in the System Properties dialog box, click the plus sign next to the category of a device installed in your computer that your computer can safely run without, such as a network adapter or scanner.

3. Click the device in the list, and click Properties.

4. On the General tab in the Properties dialog box for the device, select the Disable In This Hardware Profile check box and click OK. ▶

5. Click Close, and then restart the computer.

6. After the laptop restarts, try putting it on standby by clicking Start, clicking Shut Down, selecting Stand By, and clicking OK.

7. Press any key or move the mouse to exit standby mode.

If your laptop comes out of standby successfully, return to the Device Manager tab in the System Properties dialog box, reenable the device, and then disable a different device. Continue this troubleshooting approach until the computer is unable to return from standby, and then either remove the device or obtain an updated driver for the device that won't conflict with standby mode.

If your computer still does not resume after standby, you need to troubleshoot the video driver next.

1. Right-click My Computer, and click Properties on the shortcut menu.

2. On the Device Manager tab in the System Properties dialog box, click the plus sign next to Display Adapters, click the display adapter, and click Properties.

3. On the Driver tab in the Properties dialog box, click Update Driver, and on the first page of the Update Device Driver Wizard, click Next. (In Windows Me, click Specify The Location Of The Driver [Advanced], and then click Next.)

4. On the next page of the wizard, click the Display A List Of All The Drivers In A Specific Location, So You Can Select The Driver You Want option, and then click Next.

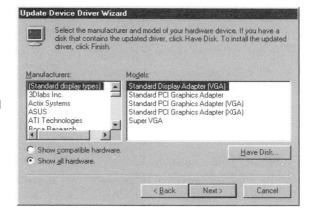

5. Click Show All Hardware, click Standard Display Types in the Manufacturers list and Standard Display Adapter (VGA) in the Models list, and then click Next. ▶

6. Click Yes at the warning that the driver was not written for the selected hardware, and then follow the instructions on the screen to complete the Update Device Driver Wizard. Restart your computer when you are asked to do so.

7. Try putting the laptop in standby mode again by clicking Start, clicking Shut Down, selecting Stand By, and clicking OK. Then try bringing the laptop out of standby by pressing a key on the keyboard.
   If the laptop comes out of standby successfully, contact the laptop's manufacturer to obtain an updated video driver that is compatible with standby mode.

If your laptop still does not resume after standby, you should repeat the steps above, but choose your original display adapter in step 5, and then try using the Power Management Troubleshooter tool, which can diagnose other conflicts. Download the Power Management Troubleshooter tool from the the Microsoft Web site by following these steps:

1. Go to *support.microsoft.com/support/kb/articles/q185/9/49.asp*.

2. Follow the instructions on the Web page to download and run Pmtshoot.exe.

A hotel room phone line or an office phone line won't work with my laptop

Source of the problem

Unlike the analog phone lines in your home, many office and hotel phone systems are digital, so they won't work with standard laptop modems. More critical is that many digital phone systems carry a higher electric current than standard phone lines, so you could damage the modem or the laptop by innocently plugging into one of these lines. You don't have to worry about plugging a modem into a jack labeled *data port* in your hotel room, but check with the front desk before you plug a modem into a wall jack. If you're not sure whether a hotel or an office phone line is digital or analog and no one can tell you for certain, here are a few workarounds.

How to fix it

- Before you plug your modem into a hotel or an office phone line, plug in a phone line tester such as the IBM Modem Saver, which tests for dangerous conditions.

  These small and inexpensive devices give a readout, usually as small status lights on the device, telling you whether the line is safe and ready for use. Search for *modem saver* on the Internet to find companies that sell these products.

- Use an adapter that can convert a digital line to an analog line suitable for your laptop's modem. These devices are available from the same companies that sell modem savers.

- If you have the flexibility to choose your own hotel, stay at a hotel that lists data ports in its rooms as one of its accommodations for travelers. In many cities, you can even stay at a hotel that offers a high-speed Internet connection in the room, but to connect you'll need to bring along a network adapter for your laptop and follow the instructions given to you by the front desk personnel.

Tip

If you're traveling outside of North America, you'll need to bring along not only an adapter for the power line, but also an adapter for the phone system. You should also clear the Wait For Dial Tone Before Connecting check box on the Connection tab in the Modem Properties dialog box, as many foreign dial tones are not recognized by domestic modems. On the General tab of a Dial-Up Networking connection, click Configure in the Connect Using section to open the Modem Properties dialog box.

My laptop can't connect to the Internet when I'm away from the office

Source of the problem

If you connect your laptop to a network in the office, or if you plug your laptop into a docking station that is connected to the network, you might find that you can't connect to the Internet when you use the laptop away from the office. A laptop that's connected to a network in an office has its network settings configured for the office network. If you can browse the Internet at your desk, you're probably connecting through the office network. But when you take the laptop home or bring it along on a trip, you need to configure the laptop's network settings for a different kind of network—the Internet. You do so by following this short procedure.

How to fix it

1. Right-click Network Neighborhood or My Network Places (in Windows Me) on the desktop, and click Properties on the shortcut menu.

2. In the list of network components in the Network dialog box, double-click TCP/IP ➜ *[the laptop's network adapter]*.

3. On the IP Address tab in the TCP/IP Properties dialog box, make a note of the IP Address and Subnet Mask settings. You'll need to restore these settings when you return to the office by returning to this dialog box and returning these settings to their previous state.

4. Click Obtain An IP Address Automatically. ▶

5. Click OK, and click OK again to close the Network dialog box.

6. Click Yes when you are asked whether you want to restart the computer.

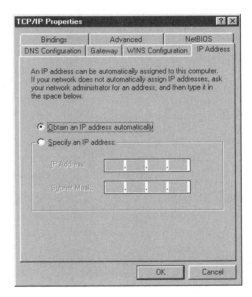

I can't transfer files between my desktop and my laptop

Source of the problem

If you need to continue the work you've started on a desktop computer while you're traveling with a laptop—or vice versa—but you don't have a system for transferring files between the two computers, you have several options. A number of products make desktop-to-laptop connections easy to establish, and Windows provides built-in support for synchronizing files between computers.

How to fix it

- If the laptop has a network adapter, ask to have an additional network connection installed in your office so that you can connect your laptop as well as your desktop. When both computers are on the network, you can copy files from one to the other.

- Set up a simple home network with a network cable and two network adapters, or use a home networking product that provides a network over your home phone lines or through USB cables. For more information about setting up a home network, see "I Don't Know How to Set Up a Home Network," on page 198.

- Upload the files you need from one computer to an online file storage Web site, such as Driveway (*www.driveway.com*) or MSN Online File Cabinets (*communities.msn.com/filecabinets*), and then download the files using the other computer.

- If the laptop has an infrared port, obtain an infrared adapter for the desktop that plugs into the desktop's serial or USB ports. Many infrared adapters come with file transfer applications, so you can beam files from one computer to another.

- If the desktop computer is at home, install the Windows Dial-Up Server component using Add/Remove Programs in Control Panel, and set up a dial-up server on the desktop so that you can dial in to the desktop and transfer files over the phone as though you were connected by a network cable.

- Connect a LapLink-style (null-modem) cable between the parallel ports on the desktop and laptop and run Direct Cable Connection on both machines.

  If you don't find Direct Cable Connection by clicking Start, pointing to Programs, pointing to Accessories, and pointing to Communications, you can install it by using Add/Remove Programs in Control Panel. Direct Cable Connection is a Communications component that you can add on the Windows Setup tab in the Add/Remove Program Properties dialog box.

- Ask your company's network administrator whether you can sign on to your company's network through Virtual Private Networking (VPN), which would allow you to use your laptop to communicate with your desktop computer through the Internet.

- Use a file synchronization program, such as Symantec's pcAnywhere or LapLink.com's LapLink, to transfer files between your desktop and laptop.

- Use a removable drive, such as a Zip drive, that you can connect to the parallel port of each computer.

Setting up programs for easy file transfer

The key to making files easy to transfer between computers is to locate your data files in an easy-to-find folder. In the My Documents folder on the desktop, for example, you can create a folder named My Laptop and then copy the files you want to take with you into this folder. Among these files would be the documents you want to take along and your Outlook data files. In Outlook, all your contacts, calendar information, e-mail messages, and other personal information are stored in a single .pst file. You can right-click Outlook Today, click Properties on the shortcut menu, and click Advanced in the Personal Folders Properties dialog box to determine the location of the .pst file. After you close Outlook and then move this .pst file to the My Laptop folder, where you can easily retrieve it along with the rest of your files, you can open the file in Outlook by clicking File, pointing to Open, clicking Personal Folders File (*.pst), and then selecting the .pst file in the Open Personal folders dialog box.

You can also take along your Outlook Express files. For more information about locating these files, see "I Can't Back Up My Outlook Express 5 E-Mail Messages," on page 73.

Using Briefcase

You can install the Briefcase accessory on your laptop to synchronize files between the laptop and a desktop computer. After you've established a connection between the computers using a network or a Direct Cable Connection, you copy folders and files from the desktop computer to Briefcase on the laptop. While you are traveling, you can work with the files in Briefcase on the laptop. When you return to your desktop, you use Briefcase to synchronize the copies between the laptop and the desktop. Briefcase copies the files with the most recent dates to the other computer, so you can always be sure that you have the most up-to-date versions of files on both computers.

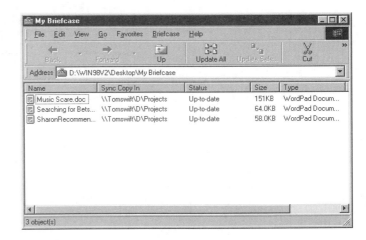

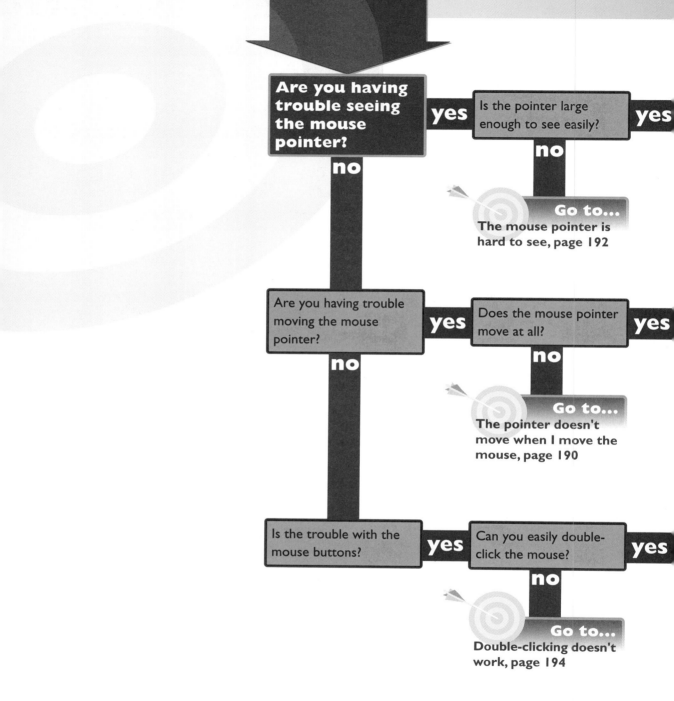

Are you having trouble seeing the mouse pointer?

yes → Is the pointer large enough to see easily?

yes →

no ↓

Go to...
The mouse pointer is hard to see, page 192

no ↓

Are you having trouble moving the mouse pointer?

yes → Does the mouse pointer move at all?

yes →

no ↓

Go to...
The pointer doesn't move when I move the mouse, page 190

no ↓

Is the trouble with the mouse buttons?

yes → Can you easily double-click the mouse?

yes →

no ↓

Go to...
Double-clicking doesn't work, page 194

Would you prefer to use an arrow for the pointer? **yes**

Quick fix

If you're using a desktop theme, the theme may have replaced the mouse pointer with a graphic that's harder to use than a simple arrow. To restore the arrow, follow these steps:

1. In Control Panel, double-click Desktop Themes.

2. In the Desktop Themes dialog box, click the Theme down arrow, click the Windows Default theme, and click Apply.

3. Click the Theme down arrow again, click the desktop theme you want, clear the Mouse Pointers check box, and then click OK.

Does the mouse pointer move too fast or slow? **yes**

Quick fix

You can adjust the sensitivity of the mouse so you don't have to move it so delicately, or pick it up and set it back down to traverse the entire screen. Follow these steps:

1. Click Start, point to Settings, and click Control Panel.

2. In Control Panel, double-click Mouse. (In Windows Me, you might need to click View All Control Panel Options before you can see the Mouse option.)

3. Drag the Pointer Speed slider on the Motion tab. (In Windows Me, it's on the Pointer Options tab.)

Do you move the mouse with your left hand? **yes**

Go to...

The buttons are backwards because I'm left-handed, page 193

If your solution isn't here

Check these related chapters:

The desktop, page 14

Desktop icons, page 24

Hardware, page 138

The screen, page 264

Or see the general troubleshooting tips on page xiii

The pointer doesn't move when I move the mouse

Source of the problem

Small children whose fingers barely reach the mouse buttons maneuver the mouse with pinpoint control. But if your mouse pointer not only won't move where you want it to but simply won't move at all, you need to follow the steps below (using the keyboard) to make sure the driver for the mouse is installed and the mouse is enabled. After all, without the mouse (or trackball, or track pad, or pointing stick), you can't take full advantage of pointing and clicking in Windows, and you'll never know the many secrets revealed by clicking that *other* mouse button.

How to fix it

1. Press Ctrl+Esc to open the Start menu.

2. Press the Up Arrow key a few times to move the highlight to Settings. Press the Right Arrow key to move the highlight to Control Panel, and then press Enter.

3. Press the Down Arrow key repeatedly until the highlight moves to System, and then press Enter. In Windows Me, you might need to press Tab to move the highlight to View All Control Panel Options, then press Enter, and then press Tab again to move the highlight to the list of icons before you can press the Down Arrow key to move the highlight to System and press Enter.

4. In the System Properties dialog box, press the Right Arrow key to move the highlight to the Device Manager tab.

5. Press Tab twice to move the highlight into the list of device categories.

6. Press the Down Arrow key to move the high-light to Mouse, and then press the plus sign key (on the numeric keypad). ▶

    If you are using a laptop that doesn't have a numeric keypad, look on the keyboard for the key combination that functions as the numeric keypad plus-sign key.

7. Press the Down Arrow key to move the highlight to the mouse, and then press Alt+R to open the Properties dialog box for the mouse.

8. On the General tab in the Properties dialog box, verify that the Disable In This Hardware Profile check box is not selected.

   If this check box is selected, press the Spacebar to clear the check box. ▶

9. Press Tab repeatedly to move the highlight to the General tab heading, and then press the Right Arrow key to move the highlight to the Driver tab.

10. Press Alt+U to open the Update Device Driver Wizard.

11. Press Enter twice. In Windows Me, press Enter only once.

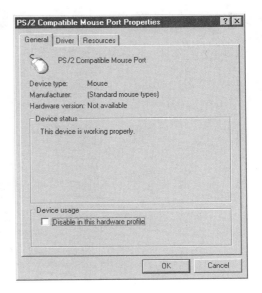

12. If your mouse or your computer came with a disk or CD containing drivers, insert the disk or CD into the drive.

13. When the wizard shows a list of compatible drivers, move the highlight to the driver that matches your mouse and press Enter.

    If the wizard doesn't show a list, press Tab to move the highlight to the check boxes for the locations you want to search for a driver, and then press the Spacebar to select the check boxes and press Enter. Move the highlight to the driver that is compatible with your mouse, and then press Enter.

14. Press Enter again and then close the dialog boxes you've opened, and press Alt+F4 when you return to Control Panel.

15. Press Alt+F4 again to open the Shut Down Windows dialog box, press the Down Arrow key to select Restart if necessary, and then press Enter to restart the computer and make the mouse work.

The mouse moves erratically

Nearly all mice require periodic cleaning. If your mouse uses a mouse ball, open the mouse ball compartment on the bottom of the mouse, remove the mouse ball, and wipe it clean. Also wipe off the gunk that may have accumulated on the rollers in the mouse ball compartment. Check your desktop for accumulated gunk too. (Don't be embarrassed. We all get gunk.)

    If your mouse seems to be slipping on the desktop, you're a perfect candidate for a mouse pad. Several companies make flat mouse pads that stick to the desktop and provide a hard, non-skid surface. Some people find that the softer, spongier variety of mouse pad can make the mouse slightly more difficult to maneuver.

The mouse pointer is hard to see

Source of the problem

Windows comes with a variety of mouse pointers you can use, some of which are larger and easier to see, especially when you're using a dim laptop screen or when the mouse pointer gets lost on a large monitor with lots of screen area. If you're using a desktop theme (a collection of icons, a background graphic, sounds, and mouse pointers) to enliven your desktop, you might be disappointed to find that your bigger mouse pointer no longer looks like a rocket ship or a ballpoint pen, but that's a small price to pay if you're struggling to use your computer. Here's how to choose a larger and more suitable mouse pointer.

How to fix it

1. Click Start, point to Settings, and click Control Panel.

2. In Control Panel, double-click Mouse. (In Windows Me, you might need to click View All Control Panel Options before you can see the Mouse option.)

3. On the Pointers tab in the Mouse Properties dialog box, click the Scheme down arrow, and then click Windows Standard (Large). ▶

4. Click Apply, and take a look at the resulting mouse pointer. If it's still not large enough, click the Scheme down arrow again, and click Windows Standard (Extra Large).

5. Click OK to close the Mouse Properties dialog box.

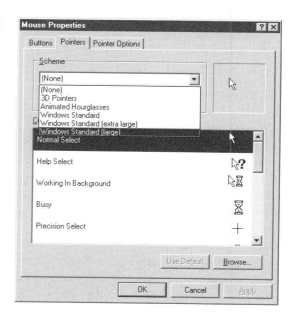

> **Tip**
>
> If you're using Windows Me or you've recently installed a new Microsoft mouse and its accompanying software, you might be able to press the Ctrl key to have Windows help you pinpoint the mouse if it's lost.

The buttons are backwards because I'm left-handed

Source of the problem

Lefties, you don't have to put up with a mouse that's backwards. By simply changing the button configuration, you can swap the functions of the left and right mouse buttons to make the mouse more suitable for you.

All models of mouse can be switched, even if one of the buttons is slightly larger than the other.

Some models of mouse come with a disk that provides setup software for the mouse. The setup software often includes an option to switch the left and right mouse buttons. But you can always use the option that is built right in to Windows in the Mouse Properties dialog box.

How to fix it

1. Click Start, point to Settings, and click Control Panel.

2. In Control Panel, double-click Mouse. (In Windows Me, you might need to click View All Control Panel Options before you can see the Mouse option.)

3. On the Buttons tab in the Mouse Properties dialog box, click Left-Handed in the Button Configuration section. ▶

4. Click OK to close the Mouse Properties dialog box.

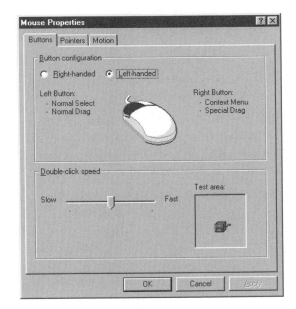

Mouse options for lefties and righties

If you've recently bought a new mouse for your computer, you can probably just plug it in, start Windows, and begin using the mouse without installing any special software. But if your mouse came with an installation disk, you should install the software it provides. The software might very well add more tabs that offer additional options in the Mouse Properties dialog box. Or it might allow you to start a special mouse settings program with options for customizing the mouse, such as assigning commands to its buttons.

Double-clicking doesn't work

Source of the problem

Double-clicking is a skill that some of us never master. Even if we usually double-click without thinking twice, we sometimes end up pushing icons around the desktop rather than starting programs with them. Whether double-clicking is always a challenge or sometimes a nuisance, you can make a few adjustments that will both reduce the need to double-click and make double-clicking easier and more reliable.

To reduce the need to double-click, you can switch to Web style, which makes Windows act like Web pages, with links you can single-click rather than icons you must double-click.

To reduce the difficulty of double-clicking, you can adjust the double-click speed and increase the double-click field, which gives you a little more latitude in case you inadvertently move the mouse a tiny bit between clicks.

How to fix it
(by switching to Web style)

1. Double-click My Computer on the desktop.

2. On the View menu or the Tools menu (in Windows Me), click Folder Options.

3. On the General tab in the Folder Options dialog box, click Custom Based On Settings You Choose and click the Settings button. If you use Windows Me, skip to the next step.

4. In the Click Items As Follows section, click Single-Click To Open An Item (Point To Select), and click OK. ▶

    The icon labels on the desktop and in folder windows will be displayed with an underline at all times unless you also click Underline Icon Titles Only When I Point At Them. Now you can just single-click these icons.

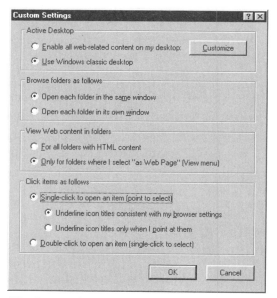

The Custom Settings dialog box in Windows Me.

How to fix it
(by adjusting double-clicking)

1. Click Start, point to Settings, and click Control Panel.

2. In Control Panel, double-click Mouse, or if you're having trouble double-clicking, press the Down Arrow key repeatedly to move the highlight to Mouse and then press Enter. (In Windows Me, you might need to click View All Control Panel Options before you can see the Mouse icon.)

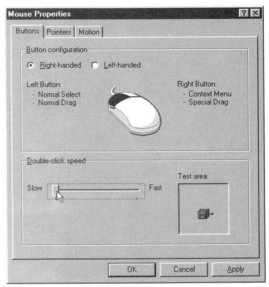

3. On the Buttons tab in the Mouse Properties dialog box, drag the Double-Click Speed slider to the left to increase the time allowed between the two mouse clicks. ▶

   Double-click the jack-in-the-box in the test area. If Jack emerges, you've double-clicked successfully.

4. Click OK to close the Mouse Properties dialog box.

You can follow these steps to use Tweak UI to decrease the precision with which you must double-click.

1. In Control Panel, double-click Tweak UI.

   If you don't see a Tweak UI icon, you need to install Tweak UI. Follow the instructions in "Where Do I Get Tweak UI?," on page 33.

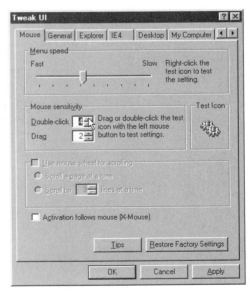

2. On the Mouse tab in the Tweak UI dialog box, increase the Double-Click value in the Mouse Sensitivity section to increase the distance allowed between the two mouse clicks in a double-click. ▶

   When you increase the Double-Click value in Tweak UI (which is different from the Double-Click Speed value in the Mouse Properties dialog box), double-clicking an object on the screen still works even if you happen to jiggle the mouse a little between clicks.

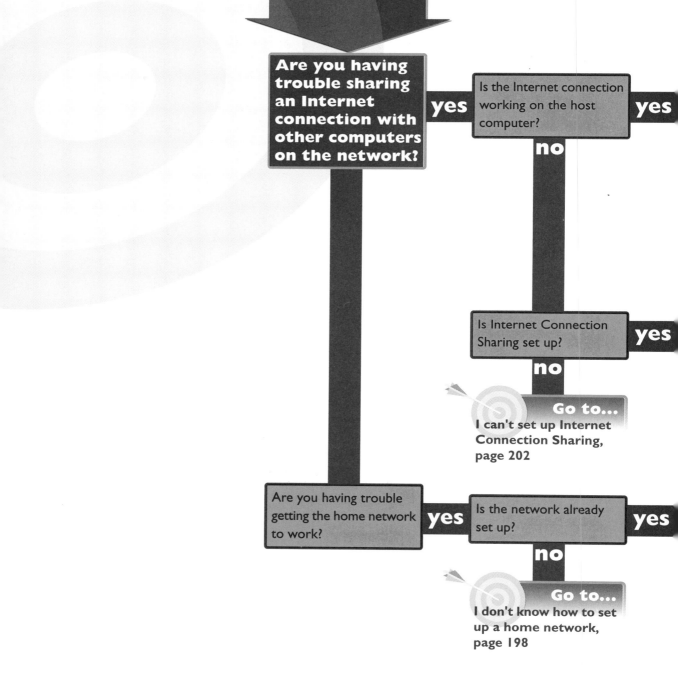

Are you having trouble sharing an Internet connection with other computers on the network?

yes → Is the Internet connection working on the host computer? **yes**

no

Is Internet Connection Sharing set up? **yes**

no

Go to...
I can't set up Internet Connection Sharing, page 202

Are you having trouble getting the home network to work? **yes** → Is the network already set up? **yes**

no

Go to...
I don't know how to set up a home network, page 198

Networks, home

Does the host computer hang up when necessary? **yes** Does the host computer refuse to dial the Internet? **yes**

no

Go to...
The Internet Connection Sharing host computer won't dial the ISP when a client computer needs an Internet connection, page 207

Quick fix

When you quit Internet Explorer on one of the other computers on a home network that has Internet Connection Sharing installed, the computer that has the Internet connection does not disconnect from your Internet service provider (ISP). The only way to end the Internet session is to end the Internet connection on the host computer.

Go to...
I can't get to the Internet from computers on the network, page 208

Are you able to use the network?

no

Go to...
I can't connect to other computers on the network, page 210

If your solution isn't here
Check these related chapters:
Dial-Up Networking, page 34
Internet, browsing, page 148
Internet, connecting to, page 164
Networks, office, page 212
Or see the general troubleshooting tips on page xiii

I don't know how to set up a home network

Source of the problem

When you have two or more computers in a single home, you should link them and gain the benefits and cost-savings of a home network. In no time, you'll be swapping files and sharing resources such as an Internet connection.

To set up a home network with two computers, you'll need three hardware devices and some cable, all of which you can buy in a single kit. All the software you need for the network is built into Windows, and Windows Me even includes a Home Networking Wizard, which configures all the software. The Home Networking Wizard even sets up Internet Connection Sharing so that all the computers on the network can use a single Internet connection. To set up a home network, follow these steps.

How to fix it

1. Get a home network kit, one that contains two Plug and Play network adapters (one for each computer), a hub, and matching cables.

   Inexpensive home network kits are available at computer stores and from online computer merchants. The network adapters plug into your computers, the hub (a small junction box) sits somewhere between the two computers, and the cables connect the computers to the hub. You can buy home network kits that contain two network adapter cards for connecting desktop computers or one regular network adapter card and one PC card or USB network adapter for connecting a desktop and a laptop. And you can buy additional network adapters and cables to add more computers.

   You can also buy kits that use your existing phone lines rather than network cables. And you can buy wireless networks that don't require cables, but they're considerably more expensive.

2. Turn off each computer and install the network adapter. Position the hub between the two computers, and connect a cable from the hub to each computer.

   The hub can be located anywhere between the two computers. If the computers are in adjacent rooms, you'll need to run the cable through the wall. If both computers are on the ground floor of your home but in different rooms, consider running the cable through the floor to a hub located in the basement. If the computers are located on different floors, you can use a phone line network kit rather than run cables between floors to take advantage of the existing phone wiring in your home.

3. Turn on each computer and wait as Windows recognizes the network adapters and installs the software for the network. Click Yes if you are asked whether you want to restart each computer.

Now that you've installed the hardware and let Windows install the underlying software for the network, you need to configure the network. Some home network kits come with setup software that configures the network for you. In Windows Me, you use the Home Networking Wizard to configure the network. (See "Using the Home Networking Wizard in Windows Me," on the next page.) In Windows 98, you need to configure the network manually by following these steps:

1. If the home network kit came with setup software, run the setup program to configure the network.

   If the home network kit came with no setup software, or if the software does not fully configure the network, continue on to the next step.

2. On each computer, right-click Network Neighborhood, and click Properties on the shortcut menu.

3. On the Identification tab in the Network dialog box on each computer, type a different computer name for each computer in the Computer Name box. ▶

4. In the Workgroup box, type the same name for each computer on the network—for example, *Workgroup* or *HomeNet*.

5. On the Configuration tab in the Network dialog box on each computer, click File And Print Sharing.

6. In the File And Print Sharing dialog box on each computer, select the I Want To Be Able To Give Others Access To My Files check box. ▶

   Also select the I Want To Be Able To Allow Others To Print To My Printer(s) check box if you want to share your printer with others on the network.

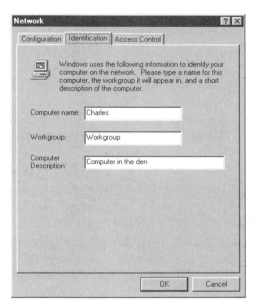

7. Click OK, and on the Configuration tab in the Network dialog box, look in the list of installed network components to find TCP/IP ➜ *[your network adapter]*.

   If you don't see any TCP/IP entries in the list, click Add, double-click Protocol, click Microsoft in the Manufacturers list, click TCP/IP in the Network Protocols list, and click OK. For information about adding a network protocol, see "I Can't See Other Computers on the Network," on page 218.

8. Click OK, and click Yes when you are asked whether you want to restart your computer.

To continue with this solution, go to the next page.

I don't know how to set up a home network

(continued from page 199)

9. Double-click My Computer on the desktop of each computer, right-click a disk drive or folder you want to share, and click Sharing on the short-cut menu. On the Sharing tab in the Properties dialog box, click the Shared As option, and replace the name in the Share Name box, if you want. In the Access Type section, click Read Only to allow only opening and copying documents, or click Full to allow changing, adding, or removing files and folders. Then type a password for the access type you've selected. ▶

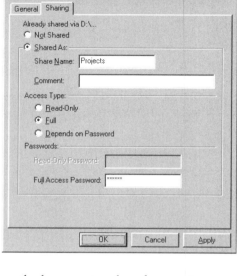

Using the Home Networking Wizard in Windows Me

Windows Me — Home networking is so popular and beneficial that Windows Me includes a special wizard devoted to setting up and configuring a home network. To run the Home Networking Wizard on each computer on the home network and set up its network connection, follow these steps:

1. Click Start, point to Programs, point to Accessories, point to Communications, and click Home Networking Wizard.

2. On the first page of the Home Networking Wizard, click Next.

3. If this computer will be used to connect to the Internet, on the Internet Connection page of the wizard, click the Yes, This Computer Uses The Following option, and click one of the two options below, depending on whether the computer will be connecting through another network computer's connection or connecting directly to an Internet service provider (ISP). ▶

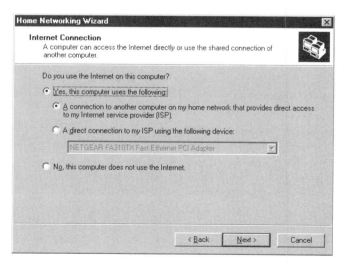

If this computer will not be used to connect to the Internet, click the No, This Computer Does Not Use The Internet option.

4. Click Next.

5. On the Computer And Workgroup Names page of the wizard, type a unique name for the computer in the Computer Name box (if one isn't already there). If you've already created a workgroup name for all the computers on the network, click Use This Workgroup Name in the Workgroup Name section and type the name in the box. Otherwise, you can click the first option, which uses MSHOME as the workgroup name. Then click Next. ▶

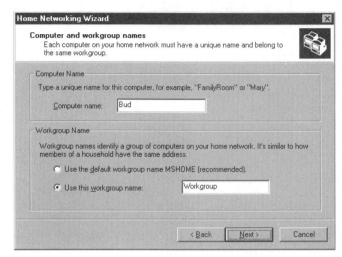

6. On the Share Files And Printers page of the wizard, select the My Documents Folder And All Folders In It check box if you want to share the My Documents folder with others in your household. Also select the check boxes for each printer you want to share. Click Next. ▶

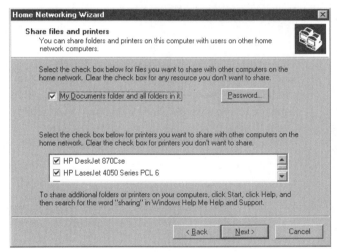

Tip

When you share a disk or folder, you can select Depends On Password as the access type and enter passwords in both password boxes so that you can control by the password entered whether someone will have full access or read-only access to the network resource.

7. On the Home Networking Setup Disk page of the wizard, click the No, Do Not Create A Home Networking Setup Disk option, and click Next.

8. Click Finish to complete the Home Networking Wizard.

9. Click Yes if you are asked whether you want to restart your computer.

I can't set up Internet Connection Sharing

Source of the problem

Internet Connection Sharing in Windows 98 Second Edition and Windows Me could be the very best reason to set up a home network. One Internet connection—one Internet service provider (ISP) account, one phone line, one monthly bill—can serve your entire household. Internet Connection Sharing works particularly well if you have an always-on Internet connection, such as a cable modem, which provides enough speed for everyone to use simultaneously. But if you don't know how to get Internet Connection Sharing up and running, follow these steps.

How to fix it

● Make sure that the computer with the Internet connection (the host computer) is running Windows 98 Second Edition or Window Me and can connect to the Internet. (If you're using Windows 98, you can determine whether you have Windows 98 Second Edition by right-clicking My Computer, clicking Properties on the shortcut menu, and looking at the System name on the General tab in the System Properties dialog box.) Other computers on the home network can be running either version of Windows 98, Windows Me, or Windows 95. If the host computer can't connect to the Internet, see "I Can't Connect to My Internet Service Provider," on page 168.

Install Internet Connection Sharing by following these steps:

1. On the host computer (the one with the Internet connection), click Start, point to Settings, and click Control Panel.

2. In Control Panel, double-click Add/Remove Programs. (In Windows Me, if Add/Remove Programs appears as an underlined link, click it once.)

3. On the Windows Setup tab in the Add/Remove Programs Properties dialog box, double-click Internet Tools (in Windows 98) or Communications (in Windows Me).

4. In the Components list, select the Internet Connection Sharing check box, and click OK.

5. Click OK again to close the Add/Remove Programs Properties dialog box.
    Windows Setup installs Internet Connection Sharing.

> **Tip**
> If you've just installed a new copy of Windows 98 Second Edition, the Internet Connection Sharing Wizard doesn't run automatically, even if you include Internet Connection Sharing as a Windows component to be installed. To manually run the wizard, click Start, point to Settings, click Control Panel, double-click Internet Options, click the Connections tab, and then click Sharing in the LAN And Internet Sharing Settings section.

If you're using Windows Me, the Home Networking Wizard opens. Read "Using the Home Networking Wizard on the Host Computer in Windows Me," on page 205, and skip steps 1 through 4 below. Here's how to use the Internet Connection Sharing Wizard that appears in Windows 98.

 Windows 98

1. Click Next on the first page of the wizard.

2. On the next page of the wizard, click the option that describes the type of Internet connection you're using, and click Next. ▶

3. If a Network Adapters list appears on the next page of the wizard, click the adapter that you're using to connect to the Internet, and click Next.

4. Insert a disk, and click Next to create the Client Configuration Disk. Remove the disk when you are prompted to, click Finish, and click Yes when you are asked whether you want to restart your computer.

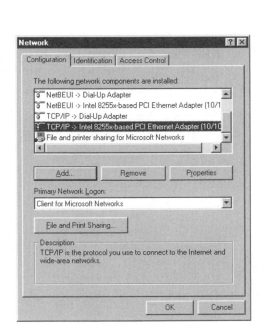

Now check the settings on the other computers:

1. On a client computer (one of the other computers on the network), right-click Network Neighborhood (in Windows 98) or My Network Places (in Windows Me), and click Properties on the shortcut menu.

2. On the Configuration tab in the Network dialog box, look for TCP/IP ➜ *[your network adapter]* in the list of installed network components. ▶

If you don't see a TCP/IP entry, click Add, double-click Protocol, click Microsoft in the Manufacturers list, click TCP/IP in the Network Protocols list, click OK, and click OK again. Click Yes when you are asked whether you want to restart your computer. For more details about installing a network protocol, see "I Can't See Other Computers on the Network," on page 218.

3. Double-click TCP/IP ➜ *[your network adapter]* in the list of installed network components.

To continue with this solution, go to the next page.

I can't set up Internet Connection Sharing

(continued from page 203)

4. On the IP Address tab in the TCP/IP Properties dialog box, make sure the Obtain An IP Address Automatically option is selected.

5. On the WINS Configuration tab, make sure the Use DHCP For WINS Resolution option is selected.

6. On the Gateway tab, make sure the Installed Gateways list is empty. If it isn't, for each gateway listed, click the gateway and click Remove.

7. On the DNS Configuration tab, make sure the Disable DNS option is selected. Click OK twice to close the Network dialog box.

8. Click Yes when you are asked whether you want to restart the computer.

> ## Setting up programs on the client computers to access the Internet
>
> Both the Client Configuration Disk and the Home Networking Wizard set up the browser on each client computer to connect to the Internet through Internet Connection Sharing, but you might need to set up other programs to connect to the Internet through your local area network (LAN) rather than a dial-up connection. For example, you need to manually configure Outlook Express 4 to connect to the Internet through your LAN. To do so, click Accounts on the Tools menu, click your mail account on the Mail tab in the Internet Accounts dialog box, and then click Properties. On the Connection tab in the Properties dialog box, click Connect Using My Local Area Network (LAN), click OK, and click Close to close the Internet Accounts dialog box. (Microsoft Outlook Express 5 shares the same Internet connection settings as Internet Explorer, so it'll work fine as is.)

Finally, you need to physically carry the Client Configuration Disk you created earlier to each of the other computers on your home network and use it to configure the Internet browser:

1. Insert the Client Configuration Disk in the disk drive of the first client computer.

2. Click Start, click Run, and in the Run dialog box, type **a:\lcsclset.exe** in the Open box and click OK.

3. On the first page of the Browser Connection Setup Wizard, click Next.

4. Click Next on the second page of the wizard to have the wizard configure the browser's connection settings.

5. On the last page of the wizard, click Finish.

6. Repeat steps 1 through 5 for each client computer.

Using the Home Networking Wizard on the host computer in Windows Me

If you're using Windows Me on the host computer, the Home Networking Wizard opens after you install Internet Connection Sharing. To use this wizard, follow these steps:

1. On the first page of the Home Networking Wizard, click Next.

2. On the Setup Options page of the wizard, click I Want To Edit My Home Networking Settings On This Computer, and click Next.

3. On the Internet Connection page of the wizard, click the Yes, This Computer Uses the Following option, click the A Direct Connection To My ISP Using The Following Device option, click the down arrow, and click the network adapter or Dial-Up Networking connection that you use to connect to the Internet. Then click Next. ▶

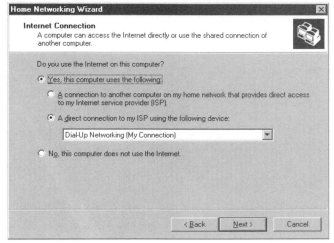

4. On the Computer And Workgroup Names page of the wizard, type a unique name for the computer in the Computer Name box (if one isn't already there). If you've already created a workgroup name for all the computers on the network, click the Use This Workgroup Name option in the Workgroup Name section and then type the name in the box. Otherwise, you can click the first option, which uses MSHOME as the workgroup name. Then click Next.

5. On the Share Files And Printers page of the wizard, select the My Documents Folder And All Folders In It check box if you want to share the My Documents folder with others in your household. Also select the check boxes for each printer that you want to share, and click Next. ▶

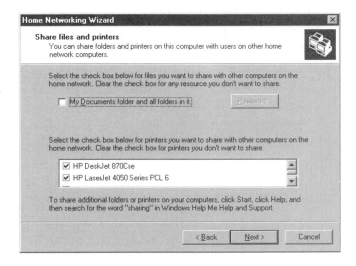

To continue with this solution, go to the next page.

I can't set up Internet Connection Sharing

(continued from page 205)

6. On the Home Networking Setup Disk page of the wizard, if other computers on the network use Windows 98 or Windows 95, click the Yes, Create A Home Networking Setup Disk option, insert a floppy disk, and click OK. Otherwise make sure No is selected, and click Next.

   You can insert the disk into the disk drive in a Windows 95 or Windows 98 computer that will be a client, and run Setup to set up the client computer.

7. Click Finish to complete the Home Networking Wizard.

   If you created a Home Networking Setup Disk, remove it from the disk drive.

Using the Home Networking Wizard on each client computer in Windows Me

Windows Me After you set up the host computer, you need to run the Home Networking Wizard on each client computer by following these steps:

1. Click Start, point to Programs, point to Accessories, point to Communications, and click Home Networking Wizard.

2. On the first page of the Home Networking Wizard, click Next.

3. On the Setup Options page of the wizard, click I Want To Edit My Home Networking Settings On This Computer, and click Next.

4. On the Internet Connection page of the wizard, click the Yes, This Computer Uses The Following option, click the A Connection To Another Computer On My Home Network option, and click Next.

5. On the Computer And Workgroup Names page of the wizard, type a unique name for the computer in the Computer Name box (if one isn't already there). If you've already created a workgroup name for all the computers on the network, click Use This Workgroup Name in the Workgroup Name section and then type the name in the box. Otherwise, click the first option, which uses MSHOME as the workgroup name. Then click Next.

6. On the Share Files And Printers page of the wizard, click the My Documents Folder And All Folders In It option if you want to share the My Documents folder with others in your household. Also select the check boxes for each printer you want to share, and click Next.

7. On the Home Networking Setup Disk page of the wizard, click the No, Do Not Create A Home Networking Setup Disk option, and click Next.

8. Click Finish to complete the Home Networking Wizard.

The Internet Connection Sharing host computer won't dial the ISP when a client computer needs an Internet connection

Source of the problem

When one of the computers that's not directly connected to the Internet (a *client computer*) needs an Internet connection, the computer with the connection (the *host computer*) should automatically dial in to the Internet service provider (ISP) and establish the connection. This is more than just courtesy. If the host computer won't establish an Internet connection when a client computer needs it, the client computers won't be able to reach the Internet at all.

When the host computer has a full-time Internet connection, such as a cable modem or a Digital Subscriber Line (DSL), you don't have to worry about the host computer dialing in—the connection is already established. But when the host computer won't dial when a client needs it to, you'll need to follow these steps.

How to fix it

1. On the host computer, click Start, point to Settings, and click Control Panel.

2. In Control Panel, double-click Internet or Internet Options. (In Windows Me, you might be able to click the Internet Options link in Control Panel instead.)

3. On the Connections tab in the Internet Properties dialog box, click Always Dial My Default Connection. ▶

   In the Dial-Up Settings list, make sure the connection you want to use is selected and designated as the default. If it isn't, click it and click Set Default.

I can't get to the Internet from computers on the network

Source of the problem

After you've installed Internet Connection Sharing, all the computers on the network should have simultaneous access to the Internet. But if you can connect to the host computer from one of the computers on the network that's not directly connected to the Internet (a *client computer*) but you can't browse the Web, there's a problem with the way Internet Connection Sharing is installed. To fix the problem, follow these steps.

How to fix it

1. Make sure the computer that has the connection to the Internet is turned on and connected to the Internet. Also make sure you can browse the Web from this computer.

If the host computer can't browse the Web, see "I Can't Connect to My Internet Service Provider," on page 168.

2. Try to browse the Web from another client computer on the home network.

If this works, Internet Connection Sharing is operational, but the network connection between your computer and the host computer isn't. See "I Can't Connect to Other Computers on the Network," on page 210.

If you can't browse the Web from any other computer, go on to the next step.

3. On the host computer, right-click Network Neighborhood or My Network Places (in Windows Me), and click Properties on the shortcut menu, and then on the Configuration tab in the Network dialog box, look for these two components in the installed network components list:

TCP/IP (Home) ➔ *[network adapter connected to the home network]*
TCP/IP (Shared) ➔ *[dial-up or network adapter connected to the Internet]* ▶

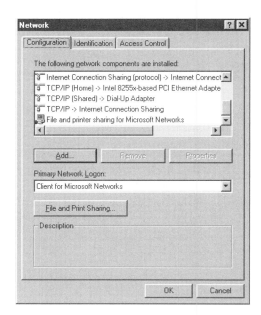

If you don't see both of these network components, Internet Connection Sharing will not work. Follow the steps in "Reinstalling Internet Connection Sharing," on the facing page.

If you do see both components but the Home and Shared connections are using the wrong adapters (for example, if the Home designation is on the dial-up adapter rather than the network adapter that's connected to the home network, or if the Shared designation is on the network adapter that you know is connected to a cable modem), follow the steps in "The Home and Shared Adapters Are Switched," below.

Reinstalling Internet Connection Sharing

If you're unable to get Internet Connection Sharing to work, your easiest and most effective option is to remove and reinstall Internet Connection Sharing by following these steps:

1. Click Start, point to Settings, and click Control Panel.

2. In Control Panel, double-click Add/Remove Programs. (In Windows Me, you might be able to click the Add/Remove Programs link in Control Panel instead.)

3. On the Windows Setup tab in the Add/Remove Programs Properties dialog box, double-click Internet Tools (in Windows 98 Second Edition) or Communications (in Windows Me).

4. Clear the Internet Connection Sharing check box, click OK, click OK again, and then click Yes if you are asked whether you want to restart your computer.

5. Repeat steps 1 through 4, but this time select the Internet Connection Sharing check box in step 4.

The Home and Shared adapters are switched

If you find that the Home and Shared designations appear on the wrong adapters, follow these steps:

1. Click Start, point to Settings, and click Control Panel.

2. In Control Panel, double-click Internet Options. (In Windows Me, you might be able to click the Internet Options link in Control Panel instead.)

3. On the Connections tab in the Internet Properties dialog box, click Sharing.

4. In the Connect To The Internet Using section of the Internet Connection Sharing dialog box, click the down arrow, and click the adapter that is connected to the Internet. ▶

5. In the Connect To My Home Network Using section of the dialog box, click the down arrow, and click the network adapter that connects to your home network.

6. Click OK, click OK again, and click Yes when you are asked whether you want to restart your computer.

I can't connect to other computers on the network

Source of the problem

After you've installed the network adapters, connected the cables, and configured the network in Windows or simply run the Home Networking Wizard in Windows Me, the computers in your home should begin talking to one another. You won't exactly hear the buzz of conversation, but you should be able to double-click Network Neighborhood or My Network Places (in Windows Me), double-click Entire Network, and find other computers listed. If not, you need to check your network settings by following these steps.

How to fix it

● First make sure you've logged on with your correct user name and password. If you press the Esc key or click Cancel in the logon dialog box, Windows will start but you won't be able to use the network because you have not logged on. To log on at this point, follow these steps:

1. Click Start, click Log Off, and then click Yes.

2. In the Enter Network Password dialog box, type your correct user name and password and click OK.

    If you're still unsuccessful at logging on, see "I Can't Log On to the Network," on page 214.

Check your computer name and workgroup name by following these steps:

1. Right-click Network Neighborhood or My Network Places (in Windows Me) on the desktop, and click Properties on the shortcut menu.

2. On the Identification tab in the Network dialog box, make sure there's a unique name for your computer in the Computer Name box and that the workgroup name in the Workgroup box is the same name used by the other computers on your network. ▶

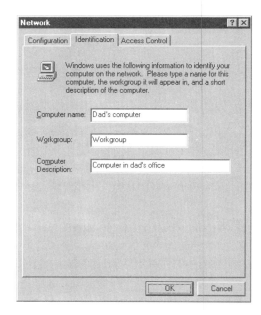

Make sure File and Printer Sharing for Microsoft Networks is installed by following these steps:

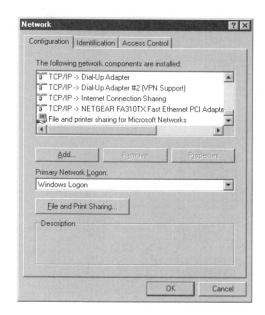

1. Right-click Network Neighborhood or My Network Places (in Windows Me) on the desktop, and click Properties on the shortcut menu.

2. On the Configuration tab in the Network dialog box, look for File And Printer Sharing For Microsoft Networks in the list of installed network components. ▶

If you find it, click OK. Otherwise, continue with this procedure.

3. Click File And Print Sharing, and in the File And Print Sharing dialog box, select the I Want To Be Able To Give Others Access To My Files check box and click OK.

4. Click Yes if you are asked whether you want to restart the computer.

If File and Printer Sharing is installed but you still can't see other computers on the network, verify that the network protocol you need is installed. The network protocol is the language that computers on the network speak. For a home network, you'll need TCP/IP on all computers for accessing the Internet and you can install the NetBEUI protocol for an easy and reliable connection among the computers on the network for transferring files and sharing resources.

1. Right-click Network Neighborhood or My Network Places (in Windows Me) on the desktop, and click Properties on the shortcut menu.

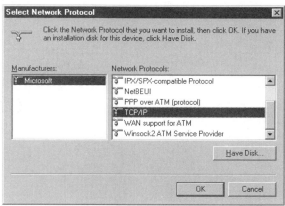

2. If the network protocol you need is not included in the installed network components list, click Add.

3. In the Select Network Component Type dialog box, click Protocol and click Add.

4. In the Select Network Protocol dialog box, click a company name in the Manufacturers list (for TCP/IP, click Microsoft), and click the protocol you need in the Network Protocols list. ▶

5. Click OK, click OK again to close the Network dialog box, and click Yes when you are asked whether you want to restart your computer.

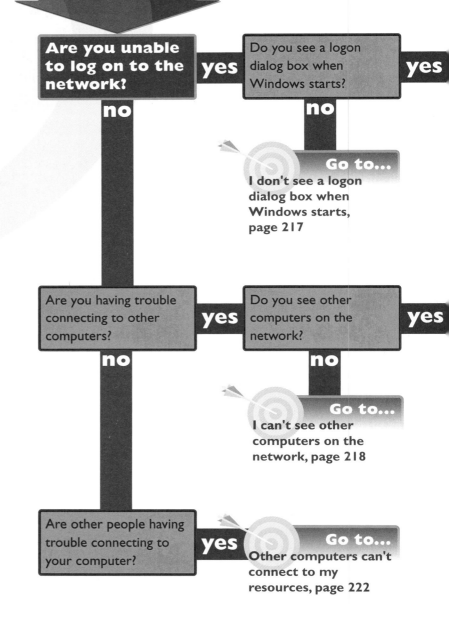

Are you unable to log on to the network? **yes** — **Do you see a logon dialog box when Windows starts?** **yes**

no

no

Go to...
I don't see a logon dialog box when Windows starts, page 217

Are you having trouble connecting to other computers? **yes** — **Do you see other computers on the network?** **yes**

no

no

Go to...
I can't see other computers on the network, page 218

Are other people having trouble connecting to your computer? **yes** — Go to...
Other computers can't connect to my resources, page 222

Do you get only one logon dialog box?

yes

Are you having trouble logging on to a domain?

yes

Go to...
I can't log on to a domain, page 221

no

Go to...
I have to enter too many passwords to log on, page 224

no

Go to...
I can't log on to the network, page 214

Are you having trouble finding a particular computer?

yes

Quick fix

If the computer you need to connect to is not visible in the Network Neighborhood or My Network Places window, search for it by following these steps:

1. Click Start, point to Find, and click Computer. In the Named box in the Find Computer dialog box, type the computer name and click Find Now.

2. In Windows Me, double-click My Network Places on the desktop, and in the My Network Places window, click Search on the toolbar. In the Computer Name box, type the name of the computer, and click Search Now.

If your solution isn't here
Check these related chapters:
The desktop, page 14
Dial-Up Networking, page 34
Networks, home, page 196
Startup, page 302
Or see the general troubleshooting tips on page xiii

I can't log on to the network

Source of the problem

Before you can exchange files, send e-mail messages on the network, or print using a network printer, you must log on to the network with your user name and password so that the network can register your presence and set up your connection. If your computer is connected to a network, you log on to the network when you log on to Windows. But if you can't log on because you get an error message about your password or logging on simply doesn't work, your first step should be to check with your network administrator to make sure your network account is valid. The network administrator might also be able to help resolve other issues that could be keeping you off the network. If you work in a small office without a network administrator or if there's nothing wrong with your account, begin troubleshooting by trying to log on again using the following steps.

How to fix it

1. Click Start, and then click Log Off.

2. Click Yes when you are asked whether you are sure you want to log off. ▶

3. In the Enter Network Password dialog box, type your user name in the User Name box and your password in the Password box. ▶

4. If you also usually enter a domain name, enter the domain name in the Domain box. ▶

   If you don't see a Domain box in the Enter Network Password dialog box, see "I Can't Log On to a Domain" on page 221.

5. Click OK.

   If you still can't log on, click Cancel and go on to the next steps.

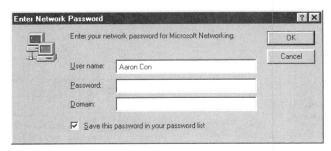

Check your computer name and workgroup name by following these steps:

1. Right-click Network Neighborhood or My Network Places (in Windows Me) on the desktop, and click Properties on the shortcut menu.

2. On the Identification tab in the Network dialog box, make sure there's a name for your computer in the Computer Name box and that the workgroup name in the Workgroup box is the same name used by the other computers on your network. ▶

    The computer name must be unique on the network, and the workgroup name must be the same as the workgroup name used by the other computers with which you need to communicate.

3. Click OK, and click Yes if you are asked whether you want to restart the computer.

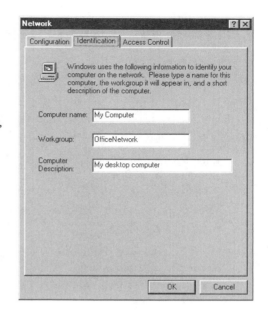

Make sure the correct network client is the primary network logon so that it is the client that's used to log on to the network.

For a Windows network, the client is Client For Microsoft Networks. Large organizations with a Novell network may require Client For NetWare Networks. If you're part of a large organization, check with the network administrator to determine the proper client.

To check the client, follow these steps:

1. Right-click Network Neighborhood or My Network Places (in Windows Me) on the desktop, and click Properties on the shortcut menu.

2. On the Configuration tab in the Network dialog box, take a look at the Primary Network Logon box. If the correct network client is not shown, or if the primary network logon is Windows Logon, click the down arrow and click the correct network client in the list. ▶

3. Click Yes if you are asked whether you want to restart the computer.

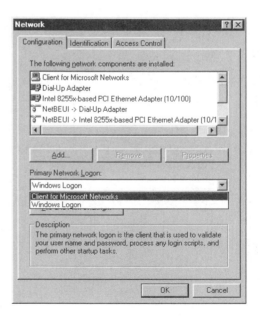

If this solution didn't solve your problem, go to the next page.

I can't log on to the network

(continued from page 215)

If you're still unable to log on to the network, your password list file might be damaged. To delete the password list file so that a new one will be created when you restart the computer, follow these steps:

1. Click Start, point to Find, and click Files Or Folders.
   In Windows Me, click Start, point to Search, and click For Files Or Folders.

2. In the Find All Files dialog box or the Search Results dialog box (in Windows Me), type ***.pwl** in the Named box (in the Search For Files Or Folders Named box in Windows Me). ▶

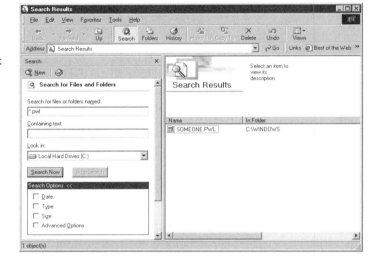

3. Click Find Now.
   In Windows Me, click Search Now.

4. Right-click the .pwl file that's found and that matches your user name.

5. Click Rename on the shortcut menu.

6. Type **temppwl** as the new name of the file, and press Enter.

7. Restart the computer.

> **Tip**
> When you share resources on a network, you can add a dollar sign ($) to the end of the name of a shared resource to make the resource available but not visible in someone else's Network Neighborhood or My Network Places window. Because others can't view your shared resources by browsing, only those to whom you've given the share name will know to connect to the resource.

I don't see a logon dialog box when Windows starts

Source of the problem

Not encountering a logon dialog box when you start Windows is either a problem or a pleasure, depending on whether you're worried about others using your computer to access the network and possibly your personal files without your permission. If you want to make sure that you're the only one who can access the network from your computer, you need to ensure that a logon dialog box appears when Windows starts. That way, someone at the computer can't log on to the network without your user name and password. To force a logon dialog box to appear, follow these steps.

How to fix it

1. Click Start, point to Settings, and click Control Panel.

2. In Control Panel, double-click Passwords. (In Windows Me, you might need to click View All Control Panel Options to see the Passwords icon.)

3. On the Change Passwords tab in the Passwords Properties dialog box, click Change Windows Password.

    If a dialog box opens asking you to specify which services you'd like to give the same password to, select the check boxes for all the services, and click OK.

4. In the Change Windows Password dialog box, type a new password in the New Password and Confirm New Password boxes, and then click OK. ▶ Leave the Old Password box blank.

5. A message box appears, informing you that your password was successfully changed. Click OK, and click Close to close the Passwords Properties dialog box.

6. Click Start, click Shut Down, and in the Shut Down Windows dialog box, click Restart and click OK.

I can't see other computers on the network

Source of the problem

Using Network Neighborhood or My Network Places (in Windows Me), you should be able to browse through the network finding other computers you can access, shared folders that you can open, and other resources you can use. To find all these resources, you double-click the Entire Network icon in the Network Neighborhood or My Network Places window (in Windows Me). But if all you see is a blank window that lists no computers, you need to make sure you are logged on to the network with the correct user name and password, and you need to ensure that all the network components are working properly. To begin, follow these steps.

How to fix it

● Make sure you have logged on with the correct user name and password.

   If you press the Esc key or click Cancel in the logon dialog box, Windows will start but you won't be able to use the network because you haven't logged on. To try logging on again, click Start, click Log Off, and then click Yes. In the Enter Network Password dialog box, type your user name and password and click OK. If you're still unsuccessful at logging on, see "I Can't Log On to the Network," on page 214.

Check your computer name and workgroup name by following these steps:

1. Right-click Network Neighborhood or My Network Places (in Windows Me) on the desktop, and click Properties on the shortcut menu.

2. On the Identification tab in the Network dialog box, make sure there's a name for your computer in the Computer Name box and that the workgroup name in the Workgroup box is the same name used by the other computers on your network. ▶

   The computer name must be unique on the network, and the workgroup name must be the same as the workgroup name used by the other computers with which you need to communicate.

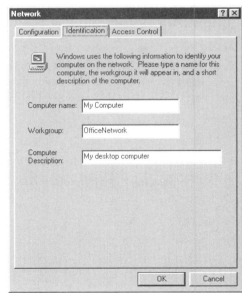

Check your network adapter and cables by following these steps:

1. Right-click My Computer on the desktop, and click Properties on the shortcut menu.

2. On the Device Manager tab in the System Properties dialog box, look in the list of devices to see whether your network adapter appears with an exclamation point, a question mark, or a red X on its icon. ▶

An exclamation point or a question mark on the icon of a network adapter indicates either a hardware problem with the adapter or a software conflict. For information about solving these problems, see "A New Device I've Installed Doesn't Work," on page 140. A red X indicates that the network adapter is disabled. To enable the adapter, double-click it, and on the General tab in the Properties dialog box, clear the Disable In This Hardware Profile check box and click OK.

3. Click OK to close the System Properties dialog box.

4. Make sure the network cable is firmly plugged in to the network card. (The cable probably looks like the cable used for cable TV.) If you can easily see the back of your computer, make sure the green light near the network cable jack is on, indicating that the network adapter is connected to the network. If the light is not on, recheck your cable connections.

If the network adapter and cable seem fine but you still can't see other computers on the network, make sure the *network protocol* you need is installed by following the steps below. The network protocol is the language that computers on the network speak. Your network administrator can confirm which protocol you need to use to connect to the network. If your network is in a small office or a small business without a network administrator, you should make sure that the TCP/IP network protocol is installed. If you're still unable to see other computers, you should install NetBEUI too.

1. Right-click Network Neighborhood or My Network Places (in Windows Me) on the desktop, and click Properties on the shortcut menu.

2. On the Configuration tab in the Network dialog box, look for the network protocol you need in the installed network components list.

If your network protocol is not listed, click Add. If your network protocol is listed, skip the rest of these steps.

> **To continue with this solution, go to the next page.**

I can't see other computers on the network

(continued from page 219)

3. In the Select Network Component Type dialog box, click Protocol in the list, and click Add.

4. In the Select Network Protocol dialog box, click a company name in the Manufacturers list (for TCP/IP, click Microsoft), and click the protocol you need in the Network Protocols list. ▶

5. Click OK, click OK again to close the Network dialog box, and click Yes when you are asked whether you want to restart your computer.

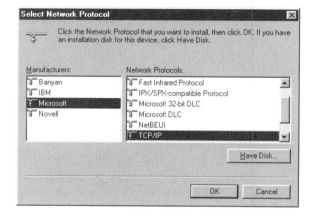

If all else fails, check the network adapter manufacturer's Web site for an updated driver for the adapter, and download and install any update that's available. If no update is available, remove and reinstall the network adapter and its driver in Device Manager by following these steps:

1. Right-click Network Neighborhood or My Network Places (in Windows Me) on the desktop, and click Properties on the shortcut menu.

2. In the list of installed network components on the Configuration tab in the Network dialog box, click the network adapter, and click Remove.

3. Click OK when you see a message asking whether you want to remove the network adapter or just disable it.

4. Click OK to close the Network dialog box, and click Yes when you are asked whether you want to restart your computer.

5. Follow the steps in the Add New Hardware Wizard, which appears after the computer restarts, to reinstall the network adapter and its driver.

Also remove and reinstall the network client and network protocols in the Network dialog box. Just by reinstalling these components, you may resolve a networking problem that's keeping your computer from connecting to the network.

I can't log on to a domain

Source of the problem

A domain is a collection of workgroups and computers, all of which can share resources on the network. If you usually enter a domain name when you log on to Windows but the Domain box doesn't appear in the Enter Network Password dialog box, you need to modify a network setting by following the procedure below.

How to fix it

1. Right-click Network Neighborhood or My Network Places (in Windows Me) on the desktop, and click Properties on the shortcut menu.

2. On the Configuration tab in the Network dialog box, click Client For Microsoft Networks in the list of installed network components, and click Properties.

3. In the Client For Microsoft Networks Properties dialog box, select the Log On To Windows NT Domain check box. ▶

4. Click OK, click OK again to close the Network dialog box, and click Yes when you are asked whether you want to restart your computer.

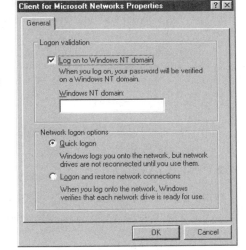

If, on the other hand, you see a Domain box in the Enter Network Password dialog box but you do not normally enter a domain name, remove the Domain box by following these steps:

1. When the computer starts, press the Esc key to close the Enter Network Password dialog box, right-click Network Neighborhood or My Network Places (in Windows Me) on the desktop, and click Properties on the shortcut menu.

2. On the Configuration tab in the Network dialog box, click Client For Microsoft Networks in the list of installed network components, and click Properties.

3. Clear the Log On To Windows NT Domain check box, click OK, click OK again to close the Network dialog box, and click Yes when you are asked whether you want to restart the computer.

Other computers can't connect to my resources

Source of the problem

Each computer attached to a network is able to share its resources with other computers on the network. But unless you specifically allow sharing of particular disk drives, folders, or printers, these resources won't be available to other people working at other computers.

Everything you learned about sharing in elementary school applies here. Sharing is letting others use your resources, and you want to be magnanimous in sharing, particularly in a small office network in which, for example, you might be the only one who's connected to the color printer that everyone wants to use. But unlike childhood sharing, you need to use some discretion in sharing your computer's resources. Rather than share an entire disk drive, for example, you should share only certain folders that you've designated for public information. Otherwise, everyone will be able to see everything that's on your computer.

To share a resource, you need to turn on the ability to share and then select a resource to share by following these steps.

How to fix it

1. Right-click Network Neighborhood or My Network Places (in Windows Me) on the desktop, and click Properties on the shortcut menu.

2. In the Network dialog box, click File And Print Sharing.

3. In the File And Print Sharing dialog box, select the I Want To Be Able To Give Others Access To My Files check box. ▶

    If you also want to share a printer, select the I Want To Be Able To Allow Others To Print To My Printer(s) check box too.

4. Click OK, click OK again to close the Network dialog box, and click Yes if you are asked whether you want to restart your computer.

5. After the computer restarts, double-click My Computer on the desktop.

6. In the My Computer window, navigate to the disk drive or folder you want to share.

7. Right-click the disk drive or folder, click Sharing on the shortcut menu, and on the Sharing tab in the Properties dialog box for the disk drive or folder, click Shared As.

8. In the Share Name box, replace the default name with any name you want. ▶

  In the Comment box, you can optionally type a brief description of the shared resource.

9. Click one of the three Access Type options, depending on your needs.

  Read-Only allows others to open and copy files or folders but won't allow anyone to change, add, or remove them. *Full* gives others the right to change, add, or remove files or folders. *Depends On Password* applies either Read-Only or Full access, depending on the password entered by someone trying to access the shared resource.

10. In the Passwords section, type a password in the Read-Only Password or Full Access Password box, depending on which Access Type option you selected.

  If you selected Depends On Password as the Access Type, type passwords in both password boxes so that you can specify by the password you give out whether someone will have full access or read-only access to the resource.

  If you want everyone on the network to have read-only or full access, you can skip this step and leave the Passwords boxes blank.

11. Click OK. The icon for the shared resource now shows a cradling hand to indicate that the resource is shared. ▶

Sharing a Printer

You can share a printer the same way you share a disk drive or folder so that others can print using the printer even though it's not physically connected to their computers. To share a printer, follow these steps:

1. Click Start, point to Settings, and then click Printers.

2. In the Printers window, right-click the icon of the printer you want to share, and click Sharing on the shortcut menu.

  If you don't see Sharing on the shortcut menu, you need to click File And Print Sharing on the Configuration tab in the Network dialog box (see the previous procedure for information about opening this dialog box) and then select the I Want To Be Able To Allow Others To Use My Printer(s) check box in the File And Print Sharing dialog box.

3. In the Properties dialog box for the printer, click the Shared As option, and then type a name for the shared printer, a comment that provides others with details about the printer, and an optional password, and click OK.

I have to enter too many passwords to log on

Source of the problem

What's more annoying than spending the morning entering passwords just so you can log on to your own computer and the network?

If you're connecting to a network in an organization with a central server that permits access through passwords, you might need to enter one password to log on to your own computer and a second password to connect to the network. Here's how to reduce that to a single password prompt, or eliminate passwords altogether if you're on a network of Windows computers without a central server.

How to fix it

1. Click Start, point to Settings, and click Control Panel.

2. In Control Panel, double-click Passwords. (In Windows Me, you might need to click View All Control Panel Options to see the Passwords option.)

3. On the User Profiles tab in the Passwords Properties dialog box, click the All Users Of This Computer Use The Same Preferences And Desktop Settings option. ▶

   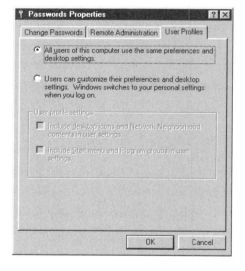

   This setting disables user profiles so that other people can no longer log on to your computer with their own user names and passwords. Without their own user names and passwords, others won't be able to restore their own desktops and personalized settings. For more information about user profiles, see "Someone Else's Desktop Appears When Windows Starts," on page 20.

4. On the Change Passwords tab in the Passwords Properties dialog box, click Change Windows Password.

   If a dialog box opens asking whether you want to change other passwords to be the same as your Windows password, select the Microsoft Networking check box. You can also select the check boxes next to other services to unify your passwords.

5. In the Change Windows Password dialog box, type your current Windows password (the password you enter to log on to Windows rather than the network) in the Old Password box, and then click OK without typing anything into the New Password and Confirm New Password boxes. This creates a blank password.

6. Click OK, and then close Control Panel.

7. Right-click Network Neighborhood or My Network Places (in Windows Me) on the desktop, and click Properties on the shortcut menu.

8. On the Configuration tab in the Network dialog box, click the Primary Network Logon down arrow and click Windows Logon in the list. ▶

9. Click OK, and then click Yes when you are asked whether you want to restart your computer.

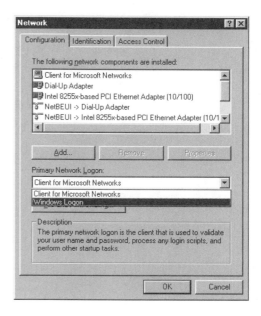

If you log on to a network with a central server (a Windows NT or Windows 2000 server), you can also store your network password so that you don't have to enter it each time. Follow these steps:

1. When the computer restarts after step 9 in the procedure above, click OK without entering a user name or password in the Welcome To Windows dialog box, and then, in the Enter Network Password dialog box, type your user name and network password.

2. Select the Save This Password In Your Password List check box, and then click OK.

Enter passwords automatically using Tweak UI

Tweak UI, a free utility that lets you change many of the settings in Windows, can enter your network password for you. In the future, you'll skip right past the logon dialog box. For more information about Tweak UI, see "What Is Tweak UI?" on page 32, and "Where Do I Get Tweak UI?" on page 33. Use Tweak UI with caution, though, as it removes your usual password protection, so others can impersonate you by starting your computer, automatically logging on to the network, and accessing all your private files. If you'd like to use Tweak UI, follow these steps:

1. Click Start, point to Settings, and click Control Panel. In Control Panel, double-click Tweak UI. (In Windows Me, you might have to click View All Control Panel Options to see the Tweak UI icon.)

2. On the Network tab in the Tweak UI dialog box, select the Log On Automatically At System Startup check box, and then enter your network user name and password in the appropriate boxes, and click OK.

3. Click Start, click Shut Down, and then select Restart and click OK to restart the computer.

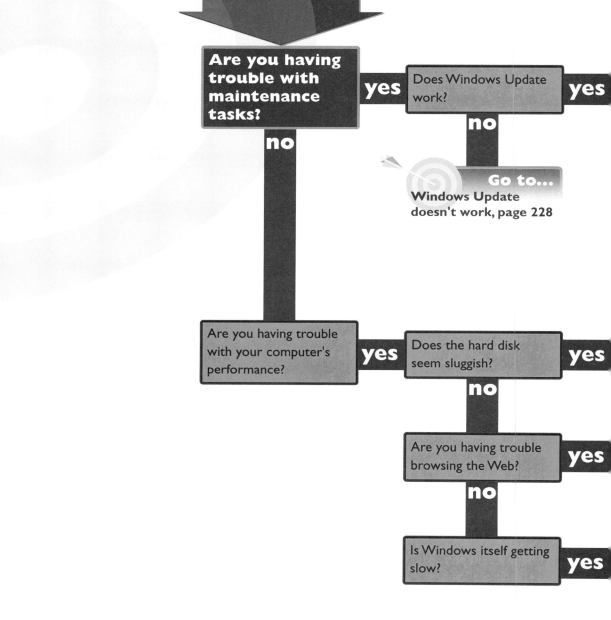

Are you having trouble with maintenance tasks?

yes → **Does Windows Update work?**

yes →

no ↓

Go to...
Windows Update doesn't work, page 228

no ↓

Are you having trouble with your computer's performance?

yes → **Does the hard disk seem sluggish?**

yes →

no ↓

Are you having trouble browsing the Web?

yes →

no ↓

Is Windows itself getting slow?

yes →

Are you having trouble with the Maintenance Wizard?

yes

Go to...
Maintenance Wizard tasks won't run, page 232

no

Is defragmenting your hard disk hanging up?

yes

Quick fix

Defragmentation of your hard disk can stall if your Internet Explorer History folder has files with names longer than 256 characters. Deleting the files in the History folder removes the current tracking of which Web sites you've visited, and a new record will begin.

1. In Internet Explorer, click Internet Options on the View menu (in Internet Explorer 4) or the Tools menu (in Internet Explorer 5).

2. On the General tab in the Internet Options dialog box, click Clear History.

Go to...
My hard disk seems slower, page 234

Go to...
Web browsing is slow, page 238

Go to...
Windows has become sluggish, page 236

If your solution isn't here
Check these related chapters:
  Hard disks, page 128
  Hardware, page 138
  Programs, page 252
  The screen, page 264
Or see the general troubleshooting tips on page xiii

Windows Update doesn't work

Source of the problem

The Microsoft Windows Update Web site checks your installation of Windows 98 or Windows Me, checks to see whether newer components or updated files are available, and then offers to install the updates for you. But if you get a blank page instead of the Windows Update Web page, or you get an error message or your computer stops responding while you use Windows Update, you might have any one of a number of problems. Here's how to solve the most common troubles. Try each solution, and continue to the next solution if you still have problems with Windows Update.

How to fix it

1. Make sure you're connected to the Internet. Windows Update must go to the Microsoft Web site to obtain the latest updates.

2. Make sure you've registered your copy of Windows. If you're not sure, click Start, click Run, and type **Regwiz /r** in the Open box to start the Registration Wizard.

   In Windows 98, you can determine whether your copy of Windows is registered by clicking Start, pointing to Programs, pointing to Accessories, pointing to System Tools, and clicking Welcome To Windows. ▶

   If Register Now doesn't have a check mark next to it, your copy of Windows 98 is not registered. Click Register Now to register.

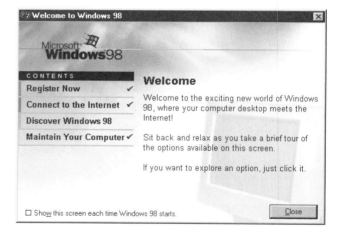

Verify that Internet Explorer's security level is set to Medium by following these steps:

1. Double-click Internet Explorer on the desktop, and on the View menu (in Internet Explorer 4) or the Tools menu (in Internet Explorer 5), click Internet Options.

2. On the Security tab in the Internet Options dialog box, make sure the Internet option is selected in the Select A Web Content Zone To Specify Its Security Settings section.

3. Verify that the Security Level For This Zone slider is set to Medium, and click OK. If the slider is set to High, drag it down to Medium and click OK. ▶

Clear the Internet Explorer cache and history by following these steps:

1. Double-click Internet Explorer on the desktop, and on the View menu (in Internet Explorer 4) or the Tools menu (in Internet Explorer 5), click Internet Options.

2. On the General tab in the Internet Options dialog box, click Delete Files, and in the Delete Files dialog box, select the Delete All Offline Content check box and click OK.

3. Click Clear History, and click OK. If you are asked whether you are sure you want to delete your history of visited Web sites, click Yes.

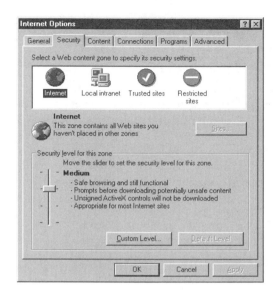

In Windows 98, clear the contents of the WindowsUpdate folder by following these steps:

1. Right-click My Computer on the desktop, and click Explore on the shortcut menu.

2. In the left pane of the My Computer window, click the plus sign next to the hard disk that contains the Windows folder.

3. Click the plus sign next to the Program Files folder, and then click the WindowsUpdate folder.

4. In the right pane of Windows Explorer, click Wuhistv3.log, and then click Invert Selection on the Edit menu. ▶

You want to save the Wuhistv3.log file because it contains a list of the updates you've down-loaded and installed.

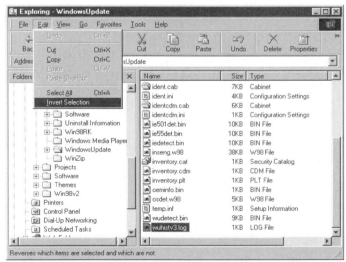

To continue with this solution, go to the next page.

Windows Update doesn't work

(continued from page 229)

5. Press the Delete key to delete everything but the Wuhistv3.log file, click Yes to confirm deletion of the files, and then close Windows Explorer.

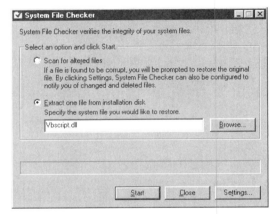

Windows 98 In Windows 98, follow the steps below to use the System File Checker to extract and install a new copy of the Vbscript.dll file, one of the files Windows Update requires in order to run. (Windows Me users can skip this procedure because the Windows Me System File Protection feature should keep the Vbscript.dll file safe.)

1. Click Start, point to Programs, point to Accessories, point to System Tools, and then click System Information.

2. On the Tools menu of the Microsoft System Information window, click System File Checker.

3. In the System File Checker dialog box, click Extract One File From Installation Disk, type **Vbscript.dll** in the Specify The System File You Would Like To Restore box, and click Start. ▶

4. In the Extract File dialog box, click OK to accept the default location source and destination for the file.

5. Click OK in the Backup File dialog box to back up the previous version of the file, and click Yes if you are asked whether you want to create a new folder.

6. Click OK, click Close, and then close the Microsoft System Information window.

Download and install the latest Microsoft Virtual Machine, which runs programs written in the JAVA language and is used by Windows Update:

1. Go to *www.microsoft.com/java/vm/dl_vm40.htm*.

2. Follow the instructions on the Web page to download and install a new Microsoft Virtual Machine.

Follow these steps to remove and reinstall Active Setup and Windows Update:

1. Double-click Internet Explorer on the desktop, and on the View menu (in Internet Explorer 4) or the Tools menu (in Internet Explorer 5), click Internet Options.

2. On the General tab in the Internet Options dialog box, click Settings, and in the Settings dialog box, click View Objects. ▶

3. In the Downloaded Program Files window, right-click the file Wuv3is.dll, and click Delete on the shortcut menu. (Ignore this step if the file doesn't exist.)

4. In the same window, right-click any one of these files: Wusysinfo, Wuredirinforb, or InstallEngineCTL Object. Then click Update on the shortcut menu. Ignore this step and skip to step 6 if these files do not exist.

5. When you are prompted to install Active Setup, click Yes, and then close the Downloaded Program Files window, click OK, and click OK again.

6. Click Start, point to Find (in Windows 98) or Search (in Windows Me), and click Files Or Folders (in Windows 98) or For Files Or Folders (in Windows Me).

7. In the Find All Files dialog box in Windows 98, type **Asctrls.ocx** in the Named box and click Find Now. (In Windows Me, type **Asctrls.ocx** in the Search For Files Or Folders Named box and click Search Now.)

8. Right-click Asctrls.ocx in the list of found files, click Delete on the shortcut menu, and click Yes in the Confirm File Delete dialog box. ▶

9. Repeat steps 6 through 8, but find and delete these files instead, if they exist: Inseng.dll, Wudetect.dll, Wupdatto.dll, and Wuredirb.dll.

10. Restart the computer.

Maintenance Wizard tasks won't run

Source of the problem

The Maintenance Wizard lets you schedule routine tasks, such as defragmenting the hard disk to keep your files quickly accessible, running ScanDisk to circumvent disk errors before they threaten your files, and running Disk Cleanup, which eliminates excess files that can clog your disks. But if the Task Scheduler won't run the tasks you've scheduled, investigate the causes by following these steps.

How to fix it

1. Verify that your computer's clock is set to the correct time. The Task Scheduler depends on the clock to determine when to start tasks.

   To change your computer's clock, right-click the clock on the taskbar, and click Adjust Date/Time on the shortcut menu. To get the exact time from the Time Service Department at the U.S. Naval Observatory, go to *tycho.usno.navy.mil/what.html*.

2. Double-click My Computer on the desktop, and in the My Computer window, double-click Scheduled Tasks. (In Windows Me, click Start, point to Programs, point to Accessories, point to System Tools, and click Scheduled Tasks.)

3. On the Advanced menu in the Scheduled Tasks window, click either Start Using Task Scheduler or Continue Task Scheduler, if either command is available. ▶

   If either of these commands is available, the Task Scheduler was either stopped or paused.

4. Make sure your computer is not turned off when the maintenance tasks are scheduled to run.

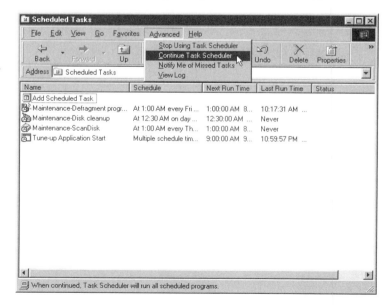

If you've set the Task Scheduler to run maintenance tasks overnight, be sure to leave the computer on overnight, at least on the night that the maintenance tasks are scheduled to run.

5. If you're using a computer without Advanced Configuration and Power Interface (ACPI) power management or with Advanced Power Management (APM) earlier than version 1.2, make sure that your computer is not in standby mode when the Task Scheduler is scheduled to run maintenance tasks. To check your level of power management, see "Checking Your Computer's Power Management Support," below.

6. Double-click My Computer, double-click the disk that contains the Windows folder, double-click the Windows folder, click Show Files if you don't see folders, and then double-click the Tasks folder. (In Windows Me, you need to click View The Entire Contents Of This Folder if you don't see folders in the Windows folder.) Each maintenance task that you've scheduled should have a file in the Tasks folder. If you don't see a file for a task, run the Maintenance Wizard again and reschedule the task. You can start the Maintenance Wizard by clicking Start, pointing to Programs, pointing to Accessories, pointing to System Tools, and clicking Maintenance Wizard.

Checking your computer's power management support

If your computer provides ACPI power management or APM version 1.2 (rather than APM version 1.1 or earlier), the Task Scheduler can wake the computer from standby mode to run its scheduled tasks. The computer's documentation can tell you the level of power management built into your computer, but if you don't have the documentation, follow these steps:

1. Right-click My Computer, and click Properties on the shortcut menu.

2. On the Device Manager tab in the System Properties dialog box, click the plus sign next to System Devices.

3. If you see Advanced Power Management Support in the list of system devices, click it and click Properties. In the Advanced Power Management Support

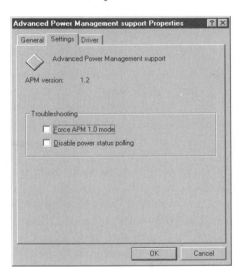

Properties dialog box, click the Settings tab to see the APM version. Remember, APM version 1.2 can wake the computer from standby mode to run scheduled tasks. ▶

> **Tip**
> To be notified if the Task Scheduler misses any tasks because the computer was turned off or the Task Scheduler was stopped or paused, double-click My Computer, double-click Scheduled Tasks, click the Advanced menu in the Schedule Tasks window, and click Notify Me Of Missed Tasks.

If you see ACPI entries in the list of system devices, your computer supports ACPI, so it will wake and perform maintenance tasks on schedule.

My hard disk seems slower

Source of the problem

If your hard disk seems to be dawdling when it used to scamper along, it's probably slowing down as it fills with files. Nothing affects the perceived performance of your computer more than the real speed at which your hard disk is working, but the more you use a hard disk, the more its files become fragmented, and the more it seems to slow down. To restore a hard disk to its full speed, you must regularly defragment the hard disk—every week, every month, or at an interval that makes sense for you. For more about fragmentation, see "Why Defragment?" on the facing page.

Here are several other procedures you can use not only to restore the speed of your hard disk, but perhaps to make it run even better than new.

How to fix it

1. Before you defragment a hard disk, see "The Disk Defragmenter Keeps Starting Over," on page 136, to learn the steps you should take in advance.

2. Double-click My Computer on the desktop, right-click the hard disk you want to defragment, and click Properties on the shortcut menu.

3. On the Tools tab in the Properties dialog box, click Defragment Now. ▶

   When the defragmentation is complete, click Yes to quit the Disk Defragmenter, and click OK to close the Properties dialog box.

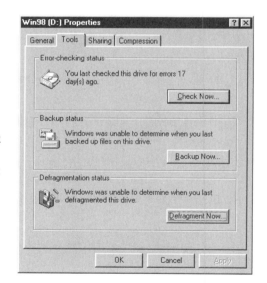

In addition to defragmenting the hard disk, you can change the Typical Role and Read-Ahead Optimization settings for the hard disk to increase its speed. If you have less than 32 MB of memory in your computer, skip this set of steps and leave the default settings, as this procedure will cause Windows to dedicate more RAM to speeding up the operation of the hard disk.

1. Right-click My Computer on the desktop, and click Properties on the shortcut menu.

2. On the Performance tab in the System Properties dialog box, click File System.

---

3. On the Hard Disk tab in the File System Properties dialog box, click the Typical Role Of This Computer down arrow and click Network Server in the list. ▶

4. Make sure the Read-Ahead Optimization slider is dragged all the way to the right, to Full.

5. Click OK, and click OK again to close the System Properties dialog box.

Why defragment?

Every time you save a file, Windows stores bits and pieces of it in the spaces that were created when you deleted other files. A large file can be scattered in dozens of small fragments on a hard disk. When you open the file, the hard disk must gather all those fragments, reassemble them into a single unit, and then deliver the reconstituted file to Windows.

By routinely defragmenting the hard disk (weekly or monthly, depending on how much you use your computer), you move the bits and pieces of files into contiguous chunks, doing the reassembly work before you need to open the file.

Defragmenting a hard disk will make it noticeably faster, so be sure to include it as a task that the Task Scheduler performs regularly. See "Maintenance Wizard Tasks Won't Run," on page 232, for more information about properly scheduling disk defragmenting.

Tip
Your hard disk will seem sluggish if it's running in MS-DOS Compatibility mode. Right-click My Computer on the desktop, click Properties on the shortcut menu, and click the Performance tab in the System Properties dialog box. If you see a message about MS-DOS Compatibility mode, see the Microsoft Knowledge Base article "Troubleshooting MS-DOS Compatibility Mode on Hard Disks," at *support. microsoft.com/support/kb/ articles/Q130/1/79.asp?LN= EN-US&SD=gn&FR=0.*

Other ways to speed up the hard disk

Adding more memory to your computer, as well as shutting down programs you aren't using, also helps speed up a hard disk because it allows Windows to create a larger cache in the computer's memory. As Windows reads files, it grabs a few more files from the hard disk and stores them in the cache. The next time Windows needs the same files or files stored nearby on the hard disk, it can get them quickly from the cache rather than retrieve them from the hard disk, which takes longer.

Windows also uses the cache to temporarily hold some of the components of the programs you are running. For example, in the cache it might store the part of the program that saves your documents. As you work, Windows finds the components it needs in the cache so that it doesn't have to tie up your hard disk with retrieving them.

Windows has become sluggish

Source of the problem

The longer you use Windows, the more encumbered it becomes by all the software and hardware you've installed. Windows must give each program and device you've added a little time and attention, and it eventually becomes noticeably bogged down and loses its crisp responsiveness to your mouse clicks and menu commands.

Some computer enthusiasts periodically start fresh with a clean, new installation of Windows. If you're not ready for that level of hassle, though, you can take a number of less drastic steps to restore a good deal of the old bounce to Windows.

How to fix it

1. Click Start, point to Settings, and click Control Panel.

2. In Control Panel, double-click Add/Remove Programs. (In Windows Me, single-click the Add/Remove Programs link, or if all the options are visible in Control Panel, double-click the Add/Remove Programs icon.)

3. On the Install/Uninstall tab of the Add/Remove Programs Properties dialog box, click a program in the list that you rarely or never use, and click Add/Remove to remove the program. ▶

   Follow the steps required by the uninstallation program, clicking Yes if you are asked whether you want to restart the computer.

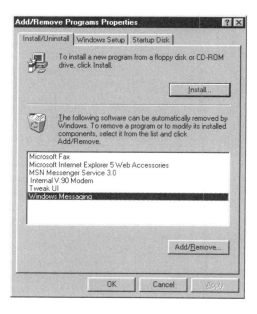

4. Repeat steps 1 through 3, continuing to remove programs until you've pared down the program list to only those programs you actually use.

5. In the same dialog box, click the Windows Setup tab, and clear the check boxes next to Windows components that you rarely or never use.

6. Click OK, and then click Yes if you are prompted to restart the computer.

Because the speed of the hard disk is so critical to the speed of Windows, follow these steps to make sure your hard disk is performing optimally:

1. Defragment the hard disk and follow the other procedures described in "My Hard Disk Seems Slower," on page 234, to optimize the speed of your hard disk.

2. Free up as much space as possible on your hard disk (at least 100 MB) to provide more space for virtual memory. For information about freeing up space, see "I've Run Out of Space on My Hard Disk," on page 130.

3. If you're using Windows 98 or Windows Me, convert the hard disk to FAT32.

4. Verify that your hard disk is not running in MS-DOS Compatibility mode by right-clicking My Computer on the desktop, clicking Properties on the shortcut menu, and clicking the Performance tab in the System Properties dialog box. If a message indicates that a disk is running in MS-DOS Compatibility mode, see the Microsoft Knowledge Base article "Troubleshooting MS-DOS Compatibility Mode on Hard Disks," at *support.microsoft.com/support/kb/articles/Q130/1/79.asp?LN=EN-US&SD=gn&FR=0*.

> **Tip**
>
> The best way to make Windows run faster is to improve the hardware on which it's running. Adding more memory, replacing your hard disk or video adapter with a newer model, or even going so far as to replace the motherboard and processor with faster versions can have huge payoffs in your productivity. Your local computer store might be able to perform one or more of these upgrades.

Tweak UI, the Control Panel program you can use to modify the Windows user interface, offers a few enhancements to try. For more information about installing Tweak UI, see "What Is Tweak UI?" on page 32, and "Where Do I Get Tweak UI?" on page 33.

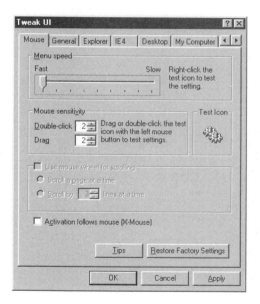

1. Click Start, point to Settings, and then click Control Panel.

2. In Control Panel, double-click Tweak UI. (In Windows Me, you might need to click View All Control Panel Options to see the Tweak UI option.)

3. On the Mouse tab in the Tweak UI dialog box, drag the Menu Speed slider all the way to the left, to Fast, to increase the speed with which the Start menu and other menus open. ▶

4. Click the General tab, and clear the Window Animation, Menu Animation, Combo Box Animation, and List Box Animation check boxes. Then click OK.

Web browsing is slow

Source of the problem

Web browsing is never rapid enough, no matter how fast your connection to the Internet. Even if you've got a high-speed Internet connection, such as a Digital Subscriber Line (DSL) or a cable modem, you can encounter Internet slowdowns, technical glitches at your Internet service provider (ISP), and busy Web servers that can't send out Web pages quickly enough. But if your connection seems slower than usual, or if you're plagued by chronically slow browsing, you can check a few things and change a few settings to make sure you're getting the most out of your modem and your browser.

How to fix it

1. Connect to your ISP as you normally do, and then verify the speed at which you're connected by double-clicking the dial-up icon, near the clock on the taskbar. ▶

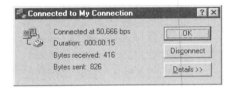

2. If you're familiar with your typical connection speed and the current connection speed is substantially slower than usual (if the connection is 19,200 bps rather than your usual 36,400 bps, for example), click Disconnect and dial the connection again; otherwise, click OK to close the dialog box.

   If you're still unable to get a connection that's as fast as usual, disconnect and restart Windows, which resets Dial-Up Networking.

Turn off the display of pictures so that your browser downloads only the text on Web pages, as follows:

1. Double-click Internet Explorer on the desktop.

2. On the View menu (in Internet Explorer 4) or the Tools menu (in Internet Explorer 5), click Internet Options.

3. On the Advanced tab in the Internet Options dialog box, clear the Show Pictures check box under Multimedia in the Settings list and click OK. ▶

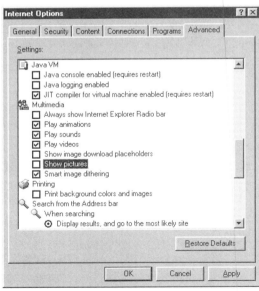

The Advanced tab in Internet Explorer 5

Turning off pictures is particularly helpful when you're using a slow connection in an office or a hotel room, but it can disable navigational features on Web pages, such as areas that you can click to move through a Web site. To view an individual picture on a page, right-click the placeholder frame that appears at the picture's position, and click Show Picture on the shortcut menu.

Disable the Content Advisor, which helps you control the Internet content that can be viewed on the computer, by following these steps:

1. In Internet Explorer, click Internet Options on the View menu (in Internet Explorer 4) or the Tools menu (in Internet Explorer 5).

2. On the Content tab in the Internet Options dialog box, click Disable in the Content Advisor section, and click OK. ▶

   If an Enable button is visible in the Content Advisor section, the Content Advisor is not running.

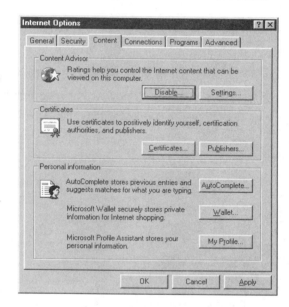

Disable page transitions, which fade Web pages in and out, by following these steps:

1. In Internet Explorer, click Internet Options on the View menu (in Internet Explorer 4) or the Tools menu (in Internet Explorer 5).

2. On the Advanced tab in the Internet Options dialog box, clear the Enable Page Transitions check box under Browsing, and click OK. ▶

Follow these steps to check your modem and its connection:

1. Visit the modem manufacturer's Web site, and look for an updated driver or software that you can download to update the modem's BIOS (also called *firmware*). The BIOS controls the operation of the modem, and updating it might enhance the modem's speed, especially if the BIOS update upgrades your modem from a V.34 model (28.8 or 33.6 Kbps) to V.90 (also referred to as 56K).

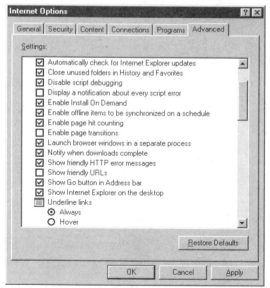

To continue with this solution, go to the next page.

Web browsing is slow

(continued from page 239)

2. Connect a regular phone to the modem line and listen for line noise. If you hear noise, ask your local phone company to clear the phone line. Be persistent with the phone company if you live in a community where your phone connections are strong and clear but the modem on a separate modem line is unable to connect at anything close to its typical speed.

3. Verify that the cords connecting your modem to the computer and to the wall jack are tightly plugged in. If the cord connections are tight and you're still having trouble, replace the cords with new ones.

Follow these steps to check your modem settings:

1. Right-click My Computer on the desktop, and click Properties on the shortcut menu.

2. On the Device Manager tab in the System Properties dialog box, click the plus sign next to Modem.

3. Click your modem, and click Properties.

4. On the Connection tab in the Properties dialog box for the modem, click Port Settings.

5. In the Advanced Port Settings dialog box, drag the Receive Buffer and Transmit Buffer sliders all the way to the right, to High. In Windows Me, click the Receive Buffer down arrow and the Transmit Buffer down arrow, and click Maximum in each list. ▶

6. Click OK, and click OK again to close the Properties dialog box for the modem.

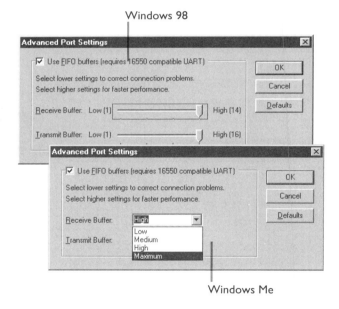

Windows 98

Windows Me

If you're using an external modem, follow these steps to check your port settings. If your modem is internal, skip these steps.

1. On the Device Manager tab in the System Properties dialog box, click the plus sign next to Ports.

2. Click the port your modem uses, and click Properties.

3. On the Port Settings tab in the Communications Port Properties dialog box, click the Bits Per Second down arrow and click 115200. ▶

4. Click the Flow Control down arrow, and click Hardware.

5. Click Advanced, and in the Advanced Port Settings dialog box, drag the Receive Buffer and Transmit Buffer sliders all the way to the right, to High. In Windows Me, click the Receive Buffer down arrow and the Transmit Buffer down arrow, and click Maximum in each list.

6. Click OK three times to close all the dialog boxes.

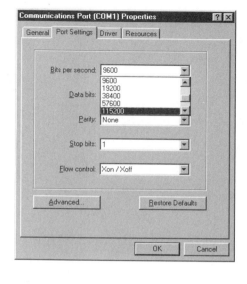

Optimize your TCP/IP communication settings by following these steps:

1. Double-click My Computer and, in the My Computer window, double-click Dial-Up Networking. In Windows Me, click Start, point to Settings, and click Dial-Up Networking.

2. Right-click the connection you use to dial the Internet, and click Properties on the shortcut menu.

3. In the dialog box for the connection, click the Server Types tab (the Networking tab in Windows Me), and select the Enable Software Compression check box.

4. Make sure the NetBEUI and IPX/SPX Compatible check boxes are cleared. ▶

5. Click TCP/IP Settings, and in the TCP/IP Settings dialog box, make sure the Use IP Header Compression check box is selected.

6. Click OK twice to close the dialog boxes, and close the Dial-Up Networking window.

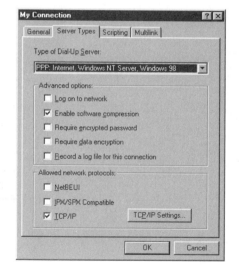

Here are two last steps to follow to obtain maximum browsing speed:

1. Make sure that you've closed all other programs that use your Internet connection, such as ICQ, AOL Instant Messenger, and MSN Messenger Service.

2. If you're using Windows 98 or Windows Me, turn off the Active Desktop by right-clicking anywhere on the desktop, pointing to Active Desktop, and making sure View As Web Page (in Windows 98) or Show Web Content (in Windows Me) is not selected. If it is, deselect it.

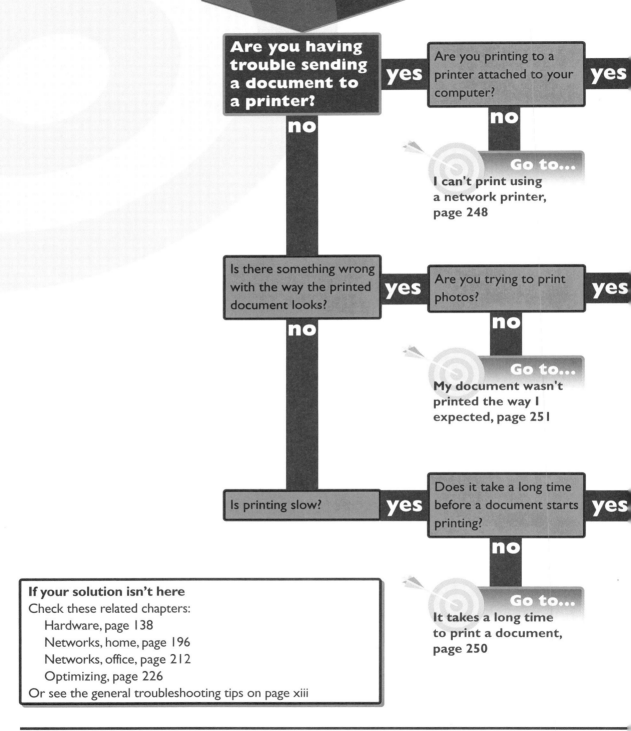

Are you having trouble sending a document to a printer? — **yes** → Are you printing to a printer attached to your computer? — **yes**

no ↓

no ↓

Go to...
I can't print using a network printer, page 248

Is there something wrong with the way the printed document looks? — **yes** → Are you trying to print photos? — **yes**

no ↓

no ↓

Go to...
My document wasn't printed the way I expected, page 251

Is printing slow? — **yes** → Does it take a long time before a document starts printing? — **yes**

no ↓

Go to...
It takes a long time to print a document, page 250

If your solution isn't here
Check these related chapters:
Hardware, page 138
Networks, home, page 196
Networks, office, page 212
Optimizing, page 226
Or see the general troubleshooting tips on page xiii

Printing

Is Windows having trouble getting status information from the printer?

yes

no

Quick fix

When your computer seems unable to get status information from the printer, such as a notification that it's out of paper or that the paper path is jammed, the most likely cause is that you're not using a bidirectional printer cable. (Note that very old printers might not be able to send status information at all.) You should replace your current printer cable with an IEEE-1284 cable, which provides bidirectional communications (that is, both to and from the printer). Also, the printer port on the computer must be set in the computer's configuration program as bidirectional, EPP, or ECP.

Go to...

I can't print my document, page 244

Go to...

The photos I print aren't clear, page 246

Quick fix

You can reduce the time it takes to start printing a document on your own printer by following these steps:

1. Click Start, point to Settings, and click Printers.

2. In the Printers window, right-click your printer, and click Properties on the shortcut menu.

3. On the Details tab in the Properties dialog box for the printer, click Port Settings.

4. Clear the Check Port State Before Printing check box, and click OK.

5. Click OK again to close the Properties dialog box.

I can't print my document

Source of the problem

A few moments after you click Print, your printer should respond, coming out of its slumber and cranking out pages in living color or in black and white. But if your printer goes on resting when it should be hard at work, the cause could be anything from a printer that's still hung up from the last job you sent its way, to a configuration problem in the part of Windows that handles printing. To investigate these possibilities and others one by one, go through this series of steps. You'll check out the most common problems and then move on to other possibilities.

How to fix it

● Make sure the printer is ready and supplied with paper and toner or ink. Most printers have a message display that reads *Ready* or *Online* or a light that is illuminated when the printer is prepared to begin printing.

If the printer appears to be ready but the document isn't printed, you may have sent the document to the wrong printer. To see whether this is your problem, follow these steps:

1. Click Start, point to Settings, and click Printers.

2. On the View menu in the Printers window, click Details.

3. Examine the Documents column to determine which printer has a document waiting in its queue (indicated by a number other than 0 in the Documents column). ▶

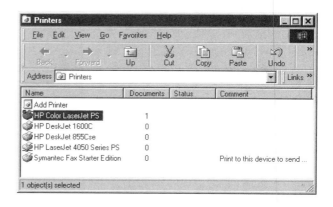

If the document was sent to the wrong printer and the printer hasn't finished printing, you can cancel the document by double-clicking the printer, right-clicking the document in the print queue window, and clicking Cancel Printing on the shortcut menu. Then select the correct printer and print the document again.

If the document is waiting to be printed by the correct printer, you might be able to determine the printer problem by examining the printer queue. Follow the steps on the facing page.

1. In the Printers window, double-click the printer that has the document waiting in its queue, and look in the Status column for information about the printer problem. ▶

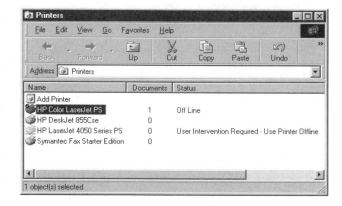

2. Correct the problem if you can. Fix a paper jam, turn the printer off and back on, reconnect the printer cable, or press the printer's Online button to put the printer in a ready state. Or put the printer back on line by clicking Use Printer Offline on the Printer menu in the Printers window.

   The print queue keeps trying to resend the document, so the document will be printed when the printer problem is resolved.

If no documents are waiting in the print queue, the document was sent through to the printer but the printer didn't print it. Try these troubleshooting steps:

1. Click Start, point to Settings, click Printers, right-click the printer you want to use, and click Properties on the shortcut menu.

2. On the General tab in the Properties dialog box for the printer, click Print Test Page.

   When a message box appears, asking whether the test page was printed correctly, click No, and follow the steps in the Print Troubleshooter Wizard or in Help And Support (in Windows Me).

You should also try to print a different document or print using a different program:

1. Try printing a different document. If the other document is printed, the original document you tried to print might be damaged. Try reopening the original document or opening a backup copy and then printing it again.

2. Try printing to the same printer from a different program. If another program is able to print successfully, you need to troubleshoot a printing problem within the program. Check the software manufacturer's Web site for support or a possible update that you can download and install to fix the problem.

If you're still unable to print, try reinstalling the printer driver. Make sure you have any disks that came with your printer, and follow these steps:

1. Click Start, point to Settings, click Printers, and in the Printers window, right-click the printer, and click Delete on the shortcut menu. Click Yes when you are asked to confirm the deletion.

2. Double-click Add Printer, and follow the steps of the Add Printer Wizard to add the same printer again.

The photos I print aren't clear

Source of the problem

Even a relatively inexpensive recent-model color printer can do a remarkably good job printing pictures you've scanned or photos you've taken with a digital camera. You must use the correct printer settings, though, and use paper that's been designed specifically for photo printing. Paper for printing digital photos is smoother and often brighter than normal paper (the type of paper you use for photocopying and every-day text printing), and it provides a dramatic improvement in the quality of photo printouts.

Two other factors can lessen print quality: an incorrect quality setting when you print a photo, and misalignment of the printer heads or ink nozzles. To fix these problems, follow these steps.

How to fix it

● Obtain paper that's made specifically for printing photos. Check your printer's documentation or the printer manufacturer's Web site for information about the brands of photo paper that are recommended for use with your printer.

Be sure to specify the correct paper type in the program's Print dialog box by following these steps:

1. On the File menu in the program you're using to view and print photos, click Print.

2. In the Print dialog box, click Properties.

3. On the Paper or Paper/Quality tab in the Properties dialog box for the printer, click the Media, Media Choice, or Paper Type down arrow and click Glossy or Photo Paper in the list. ▶
   Depending on the printer, you might need to click Advanced to get to the option that lets you specify the type of paper you're using.

4. Click OK.

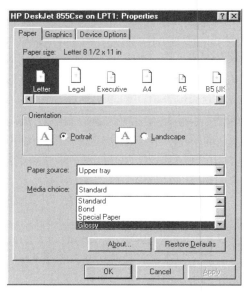

Verify the quality setting you're using to print the photo by following these steps:

1. On the File menu in the program you're using to view and print photos, click Print.

2. In the Print dialog box, click Properties.

3. On the Paper, Paper/Quality, or Device Options tab in the Properties dialog box for the printer, click the Print Quality down arrow and select the option that provides the highest quality. ▶

   For some printers, quality is listed as Good, Better, or Best. Other printers use different terminology, such as Presentation for high quality and Draft for medium quality.

   Usually, there's a trade-off between print speed and print quality, so if the Properties dialog box lists print speeds rather than print quality, choose the slowest print speed.

● Check the printer's documentation for information about how to run maintenance procedures on the printer, such as cleaning the printer heads or aligning the print cartridges or ink nozzles. Often, you can run these services from one of the tabs in the Properties dialog box for the printer. ▶

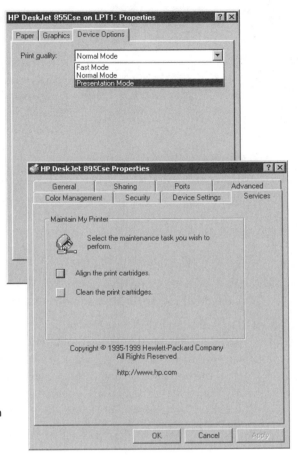

Web graphics are printed poorly no matter what I do

A photo on a Web site is intended for quick downloading and viewing on the screen rather than printing, so its *resolution* (the number of dots per inch, or dpi, in the photo) matches the fairly low resolution of most computer screens. Most screens, and most Web images, have a resolution of only 72 dpi. If you print such an image using a high-resolution printer (these days, even inexpensive color printers can produce 300 dpi resolution or better), the picture will still have only 72 dots per inch, so the image will be indistinct, and you'll notice jagged edges, particularly on diagonal or curved lines. There's really nothing you can do to fix this problem with Web graphics because the problem is in the image itself. It has nothing to do with the way you're printing it.

I can't print using a network printer

Source of the problem

If a printer that's connected to another computer on the network won't show up in the Print dialog box, you can use the Point and Print technique in Windows not only to install the network printer, but also to print the document. From then on, you'll see the network printer listed in the Print dialog box. You'll also find a shortcut to the printer in the Printers window, which you can use to check the status of the printer. To use the Point and Print technique, follow these steps.

How to fix it

1. Make a note of the make and model of the printer that's connected to the network computer.

2. Double-click My Computer on the desktop, and navigate to the folder that contains the document you want to print, and then double-click the folder to open it.

3. Double-click Network Neighborhood or My Network Places (in Windows Me) on the desktop, and in the window that shows the network resources, double-click the computer that's connected to the printer you want to use.
   If the computer is not visible, double-click Entire Network, and then double-click the workgroup icon in the Entire Network window. (In Windows Me, you might have to click View The Entire Contents Of This Folder to see the workgroup.)

4. Arrange the folder window and network computer window so that they're side by side.

5. Drag the document you want to print from the folder window to the network printer icon in the other window.

6. Click Yes when you are asked whether you want Windows to set up the printer. ▶

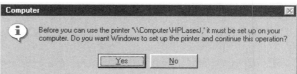

7. On the first page of the Add Printer Wizard, click Yes and click Next if you plan to use this printer for printing from MS-DOS programs. Otherwise, just click Next.

8. On the next page of the wizard, select the printer manufacturer and model.
   If the printer is not listed, click Have Disk, and in the Install From Disk dialog box, click Browse and then browse to the location of the printer driver and click OK.

---

9. Click Next, and on the next page of the wizard, type a name for the printer in the Printer Name box and click Next. ▶

If you want the network printer to be your default printer, click Yes before clicking Next.

10. On the next page of the wizard, click Finish when you are asked whether you want to print a test page.

If the test page is printed properly, click Yes; otherwise, click No to open the Print Troubleshooter, a wizard that can help you solve printing problems.

If you are asked whether you want to keep a .dll file, click Yes to make sure that the most updated software components on your computer are not overwritten by earlier versions on the printer installation disk.

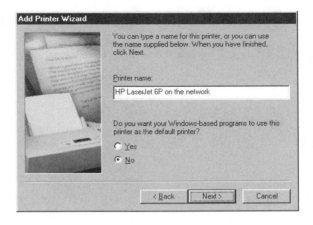

Windows installs the printer driver, opens the application you used to create the document, prints the document, and then closes the application.

Installing a network printer in advance

Point and Print is a convenience that lets you connect to and then immediately print using any shared printer on the network to which you have access. If you anticipate printing frequently using a particular network printer, you can install the printer in advance so that it will be available to you whenever you are connected to the network.

To install a network printer, follow these steps:

1. Double-click Network Neighborhood or My Network Places (in Windows Me) on the desktop, and double-click the computer that's connected to the printer you want to use.

If the computer is not visible, double-click Entire Network, and then double-click the workgroup icon in the Entire Network window. (In Windows Me, you might have to click View The Entire Contents Of This Folder to see the workgroup.)

> **Tip**
> Networks with a Windows server can provide the correct driver automatically, so you won't need to select a printer manufacturer and model.

2. Right-click the shared printer that's connected to the network computer, and click Install or Connect (in Windows Me) on the shortcut menu.

3. Follow the steps in the Add Printer Wizard to install the driver for the printer. For more information, see steps 7 through 10 above.

It takes a long time to print a document

Source of the problem

When you use a printer that's connected directly to your computer, you can tell when the printer is busy just by looking at it. But when the printer is connected to another computer on the network and a document isn't being printed as quickly as you expect, you need to check the printer's print queue to determine whether other documents are lined up to be printed ahead of yours—in which case, there's nothing you can do. Here's how to check the print queue and, if the printer is connected directly to your computer, how to take steps to speed up printing.

How to fix it

1. Click Start, point to Settings, and click Printers.

2. In the Printers window, double-click the printer you are using.

    The printer window shows the print queue, which lists any documents that are waiting to be printed. ▶

    If no documents are ahead of yours, move on to the next set of steps to continue troubleshooting.

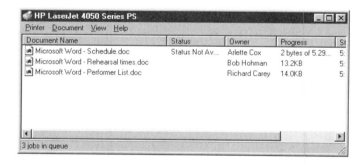

Follow these steps to speed up printing on any printer, including your own:

3. Double-click My Computer on the desktop, right-click your hard disk, and click Properties on the shortcut menu.

4. On the General tab in the Properties dialog box, click Disk Cleanup.

5. On the Disk Cleanup tab in the Disk Cleanup dialog box, select the Temporary Internet Files, Offline Web Pages, Recycle Bin, and Temporary Files check boxes in the Files To Delete list, and then click OK.

6. Click Yes when you are asked whether you are sure you want to delete files, and click OK to close the Properties dialog box for the hard disk.

My document wasn't printed the way I expected

Source of the problem

Unless you adjust settings in the Print dialog box when you choose to print a document, the document is printed with the default settings for the printer, which might not be what you expect.

Any changes you make in the Print dialog box override the default settings for the printer, so you can have finely detailed control of how the printed document will look. Some programs also have Page Setup or Print Setup options on the File menu, which give you even more control over how the document will fit the printed page.

If you'd rather avoid changing the settings in the Print dialog box each time you print, you can change the default settings for the printer in Windows. You'll be able to choose Print on the File menu of any program or click the Print button on the program's toolbar to quickly print the document. Here's how to change the default settings.

How to fix it

1. Click Start, point to Settings, and click Printers.

2. In the Printers window, right-click the printer you want to use as the default printer, and click Set As Default on the shortcut menu.

3. Right-click the printer again, and click Properties on the shortcut menu.

4. In the Properties dialog box for the printer, change the settings on the tabs to fit your needs. ▶

5. Click OK.

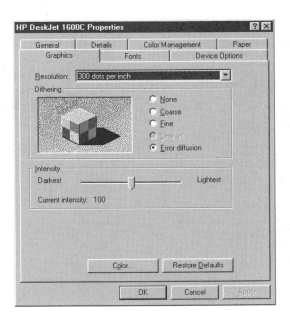

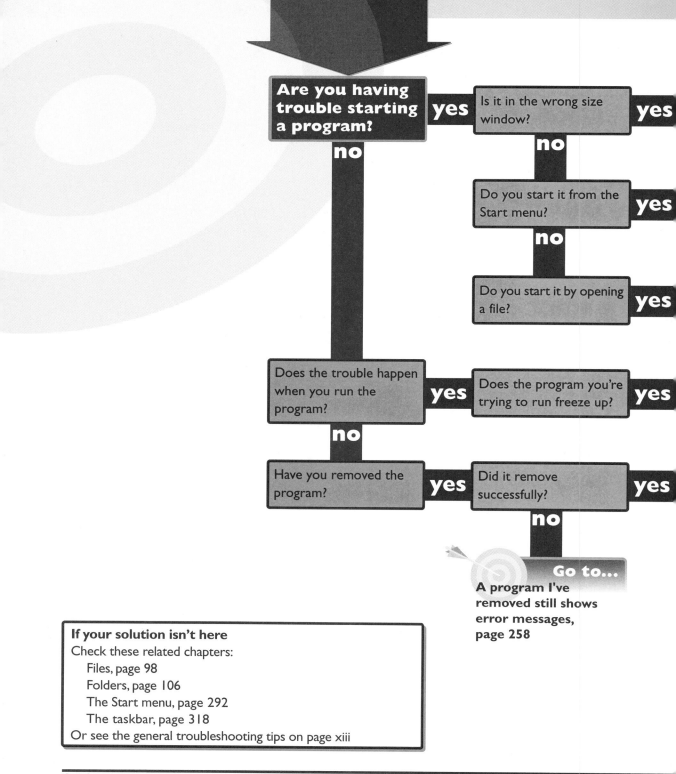

Are you having trouble starting a program? **yes** → Is it in the wrong size window? **yes**

no ↓   **no** ↓

Do you start it from the Start menu? **yes**

no ↓

Do you start it by opening a file? **yes**

Does the trouble happen when you run the program? **yes** → Does the program you're trying to run freeze up? **yes**

no ↓

Have you removed the program? **yes** → Did it remove successfully? **yes**

no ↓

Go to...

A program I've removed still shows error messages, page 258

If your solution isn't here

Check these related chapters:

Files, page 98

Folders, page 106

The Start menu, page 292

The taskbar, page 318

Or see the general troubleshooting tips on page xiii

Quick fix

By changing the properties for a command on the Start menu, you can specify whether a program should start in a regular window, in a full-screen window, or minimized as a button on the taskbar.

1. Right-click a program on the Start menu or on one of the submenus.

2. On the shortcut menu, click Properties.

3. In the Run list, click Normal Window, Minimized, or Maximized.

Go to...
It takes too many steps to start my favorite programs, page 256

Go to...
The wrong program opens when I double-click a file, page 260

Go to...
A program has stopped responding, page 254

Are the program's shortcuts gone?

yes

Is it still in the Add/Remove Programs list?

yes

no

Go to...
A program I've deleted has left broken shortcuts, page 262

Quick fix

Tweak UI (see "What Is Tweak UI?," on page 32) can remove any entry from the Add/Remove Programs list.

1. Click Start, point to Settings, and click Control Panel.

2. In Control Panel, double-click Tweak UI.

3. On the Add/Remove tab, click the program whose entry you want to remove.

4. Click Remove, and click OK to close Tweak UI.

A program has stopped responding

Source of the problem

Let's hope this doesn't happen while that unfinished novel is still unsaved. Your first thought might be "Now what have I done?" But remember that when a program just stops working, it's never your fault—programs are just not supposed to do that.

If you're wondering why programs sometimes crash, consider this: The typical computer has a library of programs on its hard disk, a handful of hardware devices installed inside and hanging off its ports (like printers, scanners, and digital cameras), and a marching parade of utility programs running in the background (such as virus checkers, Internet audio programs, and controls for speakers). All these programs and devices should interact gracefully, but they can conflict—for example, by trying to use the same resources in the computer or by giving the computer contradictory instructions. If this happens, a program that has your unfinished task might simply stare back at you without responding to any of your mouse clicks or keyboard presses, no matter how urgent they become.

How to fix it

1. Press Ctrl+Alt+Del.

2. Inspect the Close Program dialog box to see whether any of the programs listed show the text *[Not responding]*. ▶

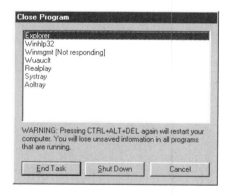

3. Click the program that's not res ponding and then click End Task.

4. Wait for at least 30 seconds, and if nothing seems to happen, wait for another 30 seconds. Windows might take time to work behind the scenes, and if you wait, you might be able to shut down only the errant program without having to restart the computer.

5. If a message box appears, telling you that you can click End Task to close the program, go ahead and do so. If nothing happens within 30 seconds or so after you've clicked End Task, press Ctrl+Alt+Del again, click the program that's not responding, click End Task, and give it another

30 seconds. If nothing happens still, click Cancel, save your work in other programs and quit those programs, and then press Ctrl+Alt+Del twice to shut down and restart the computer.

If this doesn't restart Windows, you'll need to turn off your computer using the power switch and then turn it back on. In the process, you might lose the information you haven't saved in some running programs, but others, like Microsoft Outlook, save each change as you make it, so you won't lose any work.

6. After you've shut down the frozen program, press Ctrl+Alt+Del again and verify in the Close Program dialog box that the program is no longer in the list. If it is still listed, repeat the procedure in steps 3 through 5 until the program no longer appears in the list.

7. If you now find any unusual behavior in Windows or the programs you're using, such as slow responses or features that don't work, shut down and restart Windows.

Avoiding program hang-ups in the future

You've probably noticed that hang-ups get more frequent over time. The more programs you install, the more utilities you run, and the more devices you attach, the greater the demands on Windows, which is the underlying software. Periodically, you should clean house by removing programs you rarely use, by preventing programs from starting automatically (see "Programs Start Automatically, Without My Approval" on page 312), and by running maintenance programs built into Windows, like the disk defragmenter. Some people go so far as to periodically delete Windows and reinstall it. Getting a fresh start with an unencumbered system can work wonders if you're willing to put up with the substantial hassle of backing up your data, reinstalling your hardware and software, reentering all your passwords, and setting up your favorite work or play environments all over again.

Tip

Some program hang-ups can also knock out basic Windows components that run behind the scenes and provide important services to your programs, such as Msgsrv32 and Rundll32.dll. These components will usually restart automatically after you click End Task in the Close Program dialog box, but restarting Windows yourself is always the safest bet to make sure you're working in a reliable environment.

Why won't it stop that?

Think you're busy? Windows is just as busy in its own right. It's an environment for running programs like Microsoft Word and Microsoft Excel. It's a window on the Internet. It manages every program in your computer, all your utilities, and all your fonts. It's even contending with the printers, scanners, speakers, and a few accessories—new and cooperative or old and cantankerous—that you've plugged in to soup up your computer. At the same time, it's pretending to be a plain MS-DOS computer so that decade-old, "mission-critical" programs still used by some companies won't balk. Because the demands on Windows are great, and because it must accommodate everything from state-of-the-art games to rusty old MS-DOS software, we need to tolerate its occasional mishaps. The best way to protect yourself might still be by following the old adage "Save early, and save often."

It takes too many steps to start my favorite programs

Source of the problem

There's a command somewhere on the Start menu for just about every program you've installed, but it's almost always buried several menu levels deep. You have to click submenu after submenu to find it. What's more, some setup programs for software fill the submenus for programs on the Start menu with so many utilities, accessories, uninstallers, registration programs, and readme files that you can hardly find the command that starts your program.

Here are two solutions: one for copying icons for your favorite programs to the Quick Launch toolbar, and one for excavating the Start menu entries you need and moving them to menus that are easy to reach.

How to fix it (using the Quick Launch toolbar)

1. Make sure you see the Quick Launch toolbar just to the right of the Start button. The Quick Launch toolbar is located on the taskbar and contains icons that you can click to start the programs you use most often. If the Quick Launch toolbar is not visible, see "I Don't Have a Quick Launch Toolbar," on the facing page.

2. Click Start and point to Programs.

3. Point to the correct menu and then the correct submenus until you've found the program you want to easily start.

4. Hold down the Ctrl key while you drag the icon for the program from the Start menu to the Quick Launch toolbar.

5. Continue to hold down the Ctrl key while you position the mouse pointer where you want to put the icon. (A black vertical line shows where the entry will drop.) Release the Ctrl key and then release the mouse button to drop the entry into place. ▶

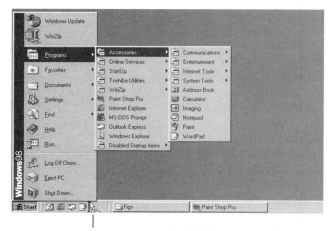

Drag an icon to the Quick Launch toolbar

How to fix it (using the Start menu)

1. Click Start and point to Programs.

2. Point to the correct menu and then the correct submenus until you've found the program you want to easily start.

3. Hold down the Ctrl key while you drag the shortcut for the program from the submenu to Programs on the Start menu.

>   Don't release the Ctrl key or the mouse button just yet.

4. When the Programs menu opens, position the mouse pointer where you want to drop the shortcut and then release both the Ctrl key and the mouse button. ▶

>   The shortcut appears where you dropped it. To reposition the shortcut, you can move it up or down on the menu simply by dragging it.

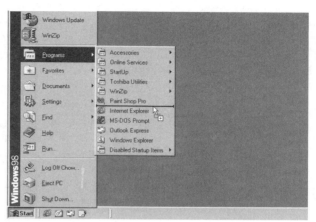

I don't have a Quick Launch toolbar

If you don't see the Quick Launch toolbar, either it's not turned on or you're using Windows 95 with Internet Explorer 3. If you're using Windows 95, you can install the latest version of Internet Explorer, which provides the Quick Launch toolbar. Download it from *www.microsoft.com/windows/ie*. Or you can upgrade to Windows 98, which provides Internet Explorer 4 (which also provides the Quick Launch toolbar).

If you have Internet Explorer 4 or Internet Explorer 5, right-click the taskbar and point to Toolbars on the shortcut menu. On the submenu, click Quick Launch.

> **Tip**
> You can rearrange the icons on the Quick Launch toolbar. You can also make the toolbar wider to accommodate more icons by dragging the handle (the vertical bar) on the right side of the toolbar farther to the right.

> **Tip**
> Right-click the Quick Launch toolbar and click Open to view its icons as shortcuts in a window. You can then manage the Quick Launch toolbar by deleting the shortcuts, dragging in new shortcuts from other windows, or dragging shortcuts to other windows.

A program I've removed still shows error messages

Source of the problem

You might see error messages that appear to emanate from the netherworld beyond the Recycle Bin. Programs that you thought you'd removed are still speaking to you. The reason for this is that you circumvented the correct method for removing programs and, in the process, left parts of the software clinging to your system. You can't just remove a program by deleting the folder for the program from your hard disk. Instead, you need to use Add/Remove Programs to remove software properly. At this point, you can still try using Add/Remove Programs, but it might be too late. If Add/Remove Programs doesn't work, you'll need to reinstall the program and then remove it the correct way, as described in the following procedure.

How to fix it

1. Have the program's installation CD handy or find the downloaded setup program you used to install the program in the first place.

2. Install the program just as you did originally. Be sure to put it in the same folder you used before. If you accepted the recommended installation folder, accept the same recommendation again.

3. Restart the computer or follow any steps that the setup program asks of you until you have a working program. Now you're ready to uninstall the program the correct way.

4. Click Start, point to Settings, and click Control Panel.

5. In Control Panel, double-click Add/Remove Programs. (In Windows Me, single-click.)

6. In the installed programs list on the Install/Uninstall tab, select the program you want to remove and click Add/Remove. ▶

7. Follow the program removal process, responding to whatever messages appear in message boxes, and restart your computer if you are prompted to do so.

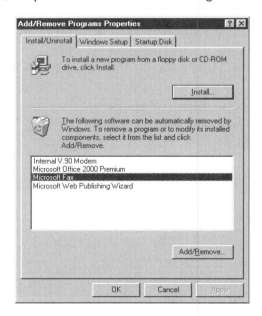

If you want to know more

During setup, many Windows programs knit themselves tightly into the fabric of your Windows installation. They copy the files they need into their own folder and the main Windows folder, and they create their own entries in the central Windows configuration file, called the registry. These changes are often all that's needed to produce error messages when you don't go through the proper uninstall process. In addition, many programs also install and run little utility programs, helpers, and monitors that you'll need to remove too. For example, a program that plays streaming audio from the Internet might install a monitor that watches for sound or music coming in on your Internet connection so that it can automatically launch its player. These modules sometimes appear as small icons in the system tray next to the clock. Other times, they run stealthily, without any visible sign.

> **Tip**
> Some programs add an uninstall shortcut to their menus on the Start menu. Choosing this shortcut is the equivalent of selecting the program in the Add/Remove Programs list.

The only way to properly untangle most programs from Windows is to run their uninstall programs. All Windows programs are supposed to list themselves in the Add/Remove Programs list and provide uninstall utilities that can properly extract every bit and piece from your system. In fact, for software manufacturers to put the *Designed for Windows* logo on their package, they must include a proper uninstall program in their software.

A message says that not all of the program could be removed

Some uninstall programs finish their business but then display a message saying that they could not remove all files or folders. When you see such a message, you know that the program has been properly extracted from Windows but not all of its files or folders have been deleted from your hard disk. This happens when the uninstall program can't tell which files and folders to delete. These folders on your hard disk won't interfere with other programs, but they take up valuable hard disk space.

When you see such a message, you can safely delete the program's installation and data folders, which are often subfolders within the Program Files folder. If you don't find these subfolders, look for them on your hard disk by viewing the list of folders in My Computer or by entering the name of the program in the Find dialog box (Search Results in Windows Me). Obviously, you shouldn't delete any folder on your hard disk unless you're sure that it belongs to the program you've deleted. You can often find a list of program-related folders in the software's documentation or on the manufacturer's Web site.

> **Tip**
> You can try selecting the program in the Add/Remove Programs list without reinstalling the program first, but by removing the program's folder, you may also have deleted its uninstall program, so this approach might not work.

The wrong program opens
when I double-click a file

Source of the problem

If you expect a particular program to open when you double-click a file in My Computer, Windows Explorer, or on the desktop but another program opens instead, you need to associate a different program with the file. For example, if double-clicking a .jpg picture file opens Internet Explorer rather than the photo editing program you want, you need to change the program associated with the .jpg file type because Windows checks the file extension at the end of the file name (.doc, .txt, .xls, .jpg, .bmp, .htm, .ppt, .gif, and so on) to determine which program to open.

Most of the time, you don't need to worry about the list of associations between file extensions and programs because the programs you install stake their claim to a file type during setup. Microsoft Excel claims .xls (spreadsheets), Internet Explorer claims .htm (Web pages), and so on. But some programs vie with each other for a file type, and you need to step in as referee.

How to fix it

1. Double-click My Computer on the desktop.

2. On the View menu (on the Tools menu in Windows Me), click Folder Options.

3. In the Folder Options dialog box, click the File Types tab, and then scroll through the Registered File Types list and click the file type you want to change, such as Address Book File. ▶

4. In Windows 95 or Windows 98, go to step 5. In Windows Me, click Change, select a program in the list in the Open With dialog box, and click OK.

5. Click Edit to open the Edit File Type dialog box.

6. In the Actions list, click Open, and then click Edit.

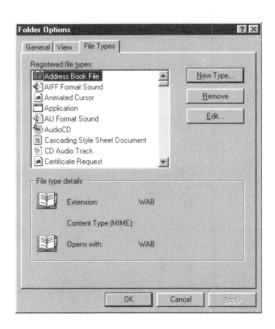

7. In the Editing Action For Type dialog box, click the Browse button and then find the program you want to use to open the file. ▶

    For more information about finding programs, see "Finding a Program," below.

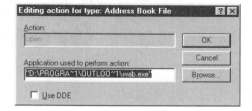

8. Click OK, click Close in the Edit File Type dialog box, and then click Close in the Folder Options dialog box to return to My Computer.

Finding a program

It would be great if Windows 98 offered a list of installed programs, as Windows Me does, so that you could simply select a program to associate with a file type. Instead, it asks for the name of the file that runs the program and the folder that file is in. Sometimes you can easily find the program folder by name just by looking in the Program Files folder. Inside the folder for the program, you'll find one file that has the name of the program or a likely abbreviation, along with the icon for the program. Here's another clue: if you click Details on the View menu in My Computer, the program associated with the file you want to choose is listed in the Type column.

    Another way to find a program is to look at its entry on the Start menu. Right-click the entry, and then click Properties on the shortcut menu. The Target box in the Properties dialog box contains the file's name and location. Copy this text and then paste it into the Application Used To Perform Action box in the Editing Action For Type dialog box.

Handling feuding programs

Usually, you need to change the program associated with a file type only after you install a new program that tries to grab the file type. That's when you need to restore the previous file association. But some programs feud and try to take over each other's file extensions each time they start up. Internet Explorer and Netscape, for example, both want to associate themselves with the file extension for a Web page (.htm), but they ask permission before usurping file types whenever they start. Programs that grab without asking aren't well-mannered enough for your PC. You don't need to tolerate such nonsense. Don't hesitate to remove these programs and replace them with others that are more considerate.

> **Tip**
> Some programs have a menu or dialog box option that you can use to specify the file types the programs are associated with. Using this option enables you to avoid having to set the file association in Windows. To find this option, look for a Preferences or Options menu command, and then check the dialog box the command leads to, or check the program's online Help for *file associations* or *file types*.

A program I've deleted has left broken shortcuts

Source of the problem

After you remove a program or a document, any shortcuts you've created to that program or its related documents on the desktop, in folders, or on the Start menu simply won't work. These shortcuts are known as *dead links*, but they're not quite as serious as the name sounds.

Dead links can't harm your computer other than to take up desktop space or fill folders and space on the Start menu. Nevertheless, they serve no purpose, so you might as well get rid of them by deleting them. Windows 98 provides a handy wizard for just that task. The wizard is part of the Windows 98 Resource Kit Tools Sampler that comes with Windows 98, so you'll need to install the kit to get to the wizard.

How to fix it

1. Insert the Windows CD.

2. If a Welcome screen appears, click Browse This CD and skip to step 3. ▶

    If a Welcome screen doesn't appear, double-click My Computer, right-click the icon for your CD-ROM drive, and on the shortcut menu, click Explore.

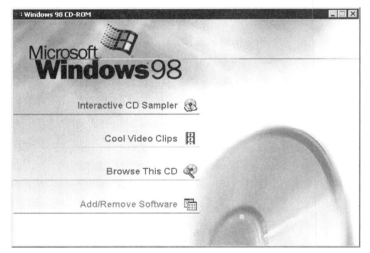

3. Double-click the Tools folder and double-click the Reskit folder.

4. In the Reskit folder, double-click Setup and proceed to install the Windows 98 Resource Kit Tools Sampler.

After you've installed the Windows 98 Resource Kit Tools Sampler, you can start it and use the Link Check Wizard by following these steps:

1. Click Start, point to Programs, point to Windows 98 Resource Kit, and then click Tools Management Console.

2. Click Close to bypass the Tip Of The Day window.

3. In the left pane of the Microsoft Management Console window, click the plus sign next to Windows 98 Resource Kit Tools Sampler.

4. Click the plus sign next to Tool Categories.

5. Click the Desktop Tools folder.

6. Double-click Checklinks in the right pane. ▶ above

7. In the Link Check Wizard window, click Next.

8. In the list of broken shortcuts, select the links to remove or click Select All, and then click the Finish button. ▶

9. Click OK to close the Information message box and then close the Microsoft Management Console.

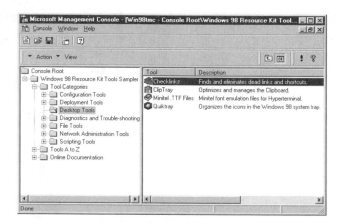

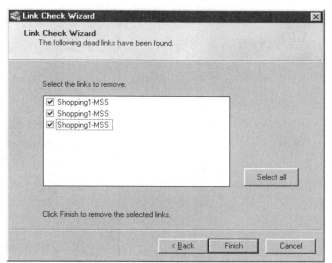

More about the Windows 98 Resource Kit Tool Sampler

The Windows 98 Resource Kit Tools Sampler provides a number of other useful tools for configuring and maintaining your Windows computer. Many of the tools in the Windows 98 Resource Kit Tools Sampler are designed for people who need to administer many computers in a corporate network environment. Nevertheless, a few of the tools are helpful to everyone. Among these, Microsoft Windiff is a great tool that compares the contents of two files or two folders and points out the differences. Microsoft File Information is another useful tool that shows all the information embedded in each file that's part of Windows.

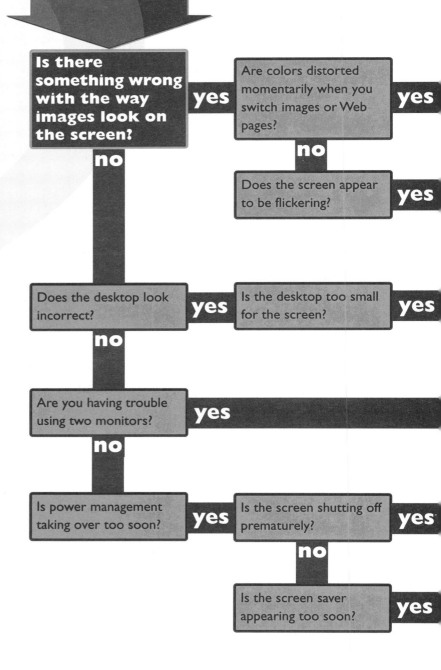

Is there something wrong with the way images look on the screen?

yes → Are colors distorted momentarily when you switch images or Web pages?

yes

no

Does the screen appear to be flickering?

yes

no

Does the desktop look incorrect?

yes → Is the desktop too small for the screen?

yes

no

Are you having trouble using two monitors?

yes

no

Is power management taking over too soon?

yes → Is the screen shutting off prematurely?

yes

no

Is the screen saver appearing too soon?

yes

Go to...
The screen has an annoying flicker, page 266

Go to...
I don't know how to get multiple monitors working, page 270

Go to...
My screen shuts off too quickly, page 268

Go to...
The screen saver appears too soon, page 269

Quick fix

If your display is set to show only 256 colors, you might find that the colors in pictures are distorted for a moment when you switch images or Web pages. This happens when Windows needs to change from one set of 256 colors to another to display the colors in the new image. To avoid these color shifts, set your display adapter to use more than 256 colors by following these steps:

1. Right-click the desktop, and click Properties on the shortcut menu.
2. On the Settings tab in the Display Properties dialog box, click the Colors down arrow and click High Color (16 Bit), True Color (24 Bit), or True Color (32 Bit), and click OK.

Quick fix

Unlike a regular monitor, an LCD screen (the screen in your laptop or a flat-panel LCD monitor) works properly at only one particular Screen Area setting because it has a fixed number of pixels, or dots, on the screen. If the Screen Area setting is lower than the LCD's screen area (for example, 800 by 600 pixels when the LCD is 1024 by 768 pixels), the Windows desktop may not fill the screen, or the image may be stretched to fit the larger screen area and look jagged. To fix this problem, follow these steps:

1. Right-click the desktop, and click Properties on the shortcut menu.
2. On the Settings tab in the Display Properties dialog box, drag the Screen Area slider to the same setting as the resolution of the LCD display. To determine this resolution, consult the documentation for the display or the laptop.

If your solution isn't here
Check these related chapters:
Or see the general troubleshooting tips on page xiii

The screen has an annoying flicker

Source of the problem

The image on your computer screen should be rock steady. But if you've recently hooked up a larger monitor or installed a new video adapter, you might find that the screen appears to be flickering rapidly instead, as if it's visually vibrating. Some people are unaware of flicker until it's removed. Others are maddened by it. Either way, flicker will ultimately tire your eyes and make your time in front of the computer less enjoyable, so eliminating it is well worth the effort.

How to fix it

1. Right-click the desktop, and click Properties on the shortcut menu.

2. In the Display Properties dialog box, click the Settings tab, and click Advanced.

3. On the Monitor tab in the Properties dialog box, note the monitor type, next to the display icon. If the monitor type is incorrect, click Change and follow the Update Device Driver Wizard steps to install the driver for your monitor.

   If clicking Change shows a list of devices instead of opening the Update Device Driver Wizard, select the manufacturer and model from the list or, if your monitor isn't listed, insert the disk that came with your monitor and click Have Disk.

4. On the Adapter tab in the Properties dialog box (on the Monitor tab in Windows Me), click the Refresh Rate or Refresh Frequency down arrow if it's available, and click Optimal in the list. ▶

   Optimal sets a *refresh rate* (the number of times the screen is refreshed each second, measured in hertz [Hz]), that's appropriate for your monitor, but you can select any value in the list. To avoid flicker, select a value greater than 60 Hz. (A rate of 70 to 80 Hz is fast enough to eliminate flicker.)

Some video adapters come with configuration programs that you use to change their refresh rates. With these video adapters, you might not find a Refresh Rate or Refresh Frequency list in the Properties dialog box.

5. Click OK. A message box might appear, telling you that Windows will adjust the refresh rate and that the screen may flicker while the settings are changing.

6. Click OK to close the message box. After the screen changes, you will be prompted with a message asking whether you want to keep the new setting. Verify that the flickering has stopped.

7. Click Yes if the refresh rate change appears to have fixed the problem. If you'd like to experiment with other refresh rates, click No and return to step 4 to select another refresh rate.

8. Click OK to close the Display Properties dialog box.

Fixing a distorted display

If you're still having display problems of any type after you verify the driver and refresh rate, try adjusting the hardware acceleration, which disables features of the display adapter that could be causing the problem you see. To do so, follow these steps:

1. Right-click the desktop, and click Properties on the shortcut menu.

2. On the Settings tab in the Display Properties dialog box, click Advanced.

3. On the Performance tab in the Properties dialog box, drag the Hardware Acceleration slider one notch to the left and click OK. Click Close in the Display Properties dialog box and click Yes when you are asked whether you want to restart your computer. ▶

Now use the computer as you normally do and see whether the problem goes away. If it does not, drag the slider another notch to the left and try again.

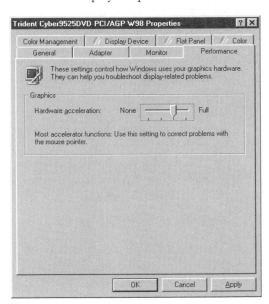

My screen shuts off too quickly

Source of the problem

Whether you're working on a desktop computer or a laptop, power management in Windows can help cut down your electricity bill or save your computer's batteries. After a period of inactivity, which can range from a few minutes to a few hours, power management can turn off the screen, which not only saves power but also helps keep a warm computer room from getting still warmer.

But if you find that the screen is shutting down prematurely, while you're just taking short breaks or making phone calls, you can instruct power management to wait longer before activating itself, or you can just plain turn off power management until you're ready to use it again. Here's how to change the power management settings in Windows.

How to fix it

1. Right-click the desktop, and click Properties on the shortcut menu.

2. On the Screen Saver tab in the Display Properties dialog box, click Settings in the Energy Saving Features Of Monitor section.

3. On the Power Schemes tab in the Power Management Properties dialog box or the Power Options Properties dialog box (in Windows Me), click the Turn Off Monitor down arrow, and click a longer interval in the list. (You must click the Turn Off Monitor down arrow in either the Plugged In or Running On Batteries column, depending on the current state of your computer.) ▶

   To disable the power management of your screen so that the screen always stays on, click Never in the list.

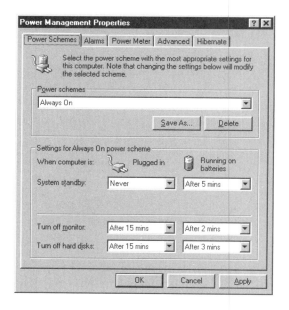

4. Click OK, and click OK again to close the Display Properties dialog box.

By making this change, you've modified the power scheme that's currently in effect, as shown in the Power Schemes section of the dialog box. In the Power Schemes list, you can choose other power schemes to enable different sets of options.

The screen saver appears too soon

Source of the problem

If you have a screen saver enabled, the screen saver will appear whenever Windows detects that you haven't moved the mouse or touched the keyboard for a certain length of time. If the screen saver appears too frequently, this interval is simply too short for your liking. You can easily lengthen it by following these steps.

How to fix it

1. Right-click the desktop, and click Properties on the shortcut menu.

2. On the Screen Saver tab in the Display Properties dialog box, click the up arrow in the Wait box to increase the number of minutes that will elapse before the screen saver is activated. ▶

    If you find that the little arrow in the Wait box is difficult to click, press Tab repeatedly until the current number in the box is highlighted, and then type a different number.

3. Click OK.

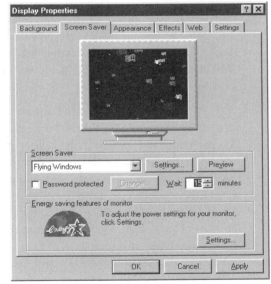

Hot Corners won't work

The screen savers you add by installing desktop themes (which provide sets of background graphics, desktop icons, sounds, and mouse pointers) have a Hot Corners feature, which is supposed to allow you to move the mouse to a corner of the screen to enable the screen saver. But this feature works only when you have Windows 95 installed rather than Windows 98 or Windows Me. The Hot Corners feature was designed to work with the System Agent software that was installed in Windows 95. Windows 98 and Windows Me have replaced the System Agent with the Task Scheduler, which causes Hot Corners not to work.

I don't know how to get multiple monitors working

Source of the problem

When you use two video cards in one Windows 98 or Windows Me computer attached to two monitors placed side by side, you can increase your work area by extending the Windows desktop across the two monitors. But to make multiple monitors work, you must have the right display adapters installed in your computer in the correct way. You also need to make Windows aware of how the monitors are physically arranged. To install multiple monitors, follow these steps.

How to fix it

1. Obtain a second display adapter and monitor.

    The second display adapter must support multiple monitors. For information about which display adapters work with multiple monitors, see the Microsoft Knowledge Base article "Hardware Requirements for Multiple Display Support," available from the Microsoft Web site, at *support.microsoft.com/support/kb/articles/Q182/7/08.ASP*.

2. Turn off the computer, and install the second display adapter and monitor.

    If you have two PCI cards (most display adapter cards plug into either PCI or AGP slots in the computer, as listed on their packaging or in their documentation), the computer will choose one to be the primary adapter. You probably want this to be the better of the two adapters as its image will be on your primary monitor. If you'd rather use the other PCI card as the primary adapter, turn off the computer and switch the order of the cards in the slots. If you have one PCI card and one AGP card, the PCI card will be the primary adapter unless the setup program for your computer's BIOS allows you to choose the primary adapter.

    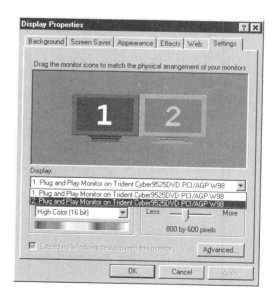

3. Start Windows and install the driver for the display adapter. Click Yes if you are asked whether you want to restart the computer.

4. Right-click the desktop, and click Properties on the shortcut menu.

5. On the Settings tab in the Display Properties dialog box, click the Display down arrow and click the secondary display adapter in the list. ▶ facing page

6. Select the Extend My Windows Desktop Onto This Monitor check box, and click OK to close the Compatibility Warning message.

7. Right-click one of the monitor icons shown on the Settings tab, and click Identify on the shortcut menu to determine which physical monitor corresponds to the monitor labeled 1. ▶

8. Drag the icons of the two monitors to reposition them so that they match the physical arrangement of the two monitors in your work area.

9. Click OK.

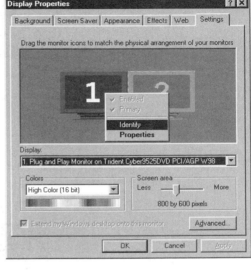

My desktop icons don't appear on the secondary monitor

If desktop icons don't appear on the secondary monitor or if they're not saved when you quit Windows, here's a fix:

1. Click Start, click Run, and in the Run dialog box, type **regedit** in the Open box and click OK.

2. In the left pane of the Registry Editor window, click the plus signs next to these folders in sequence: HKEY_USERS, .DEFAULT, Software, Microsoft, Internet Explorer, Desktop.

3. Right-click the Old WorkAreas folder in the left pane, click Delete on the shortcut menu, and then close the Registry Editor and restart Windows.

Tip
You can't drag a window from one monitor to another if the window is maximized. You must restore the window first by clicking the Restore button (next to the Close button).

Programs don't open on the secondary monitor

When you start Windows, the logon dialog box always appears on the primary monitor. The programs you start always open in windows on the primary monitor also. After a window opens on the primary monitor, you can always drag it to the secondary monitor.

To work on the secondary monitor, move the mouse pointer all the way across the desktop toward the secondary monitor and then continue dragging beyond the edge of the desktop until the pointer appears on the secondary monitor. To return to the primary monitor, drag the mouse pointer back.

To move a window from one monitor to the other, simply drag it there by dragging it off the edge of the first monitor's screen toward the other monitor.

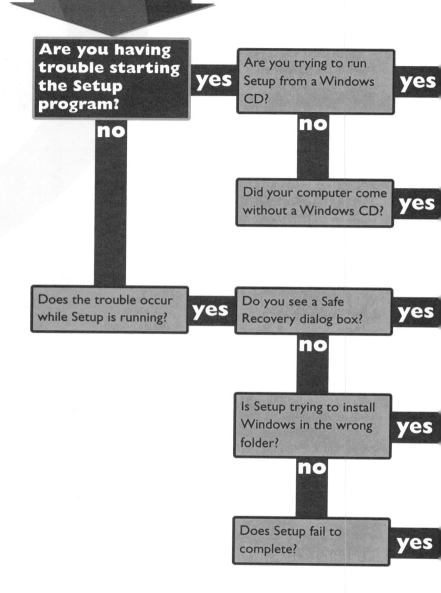

Are you having trouble starting the Setup program?

yes → Are you trying to run Setup from a Windows CD?

yes

no ↓

Did your computer come without a Windows CD?

yes

Does the trouble occur while Setup is running? **yes** → Do you see a Safe Recovery dialog box?

yes

no ↓

Is Setup trying to install Windows in the wrong folder?

yes

no ↓

Does Setup fail to complete?

yes

Go to...
I can't set up Windows because I can't use the CD-ROM drive, page 274

Did your computer come with a system recovery CD?

yes

Quick fix
If your computer came with a *configuration builder* or *system recovery* CD, the CD can be used to reinstall Windows, along with all the software, drivers, and utilities that came with your computer when it was brand new. If you want to use this CD to restore your computer to its original state, be sure to first make backup copies of your data and configuration settings on disks or on a removable disk drive.

Go to...
A Safe Recovery dialog box appears during Setup, page 279

Go to...
Setup wants to install Windows in a folder named Windows.000, page 278

Go to...
Setup stops responding, page 276

If your solution isn't here
Check these related chapters:
Or see the general troubleshooting tips on page xiii

I can't set up Windows because I can't use the CD-ROM drive

Source of the problem

So you have a Windows CD, a computer with a CD-ROM drive, and a hard disk with plenty of space. It looks like you have everything you need to get Windows set up on the hard disk. But you keep getting an *Invalid drive specification* error at the MS-DOS prompt when you try to switch to the CD-ROM drive, or you can't access the CD because your current version of Windows is no longer working. Without the proper commands in your MS-DOS startup files or some version of Windows running, which makes the CD-ROM drive usable, your computer can't read the Windows CD and its installation files.

Fortunately, this problem has several possible solutions, depending on whether you had MS-DOS or Windows 95 initially installed on the machine or whether you have another computer nearby whose services you can enlist. Here's how to proceed.

How to fix it

If you have another computer that is running Windows, make a startup disk and use it to start your computer by following these steps:

1. Insert a disk in the floppy disk drive of the other computer.

2. Click Start, point to Settings, and click Control Panel.

3. In Control Panel, double-click Add/Remove Programs. (In Windows Me, you might be able to single-click the Add/Remove Programs link.)

4. On the Startup Disk tab in the Add/Remove Programs Properties dialog box, click Create Disk, and follow the instructions on the screen. ▶

5. Carry the startup disk to the other computer, insert it in the floppy disk drive, and start the computer.

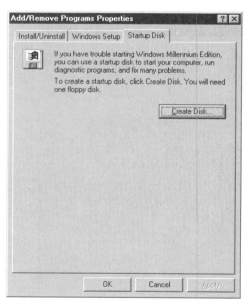

6. On the Microsoft Windows Startup Menu, which appears after the computer starts, choose the Start The Computer With CD-ROM Support option. ▶

7. With the Windows CD in the CD-ROM drive, at the MS-DOS prompt, type the drive letter of the CD-ROM drive followed by a colon (:), and press Enter to try to access the drive.

```
Microsoft Windows Millennium Startup Menu
═══════════════════════════════════════════

    1. Normal
    2. Start computer with CD-ROM support.
    3. Start computer without CD-ROM support.
    4. Minimal Boot

Enter a choice: 2
```

If you don't have access to another computer but Windows 95 was working at one time on your computer, you might be able to use the drivers in Windows 95 to reach the CD-ROM drive by following these steps:

1. Start the computer, and press F8 when you see the *Starting Windows 95* message.

2. On the Windows 95 Startup Menu, choose Command Prompt Only.

3. At the MS-DOS prompt, type **dosstart.bat**.
   When the MS-DOS prompt reappears, try accessing the CD-ROM drive again.

If Windows 95 wasn't installed on your computer but you do have MS-DOS installed on the hard disk, you must load the MS-DOS driver, which assigns a drive letter to the CD-ROM drive.

If you have the original disk that accompanied the CD-ROM drive, you can run the setup program that installs the driver in your computer's Autoexec.bat and Config.sys files. If you don't have the disk, visit the drive manufacturer's Web site for information about obtaining and installing the driver.

You may also need the Mscdex.exe file, which provides support for CD-ROM drives in MS-DOS. If you don't have this file, you can download it from the following Web page: *support.microsoft.com/support/kb/articles/Q123/4/08.ASP?LN=EN-US&SD=gn&FR=0.*

Tip
If starting the computer with the startup disk still doesn't let you access the CD-ROM drive but you have another computer (or can borrow a laptop) with a CD-ROM drive, you can copy the Windows program files from the other computer's CD-ROM drive to your hard disk. For information about how to accomplish this task, see "Performing a Clean Boot and Upgrading Windows from the Hard Disk," on page 277.

Setup stops responding

Source of the problem

If your computer has built-in virus protection, the Windows Setup program might be unable to change the boot sector, the small area on the hard disk that the computer needs to read before it can load Windows. Because altering the boot sector can prevent the computer from starting, the boot sector is a likely target for a virus program that seeks to disable your computer. To prevent viruses from altering the boot sector, many computer manufacturers have added boot sector protection to the computer's built-in software, the BIOS. If this protection is turned on, Windows won't be able to make the necessary modifications to the boot sector and the Setup program will be unable to continue. The Setup program might simply stop, or the Windows Setup Wizard might appear as a black square on the screen as the computer hangs. Or the Setup program will continue and ask whether you want to overwrite the boot sector, but because the Setup program is prevented from changing the boot sector, Windows hangs when it tries to start. To get around this problem, follow these steps.

How to fix it

1. Consult your computer's documentation to determine how to start the computer's configuration program, also sometimes called the BIOS configuration program or the CMOS setup, and then follow the instructions to start this program

    On some computers, you press Ctrl or Esc while starting the computer to start the configuration program.

    Some computers indicate how to start their configuration programs by displaying a message on the screen when they start, such as *Press Ctrl to enter setup*.

2. In the configuration program, find and disable the built-in virus detection software or antivirus feature.

3. Restart the computer.

4. Run Windows Setup.

5. After Windows is set up, run the computer's configuration program again and reenable the built-in virus detection software.

Performing a clean boot and upgrading Windows from the hard disk

If turning off the computer's antivirus feature doesn't work and Setup still fails, you should perform a *clean boot* of your computer, starting the computer without loading device drivers, utilities, or other programs. When you clean boot your computer, you will be unable to access the computer's CD-ROM drive because you won't be loading the CD driver, so before you clean boot, you must copy the Windows setup files to the computer's hard disk and then run Setup from the hard disk. Here's how to proceed:

1. Insert the Windows CD. If a Windows CD-ROM window opens, close it.

2. Double-click My Computer on the desktop, and then double-click the computer's hard disk.

3. Right-click a blank area in the window that's showing the contents of the hard disk, point to New on the shortcut menu, and click Folder.

4. Type a name for the new folder that will hold the Windows setup files, such as *Win98Files* or *WinMeFiles*, and press Enter.

5. Double-click the new folder to open it.

6. Right-click My Computer, click Explore on the shortcut menu, and arrange the folder window and the new Windows Explorer window so that they don't overlap.

7. In the left pane of the Windows Explorer window, click the plus sign next to the CD-ROM drive containing the Windows CD.

8. Click the Win98 folder (if you're upgrading to Windows 98) or the Win9x folder (if you're upgrading to Windows Me), and click any file in the right pane. ▶

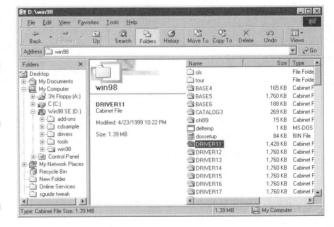

9. Press Ctrl+A to select all the files, and then drag the selected files to the window that shows the new folder you created.

10. Shut down the computer.

11. Press the F8 key repeatedly when you see the *Starting Windows* message.

12. From the Microsoft Windows Startup Menu, choose Safe Mode Command Prompt and press Enter.

13. At the MS-DOS prompt, type **CD *Win98Files*\\Setup** and press Enter to start Windows Setup (replace *Win98Files* with the name you gave your new folder).

Setup wants to install Windows in a folder named Windows.000

Source of the problem

During its installation process, Setup searches your hard disk for a valid Windows folder whose contents it can upgrade. Usually, this Windows folder contains an earlier version of Windows. But if Setup determines that the Windows folder is damaged, or if it determines that important files are missing from the Windows folder, Setup by default installs Windows in a separate folder named Windows.000. If you proceed with the installation as is and try to rename the folder (from *Windows.000* to *Windows*) after setup is complete, Windows will no longer work because it will be looking for its files in a folder whose name no longer exists. You can solve this problem by installing Windows in a folder with a name of your choice.

How to fix it

1. When the Windows Setup Wizard asks you to select the directory in which you want to install Windows and suggests C:\WINDOWS.000, click Other Directory, and click Next. ▶

2. On the Change Directory page of the wizard, type the name of the folder you want to use, such as *Win98* or *WinMe*, and click Next.

   A warning message informs you that you must reinstall all your Windows programs to make them work properly under Windows. Click Yes to continue.

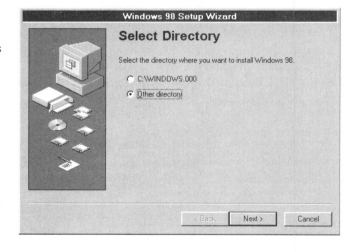

   If Windows has suggested Windows.000, it detected a problem with the Windows folder that might prevent the new installation of Windows from operating properly. If you want to use *Windows*, you should quit Windows Setup by clicking Cancel, delete the Windows folder by typing **Deltree C:\Windows /Y** (replace the *C:*, if necessary, with the drive letter of the hard disk that contains the Windows folder) at the MS-DOS prompt, and then restart Setup. You will still need to reinstall all your Windows programs after you set up Windows.

A Safe Recovery dialog box appears during Setup

Source of the problem

If Setup grinds to a halt because of a problem along the way, such as a failure to communicate with a hardware device it's trying to detect, you might have to exit Setup and start again. This time, Setup displays a Safe Recovery dialog box, giving you the option of bypassing the task that caused Setup to fail during the previous attempt. Choose Safe Recovery to continue, as described here. After Windows is running, you can determine which hardware device Windows couldn't detect and properly install the device or replace its driver.

How to fix it

1. After Setup stops working and you've waited a few minutes to see whether it will continue, press F3 or click the Exit button.

    If the computer doesn't respond, you might need to press Ctrl+Alt+Del to restart the computer. If that doesn't work, turn off the computer, and then turn it on again.

2. Start Setup again, and when the Safe Recovery dialog box appears, click Safe Recovery and click Continue. ▶

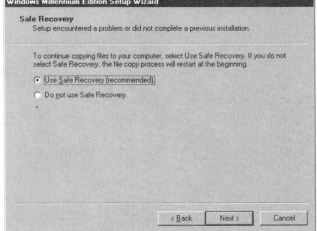

3. After Setup is complete and Windows starts, right-click My Computer on the desktop, and click Properties on the shortcut menu.

4. On the Device Manager tab in the System Properties dialog box, look in the list for a device with a question mark or exclamation point on its icon or for a device that's missing from the list

    You might need to expand a category of devices, such as Network Adapters, by clicking the plus sign next to it to check each device. If the entire category is missing, the device won't be listed.

5. Follow the steps in "A New Device I've Installed Doesn't Work," on page 140, to troubleshoot the device.

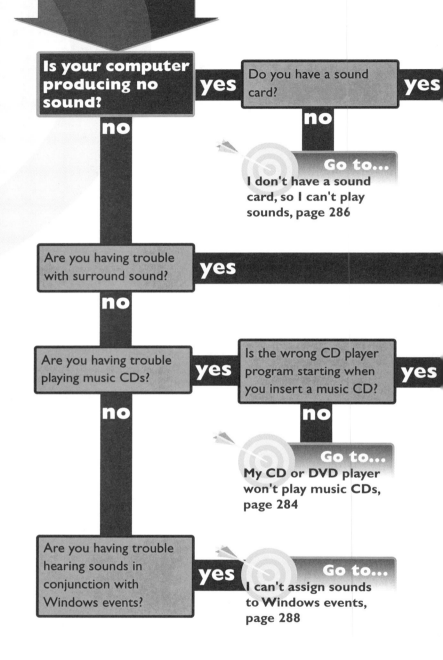

Is your computer producing no sound?

yes → Do you have a sound card?

yes →

no ↓

no ↓

Go to...
I don't have a sound card, so I can't play sounds, page 286

Are you having trouble with surround sound?

yes →

no ↓

Are you having trouble playing music CDs?

yes → Is the wrong CD player program starting when you insert a music CD?

yes →

no ↓

no ↓

Go to...
My CD or DVD player won't play music CDs, page 284

Are you having trouble hearing sounds in conjunction with Windows events?

yes

Go to...
I can't assign sounds to Windows events, page 288

Is the volume or balance wrong?

yes → **Go to...**
The volume or balance is wrong, page 285

no → **Go to...**
I don't hear sound, page 282

Go to...
I want to use my CD player instead of the one in Windows, page 290

Quick fix

If you've got four speakers but you're not hearing surround sound, follow these steps:

1. Click Start, point to Settings, and click Control Panel.

2. In Control Panel, double-click Multimedia or Sounds And Multimedia (in Windows Me). (In Windows Me, you might need to click View All Control Panel Options to see the Sounds And Multimedia icon.)

3. On the Audio tab in the Properties dialog box, click Advanced Properties in the Playback section or click Advanced in the Sound Playback section (in Windows Me).

4. Click the Speaker Setup down arrow, and click Surround Sound Speakers in the list. Click OK twice to close the dialog boxes.

If your solution isn't here

Check these related chapters:

Games, page 116

Hardware, page 138

Optimizing, page 226

Programs, page 252

Or see the general troubleshooting tips on page xiii

I don't hear sound

Source of the problem

If you're trying to play a game, assign sounds to Windows events such as exiting Windows, watch a DVD movie, or play a music CD, and you're not hearing sound from your computer, Windows might not be set to use your sound card, the speakers might not be turned on or connected correctly, some of the software components that Windows needs to play sounds might not be installed, your hardware and software could be conflicting with each other, or your sound card might not be set up properly. You'll need to try a few things until the problem is solved.

How to fix it

1. If your computer's speakers are external, verify that they're powered up, that their volume is turned up, and that they're connected to the correct jacks on the back of the computer.
     The sound card or computer documentation should show the location of the speaker jacks.

2. If the speakers are built into the monitor, adjust their volume using the controls on the monitor or keyboard. Some monitors have a rotary dial on their front panel. Others have controls hidden behind a door panel you can open, usually on the front face of the monitor.

3. Set the volume in Windows to at least midrange, and make sure that muting is not turned on. For information about changing the volume, see "The Volume or Balance Is Wrong," on page 285.

If checking the volume and connections didn't work, your sound card might not be turned on or designated as the device to play sounds. To enable the sound card and set it as the preferred device (the device that plays sounds), follow these steps:

1. Right-click My Computer on the desktop, and click Properties on the shortcut menu.

2. On the Device Manager tab in the System Properties dialog box, click the plus sign next to Sound, Video And Game Controllers, and then click your sound card in the list.

3. Click Properties, and in the Properties dialog box, verify that the Disable In This Hardware Profile check box is cleared. If the check box is selected, clear it. ▶

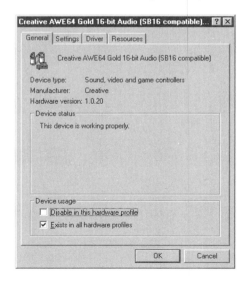

4. Click OK, click OK again, and click Yes if you are asked whether you want to restart your computer. After Windows restarts, continue to the next step.

5. Click Start, point to Settings, and click Control Panel.

6. In Control Panel, double-click Multimedia or Sounds And Multimedia (in Windows Me). In Windows Me, you might need to click View All Control Panel Options to see the Sounds And Multimedia option.

7. In the Playback section or the Sound Playback section (in Windows Me) of the Audio tab, click the Preferred Device down arrow and click your sound card in the list. Also verify that the Use Only Preferred Devices check box is selected, and then click OK. ▶

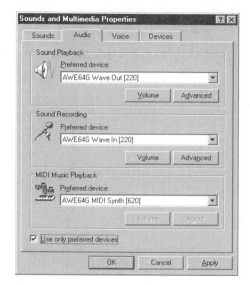

8. Click the Devices tab, click the plus sign next to Audio Devices, click your sound card, and then click Properties.

9. In the Properties dialog box for your sound card, verify that Use Audio Features On This Device option is selected, and click OK until you get back to Control Panel. ▶

10. Close Control Panel, and restart your computer.

If you still don't hear sound, or if you see a message such as *Mmsystem326 No wave device that can play files in the current format is installed,* the software components that Windows requires to play sound are probably not installed. You can install them by following these steps:

1. Click Start, point to Settings, and click Control Panel.

2. In Control Panel, double-click Add/Remove Programs. (In Windows Me, you might be able to single-click the Add/Remove Programs if it's an underlined link.)

3. On the Windows Setup tab in the Add/Remove Programs Properties dialog box, double-click Multimedia in the Components list. In the Multimedia dialog box, select the Audio Compression check box and click OK.

    If Audio Compression is already selected, it might not be installed correctly. Remove it by clearing the check box and clicking OK twice. Then repeat steps 1 through 3 to reinstall it.

4. Click OK again, and follow the instructions on your screen if you're prompted to insert the Windows CD or disk.

My CD or DVD player won't play music CDs

Source of the problem

Whether you're relaxing at home or stuck on a long flight, the CD or DVD drive in your computer might be just the ticket to keep you entertained. You can pass the time by listening to music or watching your favorite movie. But if you don't hear your favorite music CDs or the sound track of movies even though you do hear other sounds through your speakers or headphones, you should investigate a few causes.

How to fix it

1. Give the CD or DVD drive at least five seconds to read the disc before you try to eject it. The player can take a few moments to start producing sound.

2. Try cleaning the disc with a lint-free cloth or play a different disc altogether to make sure the problem isn't the disc itself rather than the computer.

3. Check the volume and mute settings in Windows. For information about checking these settings, see "The Volume or Balance Is Wrong," on the facing page.

4. If you installed the CD or DVD drive yourself in a desktop computer, make sure that you ran a cable from the drive's audio-out jack to the audio-in jack on the sound card or on the computer's main circuit board (the *motherboard*).

If you're using Windows 98, try using Windows Media Player instead of CD Player. In Windows Me, you must use Windows Media Player because CD Player isn't installed. ▶

To switch to Windows Media Player, follow these steps:

1. Click Start, point to Programs, point to Accessories, and point to Entertainment.

2. Click Windows Media Player.

The volume or balance is wrong

Source of the problem

Whether you find yourself straining to hear the sounds coming from your computer or you're blasted out of your seat, that little Volume icon nestled on the taskbar near the clock is the answer. Clicking it once opens a simple slider that you can drag for overall volume control. Clicking it twice opens a full control panel you can use to change the volume levels of individual sound sources and adjust their balance between left and right.

How to fix it

1. Single-click the Volume icon on the taskbar, near the clock, and drag the slider up or down to change the overall volume of all sound; or double-click the Volume icon to open the Volume Control dialog box so that you can adjust individual sound sources in the computer.

2. In the Volume Control dialog box, drag the Balance sliders left or right and drag the Volume sliders up or down to adjust the levels of each sound source. ▶

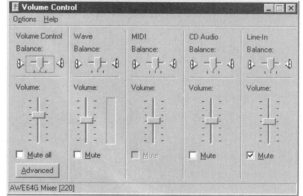

   The Volume Control slider at the left is the master control. If it's set too low, none of the other sources will be heard.

   Depending on the devices you have installed, the sliders you can drag are Wave (general sounds from sound files), MIDI (synthesized music and sounds from the sound card), and Line-In (sounds from another device, such as a CD drive, that's connected to the audio input jack on the sound card).

   If the Mute check box for a device is selected, the device is temporarily turned off. To turn the device back on, clear the Mute check box.

   If a slider for the device you want to control isn't available, click Properties on the Options menu, click the Playback option in the Adjust Volume For section, select the check box for the device in the Show The Following Volume Controls list, and then click OK.

I don't have a sound card, so I can't play sounds

Source of the problem

If you don't have a sound card, you still can play certain sounds in Windows with the help of a small program named PC Speaker Driver, which enables you to use the PC's speaker.

The quality of the sound produced by the PC Speaker Driver won't be great because computer speakers are designed just to beep rather than to play music. In addition, the PC Speaker Driver can play only one type of sound file (.wav files). Downloaded music files are often .mp3 files, so if you really want to play music, you should add a sound card to your computer.

To use the PC Speaker Driver, you need to download it from the Microsoft Web site and install it by following this procedure.

How to fix it

1. To download the PC Speaker Driver, go to the Microsoft Download Center, at *www.microsoft.com/downloads/search.asp*.

2. At the Microsoft Download Center Web page, click Keyword Search, and type **PC Speaker Driver** in the Keywords box.

3. Click the Operating System down arrow, click Windows 98 in the list (no matter which version of Windows you're using), and click Find It. ▶

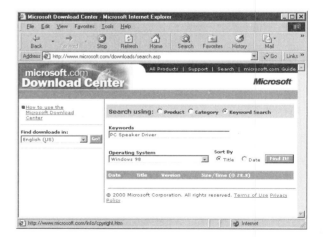

4. Click the PC Speaker Driver for Windows 95/98 link.

5. On the next Web page, click the Speak.exe link.

6. In the File Download dialog box, click Save This Program To Disk, and click OK.

7. In the Save As dialog box, select a destination folder for the file, and click Save.

8. Navigate to the folder in which you saved the downloaded Speak.exe file, double-click Speak.exe, and when prompted, press Y to extract the installation files.

Now that you've downloaded the driver, you need to install it by following these steps:

1. Click Start, point to Settings, and click Control Panel.

2. In Control Panel, double-click Add New Hardware. (In Windows Me, you might have to click View All Control Panel Options to see the Add New Hardware icon.)

3. On the first two pages of the Add New Hardware Wizard, click Next.

4. Click the No, The Device Isn't In The List option, and click Next.

5. Click the No, I Want To Select The Hardware From A List option, and click Next.

6. In the Hardware Types list, click the Sound, Video, And Game Controllers option, click Next, and then click Have Disk to open the Install From Disk dialog box.

7. In the Install From Disk dialog box, click the Browse button, and in the Open dialog box, navigate to the folder in which you saved the Speak.exe file.

8. Click OK. Click OK again. And then click OK in the Select Device dialog box, which shows the Sound Driver For PC-Speaker option selected in the Models list.

9. Click Finish, follow the instructions on the screen, and then click Yes if you are asked whether you want to restart the computer.

   If the Copying Files dialog box displays a message saying that the file Speaker.drv cannot be found, click Browse, navigate again to the folder in which you saved the Speak.exe file, and then click OK.

Configuring the PC Speaker Driver

To set up the PC Speaker Driver to play .wav files, follow these steps:

1. Click Start, point to Settings, click Control Panel, and then double-click Multimedia or Sounds And Multimedia (in Windows Me). In Windows Me, you might need to click View All Control Panel Options to see the Sounds And Multimedia option.

2. On the Devices tab in the Properties dialog box, click the plus sign next to Audio Devices, and then double-click Audio For Sound Driver For PC-Speaker.

3. In the Properties dialog box, click Settings. ▷

4. In the PC-Speaker Setup dialog box, adjust the Speed and Volume sliders, click Test, and repeat until the sound is right, and then click OK.

To play .wav files, you must use the Sound Recorder because Windows Media Player doesn't work with the PC Speaker Driver.

I can't assign sounds to Windows events

Source of the problem

A *sound scheme* provides a suite of sounds for Windows events, such as a chime for an error message or a fanfare to proclaim the excitement of emptying the Recycle Bin. But if you don't hear sounds, you can try attaching sounds from a sound scheme to individual Windows events by using the Sound Properties dialog box. (For instructions, see "Assigning Sounds to Events," on the facing page.) If you find that you can't choose any of the Multimedia Sound Schemes in the Sound Properties dialog box, either you skipped adding the schemes during Windows setup or they were deleted from the Media folder on your hard disk. Using Windows is infinitely more fun when you use the Multimedia Sound Schemes, so here's how to install them and get them working.

How to fix it

1. Click Start, point to Settings, and click Control Panel.

2. In Control Panel, double-click Add/Remove Programs. (In Windows Me, you might be able to single-click the Add/Remove Programs underlined link.)

3. In the Add/Remove Programs dialog box, click the Windows Setup tab.

4. In the Components list, select the Multimedia check box, and then click Details to open the Multimedia dialog box and see the Multimedia options you can select.

5. In the Components list in the Multimedia dialog box, select the Multimedia Sound Schemes check box. ▶

6. Click OK, and click OK again to close the Add/Remove Program Properties dialog box.

   If you installed Windows using a CD-ROM, you may be prompted to insert the Windows CD.

Assigning sounds to events

Once you install the Multimedia Sound Schemes, you can assign sounds to Windows events. You can change the sound that plays every time Windows starts, for example, or even assign a sound to play whenever a menu pops up.

1. Click Start, point to Settings, and click Control Panel.

2. In Control Panel, double-click Sounds or Sounds And Multimedia (in Windows Me). (In Windows Me, you might need to click View all Control Panel Options first.)

3. In the Sounds Properties dialog box or the Sound And Multimedia Properties dialog box (in Windows Me), click the event you want in the list of events.

4. In the Sound section (the Sound Events section in Windows Me), click the Name down arrow and then click a sound in the list. ▶

   You can preview the sound by clicking the Play (right-arrow) button in the Preview section (next to the Name list in Windows Me).

5. Repeat steps 3 and 4 for each event to which you want to attach a sound.

6. After you've assigned sounds to all the events you want, click Save As.

7. In the Save Scheme As dialog box, type a name for your new sound scheme and click OK.

8. Click OK again, and start using your new sounds.

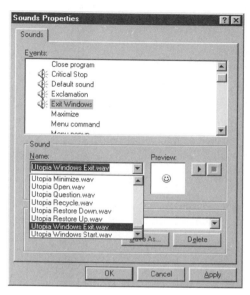

Tip

To choose an entirely different set of sounds, click the Scheme down arrow after step 3, and click a different scheme in the list.

Getting better sounds

There's nothing wrong with the sounds that come with Windows, but after a while, you'll probably be ready for a change. You can also install desktop themes (using the Windows Setup tab in the Add/Remove Programs dialog box), which provide their own sets of sounds, or you can download thousands of sounds from file download sites on the Web to create entirely new sound schemes.

After you download sounds (as .wav files), copy them to the C:\Windows\Media folder. Now when you open the Sound Properties or Sounds And Multimedia Properties dialog box, you'll see your new sounds in the Name list.

I want to use my CD player instead of the one in Windows

Source of the problem

Windows comes with a perfectly fine program you can use to play your favorite CDs, and Windows Media Player plays sound files in addition to sounds and video from the Internet. But you still might want to use a CD player that you can download for free from the Web. These players show animated control panels, they record music from CDs onto your hard disk, and they can go to the Web and get a list of the songs on a CD so that you can choose a song by name rather than track number.

If you've installed one of these programs and find that another program still starts whenever you insert a music CD in the CD-ROM drive, you need to change the program that's associated with the AudioCD file type by following these steps.

How to fix it

1. Double-click My Computer on the desktop.

2. On the View menu of the My Computer window (on the Tools menu in Windows Me), click Folder Options.

3. On the File Types tab in the Folder Options dialog box, click AudioCD in the Registered File Types list. ▶

4. Click Edit (or click Advanced in Windows Me) to open the Edit File Type dialog box, click Play in the Actions list, and click Edit.

5. In the Editing Action For Type: AudioCD dialog box, enter the file name and the entire path to the CD player program you want to use in the Application Used To Perform Action box.

   This overwrites the text that points to the current default audio player. (An appropriate path and file name for the MusicMatch Jukebox program, for example, would be *C:\Program Files\MusicMatch\MusicMatch Jukebox\mmjb.exe*.)

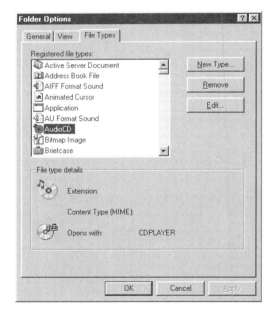

If you're not sure what the exact path to the program is, click Browse, use the Open With dialog box to locate the application's executable file (the file with the .exe extension), click Open, click OK, and then close the remaining dialog boxes.

6. Click OK, and close any open dialog boxes if necessary.

Removing CD Player

Windows 98 If you're using Windows 98, and you don't want to change the program that starts when an audio CD is inserted, and you know you don't want to use CD Player in Windows 98, you can remove it from your computer and then install the audio CD player of your choice. To remove CD Player, simply follow these steps:

1. Click Start, point to Settings, and click Control Panel.

2. In Control Panel, double-click Add/Remove Programs.

3. On the Windows Setup tab in the Add/Remove Programs dialog box, click Multimedia in the Components list, and click Details.

4. In the Multimedia dialog box, clear the CD Player check box in the Components list. ▶

5. Click OK twice to confirm your selection, and close the Add/Remove Programs dialog box.
    You may be prompted to insert the Windows CD.

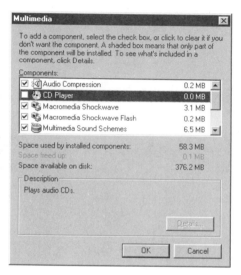

Installing Windows Media Player

Windows Media Player is a sophisticated player for all types of multimedia, such as music CDs, Internet radio, streaming video from the Web, and downloaded music from the Internet. Windows Media Player is built into Windows Me, but it's also a free download that you can obtain from the Windows Update Web page if you're using Windows 98. (Connect to the Internet, and click Windows Update on the Start menu.)

After it's installed, Windows Media Player will open whenever you insert an audio CD. Windows Media Player can even copy the music from your music CDs onto your hard disk so that you can create a library of music to play whenever you're using your computer.

Warning

Windows Media Player is not compatible with Windows 95, so you should not install it if you're running Windows 95 on your computer.

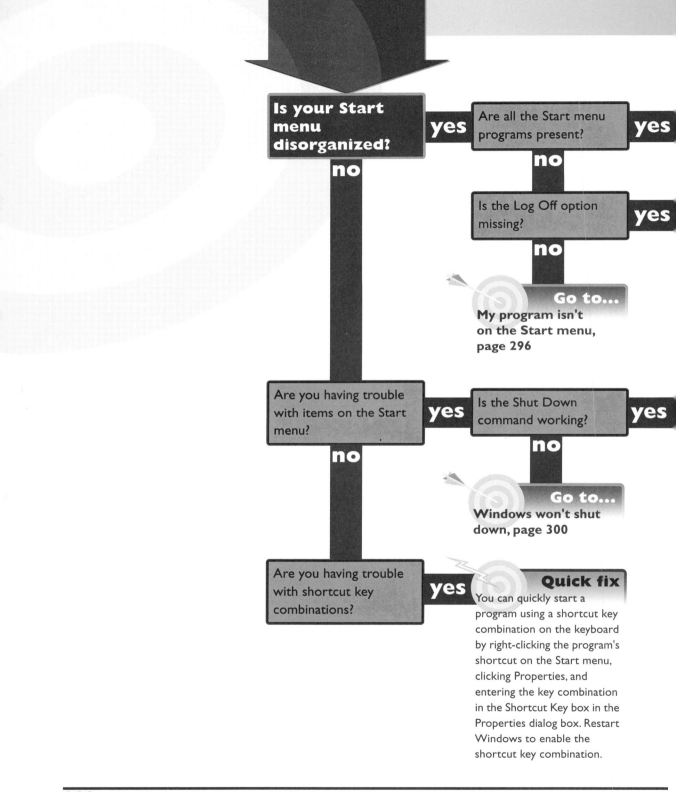

Is your Start menu disorganized?

yes → **Are all the Start menu programs present?** yes →

no ↓

Is the Log Off option missing? yes →

no ↓

Go to...
My program isn't on the Start menu, page 296

Are you having trouble with items on the Start menu?

yes → **Is the Shut Down command working?** yes →

no ↓

Go to...
Windows won't shut down, page 300

Are you having trouble with shortcut key combinations?

yes → **Quick fix**
You can quickly start a program using a shortcut key combination on the keyboard by right-clicking the program's shortcut on the Start menu, clicking Properties, and entering the key combination in the Shortcut Key box in the Properties dialog box. Restart Windows to enable the shortcut key combination.

Are there too many entries on the Start menu?

yes

Go to...
My Start menu is too long or too disorganized, page 294

Quick fix

If you've seen a Log Off option on the Start menu of other computers, but it doesn't appear on the Start menu of your computer, don't worry. You don't have a problem that needs to be fixed. The Log Off option appears only if you're part of a network or if you have multiple-user profiles activated (so that each person who works at your computer can use a personalized set of options for the desktop, Start menu, and other Windows features). The Log Off option also appears if you've used a Direct Cable Connection to connect two computers with a cable through their serial or parallel ports, creating a miniature home network.

Do programs you add to the Start menu appear where you want?

yes

Does the Documents list show files you want hidden?

yes

Go to...
The Documents list shows a file I don't want others to see, page 299

no

Go to...
The shortcuts I add are listed at the top of the Start menu, page 298

If your solution isn't here
Check these related chapters:
The desktop, page 14
Folders, page 106
Programs, page 252
The taskbar, page 318
Or see the general troubleshooting tips on page xiii

My Start menu is too long or too disorganized

Source of the problem

Little by little, the Start menu grows as you install new software, until its purpose—to provide quick and easy access to your programs—is nearly defeated. If, like many people, you click Start, point to Programs, and watch a mile-long menu struggle to find space on your screen, it's time to shorten and organize the Start menu.

In the following steps, you'll create folders in the Start menu folder for categories of programs, and then you'll group shortcuts and folders in the category folders.

How to fix it

1. Right-click Start, and click Explore on the shortcut menu.

2. In the left pane of the Windows Explorer window, click the Programs folder under Start Menu.

3. Right-click a blank area in the right pane of the Windows Explorer window, point to New on the shortcut menu, and then click Folder.

4. Type a name for the new folder that best describes a category of programs you have installed, such as Games or Graphics, and press Enter.

5. Repeat steps 3 and 4, creating additional folders for other categories of programs.

6. Drag a shortcut or folder from the right pane to one of the new category folders you've created. For example, drag all the shortcuts and folders related to graphics to the new Graphics folder.

7. After you finish arranging shortcuts and folders, close the Windows Explorer window. The changes to the Start menu are immediate.

Dragging shortcuts on the Start menu

Another way to rearrange your shortcuts and menus is to drag them around right on the Start menu. This method is simple and direct and you see the results instantly, but it doesn't enable you to create new menus. You can drag shortcuts and menus only onto menus that already exist. To create a new menu, you must follow the procedure above. To reorganize your Start menu using this technique, follow these steps:

1. Click Start and, on the Start menu, position the mouse pointer on a shortcut or menu you want to move. Drag the shortcut or menu to a different menu on the Programs menu, and pause until the menu opens.

If you're using Windows Me and you find that you can't drag a shortcut or menu, right-click the taskbar, and click Properties on the shortcut menu. On the Advanced tab in the Taskbar And Start Menu Properties dialog box, select the Enable Dragging And Dropping check box in the Start Menu And Taskbar list.

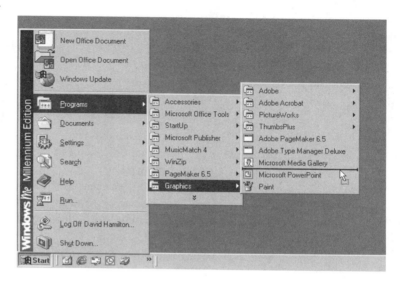

2. Drag the shortcut or menu onto the submenu, and release the mouse button. ▶

When you drag the shortcut or menu onto the submenu, a horizontal black bar appears on the submenu to indicate where the shortcut or menu will drop when you release the mouse button.

Personalized Menus in Windows Me

Windows Me

Personalized menus in Windows Me hide shortcuts and menus on the Start menu that you haven't used for a while so that you see only those items you use regularly. This keeps the Start menu shorter. To indicate that shortcuts and menus are hidden, menus and submenus on the Start menu show a double down arrow that you can click to open the full menu. ▶

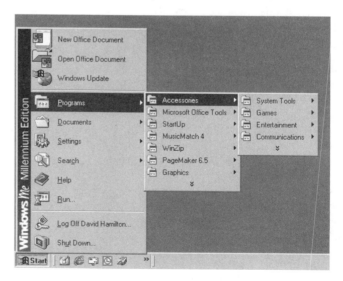

Tip

You can also reorganize the Start menu by right-clicking the taskbar, clicking Properties on the shortcut menu, and clicking the Start Menu Programs tab or the Advanced tab (in Windows Me) in the Properties dialog box. Click Advanced to open the Start menu in Windows Explorer. Drag shortcuts from folder to folder to move them on the Start menu.

My program isn't on the Start menu

Source of the problem

It was there last week. It was even there yesterday. But now the shortcut for a program has disappeared from the Start menu. Has something gone wrong? Is someone tampering with your settings? No, not if you're using Personalized Menus, a feature in Windows Me that simplifies menus, including the Start menu, by hiding items that you use infrequently.

To solve the case of the disappearing items, you can disable Personalized Menus, or you can learn to use them to your advantage. Here's how to disable Personalized Menus, along with information about using them if you'd rather become accustomed to this new feature in Windows Me.

How to fix it

1. To disable Personalized Menus in Windows Me, right-click the taskbar, and click Properties on the shortcut menu.

2. On the General tab in the Taskbar And Start Menu Properties dialog box, clear the Use Personalized Menus check box. ▶

3. Click OK.

    Now when you click Start and point to Programs, all the items on the Programs menu and its submenus are always visible.

Using Personalized Menus

When Personalized Menus are turned on, Windows keeps track of the items that you've selected on the Start menu and hides the items that you haven't recently used. The result is shorter, cleaner menus and submenus that display only the items you really use and hide all the rest.

To find an item that's hidden, you have two options: you can pause the mouse pointer on a menu and wait for the hidden items to appear, or you can click the double down arrow at the bottom of a menu to reveal the full menu. The items that were hidden by the Personalized Menus feature appear on the Start menu against a lighter, flatter background. ▶ facing page

Other ways to customize the Start menu in Windows Me

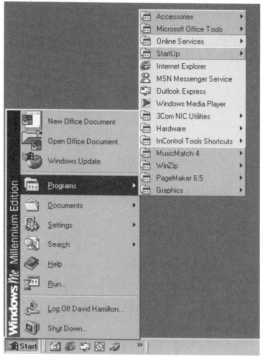

The Personalized Menus feature is not the only way to personalize the Start menu in Windows Me. By making some of the submenus on the Start menu expandable, you gain more direct access to Windows features, such as the options in Control Panel. For example, when you make the Printers submenu expandable, you can click Start, point to Settings, and point to Printers to select a printer rather than clicking Start, pointing to Settings, clicking Printers to open the Printers window, and then selecting a printer.

To make some of the key submenus on the Start menu expandable, follow these steps:

1. Click Start, point to Settings, and click Taskbar And Start Menu.

2. In the Taskbar And Start Menu Properties dialog box, click the Advanced tab.

3. In the Start Menu And Taskbar list on the Advanced tab, scroll to the five Expand options, and select the check box next to each menu that you want to be able to expand. ▶

You can expand the Control Panel, Dial-Up Networking, My Documents, My Pictures, and Printers menus.

4. Click OK to close the Taskbar And Start Menu Properties dialog box.

To further customize the Start menu, you can also select any of the three Display check boxes in the Start Menu And Taskbar list on the Advanced tab in the Taskbar And Start Menu Properties dialog box. You can choose to display the Favorites item, the Logoff command, and the Run command.

> **Tip**
>
> To show the Start menu as a scrollable list rather than a multiple-column list, select the Scroll Programs check box in the Start Menu And Taskbar list on the Advanced tab in the Taskbar And Start Menu Properties dialog box.

The shortcuts I add are listed at the top of the Start menu

Source of the problem

Almost every setup program that installs a Windows program also installs a shortcut to the program on the Start menu. Being a good citizen, the setup program creates a new submenu on the Programs menu and places a shortcut to the program on the submenu. Some programs also add a few more shortcuts to the submenu, such as a shortcut to a Readme file or to the program's product registration routine.

You can create your own shortcut to a program by dragging the icon for the program to the Start button on the taskbar. But the shortcut you create appears on the Start menu itself, near the top, rather than on the Programs menu. At least you've gotten the shortcut to the Start menu, but now you must drag it to where you want it on the Programs menu by following these steps.

How to fix it

1. Click Start.

2. On the Start menu, drag the shortcut you want to move to the Programs menu and pause until the Programs menu opens.

3. Drag the shortcut to the position on the Programs menu where you'd like it to appear, and then release the mouse button. ▶

    To position the shortcut on a submenu of the Programs menu, drag the shortcut to the submenu, pause until the submenu expands, and then drag the shortcut onto the submenu and drop it wherever you want.

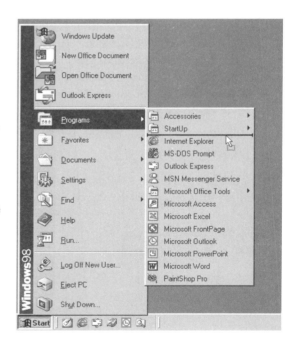

The Documents list shows a file I don't want others to see

Source of the problem

The Documents list on the Start menu makes the files you've used recently readily available. But it also leaves a trail that others can follow to see the files you've worked on. If you'd occasionally prefer to sacrifice a little convenience to maintain your privacy, here's how you can either clear the entire Documents list or selectively delete documents from it.

How to fix it

1. Click Start, point to Settings, and click Taskbar & Start Menu or Taskbar And Start Menu (in Windows Me).

2. On the Start Menu Programs tab in the Taskbar Properties dialog box or on the Advanced tab of the Taskbar And Start Menu Properties dialog box (in Windows Me), click Clear in the Documents Menu area to clear the entire Documents list. ▶

3. Click OK.

Deleting a single entry

To remove a single entry from the Documents list, you can delete its shortcut from the Recent folder within the Windows folder on the hard disk. The Recent folder is a hidden folder, though, so to see it you must first double-click My Computer on the desktop, click Folder Options on the View menu or the Tools menu (in Windows Me), and in the Folder Options dialog box, click Show All Files on the View tab or click Show Hidden Files And Folders in the Advanced Settings list (in Windows Me). Now you can open the Windows folder, open the Recent folder within the Windows folder, and delete shortcuts. Be sure to change the Show All Files or Show Hidden Files option back after deleting the shortcut.

Windows won't shut down

Source of the problem

If you click Shut Down and find that the computer hangs up when it should either turn itself off or display the message *It is now safe to turn off your computer,* you need to look into several common causes of shutdown problems. Among these are a faulty Fast Shutdown option, problems with installed hardware devices, and a BIOS that needs updating. (The BIOS is the software built into the computer that controls its most basic operations.) Follow the steps below to take care of all these potential problems.

If you use Windows 98 Second Edition, you should first try downloading and installing two updates, as described below, that correct a number of possible causes.

How to fix it (in Windows 98 Second Edition)

1. In Windows 98 Second Edition, connect to the Internet and go to *www.microsoft.com/windows98/downloads/corporate.asp*.

2. In the Recommended Updates section of the Windows Update Web page, click both Windows 98 Second Edition Shutdown Supplement and Windows 98 Second Edition Mapped Drives Shutdown Update, and install each update according to the instructions on the screen.

   If the updates don't solve the shutdown problem, follow the steps in "How to Fix It (in Windows 98 and Windows Me)," below.

How to fix it (in Windows 98 and Windows Me)

If you're using Windows Me, skip steps 1 through 4 below, as they apply only to Windows 98.

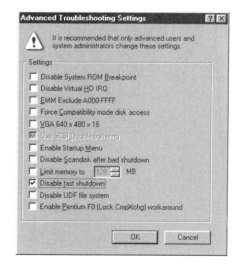

1. Click Start, click Run, and in the Run dialog box, type **msconfig** in the Open box.

2. On the General tab in System Configuration Utility, click Advanced.

3. In the Advanced Troubleshooting Settings dialog box, select the Disable Fast Shutdown check box. ▶

4. Click OK, click OK again to close the System Configuration Utility, and try shutting down again.

If the computer still won't shut down, see whether a program is failing to respond by following these steps:

1. Press Ctrl+Alt+Del and look in the list in the Close Program dialog box for a program that is accompanied by a *Not responding* message. ▶

If you see such a program, click it and click End Task. If a message box appears telling you that the program is not responding, click End Task to close the dialog box and quit the program.

2. Try shutting down again.

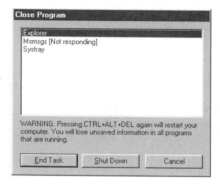

If the computer still won't shut down properly, use Device Manager to verify that no devices in your computer are having trouble by following these steps:

1. Right-click My Computer on the desktop, and click Properties on the shortcut menu.

2. On the Device Manager tab in the System Properties dialog box, look for devices whose icons show a yellow exclamation point. A problem with one of these devices may be preventing Windows from properly shutting down.

If you find that one of your devices is reporting trouble, see "A New Device I've Installed Doesn't Work," on page 140, for further troubleshooting steps.

If the computer still won't shut down properly, contact the computer manufacturer or go to the manufacturer's Web site to look for a program that you can download and run to update the computer's BIOS. Computer manufacturers frequently post BIOS update programs to fix problems that are found only later.

> **Tip**
>
> To determine whether you're using Windows 98 Second Edition, right-click My Computer on the desktop, click Properties on the shortcut menu, and see whether "Second Edition" appears under "Microsoft Windows 98" in the System Properties dialog box.

My computer won't turn itself off when I use Shut Down

Some computers are able to turn themselves off after you click Shut Down, just as if you turned off their power switch. If your computer has never turned itself off (you've always seen the *It is now safe to turn off your computer* message), you probably can't get it to do so now because the computer is not designed for this feature. But if your computer has turned itself off in the past, the computer has this capability but it's probably been deactivated. To restore automatic shutdown, run the setup program for the computer (usually, to start the setup program, you press a key while the computer is starting), and look for an option that turns on Advanced Power Management (APM). For additional information about APM, see "The Battery Runs Down Too Fast," on page 180.

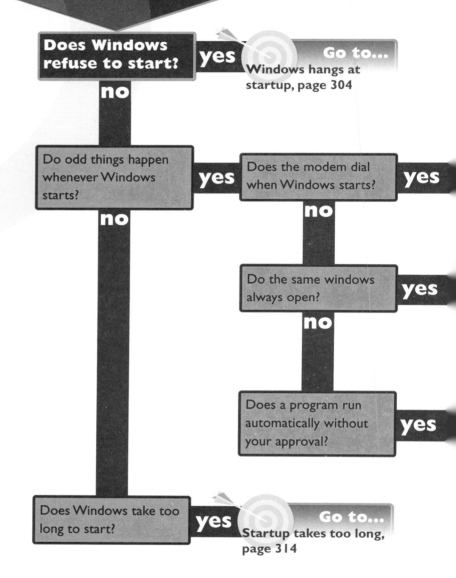

Does Windows refuse to start? yes → **Go to...** Windows hangs at startup, page 304

no

Do odd things happen whenever Windows starts? yes → **Does the modem dial when Windows starts?** yes →

no

Do the same windows always open? yes →

no

Does a program run automatically without your approval? yes →

Does Windows take too long to start? yes → **Go to...** Startup takes too long, page 314

Go to...

The modem dials whenever Windows starts, page 317

Go to...

The same windows open whenever Windows starts, page 316

Is ScanDisk the program that runs?

yes

Quick fix

Be sure to click Shut Down on the Start menu when you want to shut down Windows; otherwise, ScanDisk runs the next time you start Windows.

no

Go to...

Programs start automatically, without my approval 312

If your solution isn't here
Check these related chapters:
   The desktop, page 14
   Optimizing, page 226
   The Start menu, page 292
   Window, working with a, page 328
Or see the general troubleshooting tips on page xiii

Windows hangs at startup

Source of the problem

If you're ready to start, but Windows just stops—it gets stuck at the logo screen, never gets to the desktop, and displays no error messages—you could be encountering any one of several problems that can keep Windows from starting properly. You might have a bad device driver, a network error, a registry problem, or a program that hangs when it loads automatically at startup. To fix the problem, you'll investigate possible causes until you've determined what's going on, and then you'll take different steps to fix the problem depending on the cause.

How to fix it

1. Turn on your computer, and press F8 repeatedly while the computer is starting.

2. When the Microsoft Windows Startup Menu appears, press the Down Arrow key to move the highlight to Safe Mode, and then press Enter.

   If Windows won't start even in safe mode, skip to "Safe Mode Doesn't Work Either," on the facing page.

3. When Windows starts in safe mode, click Start and click Run on the Start menu.

   In Windows 95 and Windows 98, you need to click OK when a message tells you that you're running in safe mode. After Windows starts, you see the words *Safe Mode* in each corner of the desktop. In Windows Me, the Safe Mode Troubleshooter opens in the Microsoft Help And Support window. Close this window so that you can follow the steps here.

4. In the Run dialog box, type **Msconfig** in the Open box, and press Enter.

5. In Windows 95 and 98, on the General tab in the System Configuration Utility, click Create Backup, and then click OK when you see a message that says your files have been backed up. In Windows Me, skip this step.

6. Click Selective Startup, also on the General tab. ▶

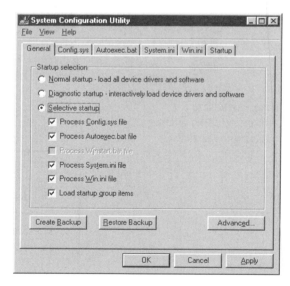

7. Clear the Process System.ini File and Process Win.ini File check boxes, click OK, and click Yes when you are asked whether you want to restart your computer. In Windows Me, when the computer restarts, enter your password if necessary, and click OK in the message box telling you that you are using Selective Startup. In Windows 95 or Windows 98, you won't get this message.

　　If Windows starts normally, skip to "My Configuration Files Are Keeping Windows from Starting," on page 306.

If Windows does not start normally, turn off the computer and follow steps 1 and 2 above. After Windows starts in safe mode, follow these steps:

1. Click Start, click Run, and type **Msconfig** again and press Enter to restart the System Configuration Utility.

2. On the General tab, reselect the Process System.ini File and Process Win.ini File check boxes.

3. In Windows 95 or Windows 98, clear the Process Config.sys File and Process Autoexec.bat File check boxes, click OK, and click Yes when you are asked whether you want to restart your computer. In Windows Me, skip to "My Configuration Files Are Keeping Windows from Starting," on page 306.

　　If Windows now starts normally, skip to "My Config.sys or Autoexec.bat File Is Keeping Windows 95 or Windows 98 from Starting," on page 308. If Windows doesn't start normally, follow steps 1 through 4 on the previous page to start the computer in safe mode again, reselect the Process Config.sys File and Process Autoexec.bat File check boxes, and then skip to "My Configuration Files Are Keeping Windows from Starting," on page 306.

Safe mode doesn't work either

If Windows won't start even in safe mode, you may have a registry problem that you can solve by running the Microsoft Registry Checker. Follow these steps:

1. Turn off the computer, insert the Windows startup disk you made when you set up Windows, and start the computer.

2. At the Microsoft Windows Startup Menu, press the Down Arrow key to select Start Computer With CD-ROM Support, and then press Enter.

3. At the MS-DOS prompt, type **scanreg** and press Enter. If a message asks whether you want the Registry Checker to begin, press Enter.

　　The Microsoft Registry Checker detects and fixes any errors. If you are asked whether you want to back up the registry, click No. ▶

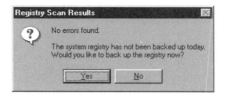

If this solution didn't solve your problem, go to the next page.

Windows hangs at startup

(continued from page 305)

If Microsoft Registry Checker reports that it found no errors, exit the Registry Checker and look into these possibilities:

- Check your computer's hardware settings for possible conflicts. If you've just installed a new hardware device, remove it and try to start Windows again. If that works, try to install the device again but make sure you follow the installation instructions precisely so that you don't skip or deviate from any steps. Check the support area on the hardware manufacturer's Web site too, in case there's something special you should be doing, such as running a setup program before you plug in the device.

- Run the configuration program for the computer itself, which sets the configuration of the computer's hardware. Look for a conflict such as two devices that have the same IRQ setting, and then change the IRQ setting for one of the devices. Your computer's manual, or the manufacturer's Web site, may help you decipher all the options and settings. If not, give the manufacturer's tech support line a call.

- Use an antivirus program to determine whether a virus has infected your system. Most antivirus programs either come with or help you create a bootable disk you can use to start your computer and then detect and clean out viruses.

My configuration files are keeping Windows from starting

The System.ini and Win.ini files contain configuration information that Windows uses to start itself properly. Included in this information are two lines in the Win.ini file: one that loads programs, such as utilities used by devices or applications in your computer, and another that runs programs. If any of these programs or utilities has trouble running or conflicts with another program, Windows might not start. To fix this problem, follow these steps:

1. Start Windows in safe mode by pressing F8 repeatedly while your computer is starting and then choosing Safe Mode from the Microsoft Windows Startup Menu.

2. In safe mode, click Start, click Run, and in the Run dialog box, type **Msconfig** in the Open box and press Enter.

3. On the Win.ini tab in the System Configuration Utility window, double-click the [Windows] folder. ▶ facing page

   If there isn't anything on the Load= and Run= lines and you're using Windows 95 or Windows 98, skip to "My Config.sys or Autoexec.bat File Is Keeping Windows 95 or Windows 98 from Starting," on page 308. If you're using Windows Me, skip to "A Startup Program Is Keeping Windows from Starting," on page 309.

4. Clear the Load= and Run= check boxes, click OK, and click Yes when you are asked whether you want to restart your computer.

If Windows does not start normally, skip to "My Config.sys or Autoexec.bat File Is Keeping Windows 95 or Windows 98 from Starting," on the next page, or to "A Startup Program Is Keeping Windows from Starting," on page 309, if you're using Windows Me.

If Windows starts normally again, follow these steps:

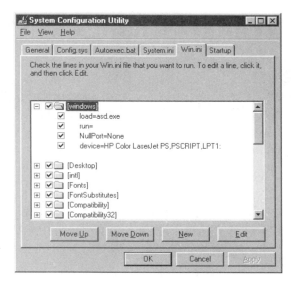

1. In Windows Me, click OK to close the System Configuration Utility dialog box, and click Start, click Run, type **Msconfig** in the Open box and press Enter.

2. On the Win.ini tab in the System Configuration Utility window, double-click the [Windows] folder again, select the Load= check box and click OK, and then click Yes when you are asked whether you want to restart your computer.

    If Windows doesn't start, the problem is a program that's listed on the Load= line. Fix the Load= line by returning to safe mode and running the System Configuration Utility (Msconfig) again. On the Win.ini tab, double-click [Windows], select the Run= line, click the Load= line, and then click Edit. Remove programs listed on the Load= line one by one, restarting the computer after you remove each program, until the computer starts normally.

If Windows started normally when you selected the Load= check box, follow these steps:

1. Click Start, click Run, and in the Run dialog box, type **Msconfig** in the Open box and press Enter.

2. On the Win.ini tab in the System Configuration Utility window, double-click [Windows], select the Run= check box, click OK, and then click Yes when you are asked whether you want to restart your computer.

    If Windows doesn't start, the problem is a program that's listed on the Run= line. Fix the Run= line by returning to safe mode and running the System Configuration Utility (Msconfig) again. On the Win.ini tab, double-click [Windows], click the Run= line, click Edit, and remove programs one by one, restarting the computer after you remove each program, until the computer starts normally.

If this solution didn't solve your problem, go to the next page.

Windows hangs at startup

(continued from page 307)

My Config.sys or Autoexec.bat file is keeping Windows 95 or Windows 98 from starting

These two files are vestiges of the days before Windows. If you have never dealt with MS-DOS and have never edited a Config.sys or an Autoexec.bat file, consider yourself lucky.

The Config.sys and Autoexec.bat files load drivers and start utility programs before Windows 95 or Windows 98 starts. (Windows Me doesn't use the Config.sys or Autoexec.bat file.) The Windows setup process usually cleans out anything from these files that Windows either doesn't need or provides on its own, but the installation program for a device or piece of software that you've added, especially if the device or software is old (pre–Windows 95), may have inserted a reference to a driver or program in these files that is keeping Windows from starting.

1. Start Windows in safe mode by pressing F8 repeatedly while your computer is starting and choosing Safe Mode from the Microsoft Windows Startup Menu.

2. Run the System Configuration Utility (by clicking Start, clicking Run, typing **Msconfig** in the Open box, and pressing Enter). On the General tab, click Selective Startup, select the Process Config.sys File check box, click OK, and click Yes when you are asked whether you want to restart your computer.

If Windows starts, the problem is in the Autoexec.bat file. If Windows does not start, the problem is most likely in the Config.sys file. To pinpoint the problem, continue with these steps:

1. Run the System Configuration Utility (Msconfig) again.

2. On the General tab, select both the Process Config.sys File and Process Autoexec.bat File check boxes, and then click the Autoexec.bat tab or the Config.sys tab, depending on which file contains the problem.

3. Clear all the check boxes in the list. ▶

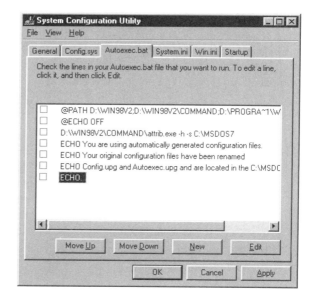

4. Click OK, and click Yes when you are asked whether you want to restart your computer.

5. If Windows starts, run the System Configuration Utility (Msconfig) again.

6. Click the same tab as you did in step 2, select the first check box in the list, click OK, and restart the computer.

7. Keep repeating steps 5 and 6, selecting the next check box in the list each time, until Windows does not start. ▶

8. Start Windows in safe mode.

9. Run the System Configuration Utility (Msconfig) again, and clear the last check box you selected.

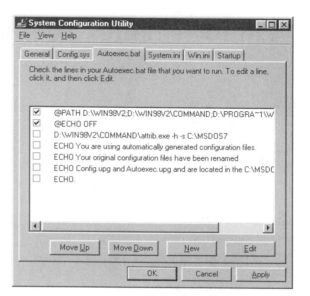

10. Select all the other check boxes and click OK.

11. Restart Windows once again just to confirm that you've really found the offender.

If Windows still won't start, skip to "A Startup Program Is Keeping Windows from Starting," below. But if Windows starts, the last check box you selected before Windows stopped working represents the line in Config.sys or Autoexec.bat that's preventing Windows from starting. Try to determine which device or program added this line. If a device won't work properly without the line, you'll need to upgrade to a newer model or software version or switch to a version made by a different manufacturer. Make sure the new device is Plug and Play compatible.

A startup program is keeping Windows from starting

If Windows seems to hang just as it's finally getting started—when the desktop starts to appear, or as the icons on the taskbar next to the clock fall into place—a program that launches automatically at startup may be keeping Windows from starting. You can determine whether this is the cause and isolate the program and prevent it from starting.

1. Start Windows in safe mode by pressing F8 repeatedly while your computer is starting and then choosing Safe Mode from the Microsoft Windows Startup Menu.

2. Click Run on the Start menu, and in the Run dialog box, type **Msconfig** in the Open box and click OK.

> **To continue with this solution, go to the next page.**

Windows hangs at startup

(continued from page 309)

3. On the Startup tab in the System Configuration Utility window, clear each of the check boxes in the list. ▶

4. Click OK, and click Yes when you are asked whether you want to restart your computer.

5. Start the System Configuration Utility (Msconfig) again.

6. On the Startup tab, select the first check box in the list. ▶ below

7. Click OK, and click Yes when you're asked whether you want to restart the computer.

8. If Windows starts normally, start the System Configuration Utility (Msconfig) again.

9. Select the next check box in the list on the Startup tab and click OK.

10. Click Yes when you are asked whether you want to restart your computer.

11. Continue this process until Windows hangs when it tries to restart.
 The last program you selected is the one that's keeping Windows from starting.

12. Clear the check box next to the last program you selected, but select all the other check boxes in the list, including the untested programs below this program, and restart Windows once again just to confirm that you've really found the offender.

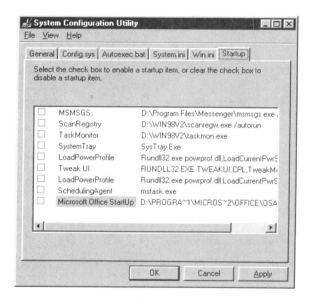

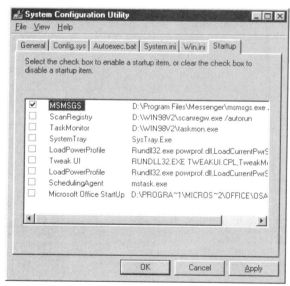

Startup entries on the Startup tab

Some of the items in the list on the Startup tab are easy to identify. ▶

ScanRegistry, for example, refers to the Microsoft Registry Checker, which runs during the startup process, checks the registry for errors, and restores a backup copy of the registry if it finds that the main registry file is corrupted. Other programs may have far more cryptic names and descriptions. Here are some of the more common programs you might encounter:

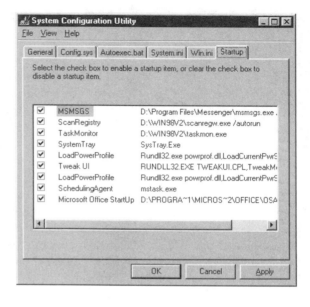

- **SystemTray** Runs the system tray, where the clock and other icons reside

- **StillImageMonitor** Provides support for scanners and cameras

- **LoadPowerProfile** Loads your profile for power management

- **COMSMDEXE** Operates 3Com networking

- **HP JetDiscovery** Provides support for Hewlett-Packard network printing

- **HPSCANMonitor** Provides support for Hewlett-Packard scanners

- **Tweak UI** Runs Tweak UI, an add-on Control Panel utility for modifying the user interface

If you can readily identify the startup program you've disabled, check the manufacturer's Web site for updated software or technical support. If you are unable to easily determine the program you've disabled, you may find out only when a device no longer works, a program fails, or a capability (such as a special shortcut key combination that starts your Web browser) is no longer available.

Tip

When you temporarily disable items in the list on the Startup tab, they're moved to a folder in the Program Files folder named Disabled Startup Items. To reenable these items, you can drag them from this folder to the StartUp folder.

Programs start automatically, without my approval

Source of the problem

You can stop some programs from running when Windows starts, such as companion programs for Webcams and other devices, just by changing one of their options. These are polite programs. Others need to be yanked out by the roots.

Programs start themselves by putting a shortcut that starts their main program file in the StartUp folder on the Start menu. Each time Windows starts, the programs in the StartUp folder start too. That makes the StartUp folder the first place to look for unwanted software that launches itself. But not all programs use the StartUp folder. Some software setup programs put a startup command in the Windows registry. A registry entry is harder to remove than a simple StartUp folder shortcut. Here's how to go through and systematically prevent all unwanted programs from starting up without your express permission—regardless of whether they have shortcuts in the StartUp folder or startup commands in the registry.

How to fix it

1. Right-click Start, and click Explore on the shortcut menu.

2. In the left pane of the Windows Explorer window, click the plus sign next to the Programs folder under Start Menu, and then click the StartUp folder. ▶

3. In the right pane, drag the icons for the programs you want to prevent from starting to the Recycle Bin on the desktop.

4. Close the Windows Explorer window.

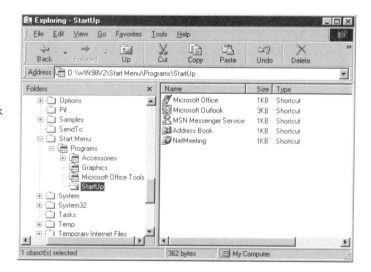

That takes care of the StartUp folder shortcuts. Now here's how to fix the programs that start by using registry settings:

1. Click Start, click Run, and in the Run dialog box, type **Msconfig** in the Open box and click OK.

2. Click the Startup tab in the System Configuration Utility window, and clear the check box next to any program that you want to prevent from loading. ▶

3. Click OK, and then click Yes when you are asked whether you want to restart the computer.

4. After the computer restarts, click Start, click Run, and in the Run dialog box, type **Msconfig** in the Open box and click OK to start the System Configuration Utility.

5. Click the Win.ini tab, and then double-click the [Windows] folder. ▶ below

6. Click the Load= line, click the Edit button, and then remove the entries for programs that you do not want loaded.

7. Click the Run= line, click the Edit button, remove the entries for programs you do not want loaded and run, and then click OK.

8. Click Yes if you are asked whether you want to restart the computer.

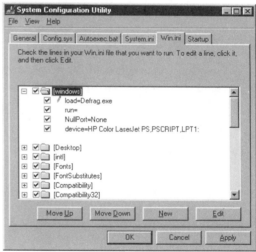

More about the StartUp folder

You may be surprised to find how many icons your StartUp folder contains. Each icon corresponds to a program that starts when Windows does. Some programs in the StartUp folder open a window and announce their presence. Your Internet service provider's (ISP's) dialer program may be an example. Other programs run without fanfare, waiting quietly in the background until it's their time to provide a service. Some printers have special programs, for example, that pop open to show you the printer's progress through queued-up documents.

How did all those icons get there? Some software setup programs rudely drop icons into the StartUp folder without asking. Others have a little more courtesy and ask whether you want their program started each time you start Windows.

Tip
You can specify whether a program opens in a regular window, a full-screen window, or as a button on the taskbar by right-clicking its icon in the StartUp folder, clicking the Run down arrow in the Properties dialog box, and then clicking Normal Window, Maximized, or Minimized in the list.

Startup takes too long

Source of the problem

Windows is ready to go when the desktop appears, when all the little icons on the taskbar are visible, and when the mouse pointer no longer shows that wait-just-a-minute hourglass. But if getting to that point requires nothing short of endurance when it used to require just a little patience, Windows startup is taking too long.

Startup takes time because Windows has a lot of devices to set up, a ton of programs to load, a slew of fonts to install, and a full roster of housekeeping to do before it's ready to go to work for you. Windows Me has made a few strides toward a shorter startup time. You'll find that it gets up and running noticeably faster than previous versions of Windows. But here are steps you can take to minimize startup time no matter which version of Windows you use.

How to fix it

1. Follow the procedure in "Programs Start Automatically, Without My Approval," on page 312, to remove programs that automatically start whether you want them or not.

2. Right-click My Computer on the desktop, and click Properties on the shortcut menu.

3. On the Performance tab in the System Properties dialog box, click File System.

4. On the Floppy Disk tab in the File System Properties dialog box, clear the Search For New Floppy Disk Drives Each Time Your Computer Starts check box. ▶

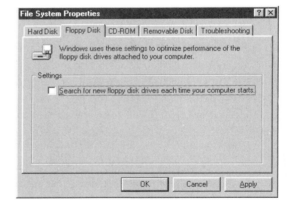

5. Click OK, and then click OK again to close the dialog box.

In addition, follow these steps to remove unnecessary fonts:

1. Double-click My Computer on the desktop, and then double-click your hard disk in the My Computer window.

2. Right-click in any blank space in the My Computer window, point to New on the shortcut menu, and click Folder.

3. Type a name for the folder, such as *Extra Fonts*, and press Enter.

4. Double-click the new folder to open it.

5. Click Start, point to Settings, and click Control Panel.

6. In Control Panel, double-click Fonts. (In Windows Me, you might need to click View All Control Panel Options to see the Fonts option.)

7. In the Fonts window, double-click any font whose name does not seem familiar to you to preview the font, and then, after you've taken a look at the font, click Done to close the preview window.

8. Drag any font you do not need from the Fonts window to the new window (named Extra Fonts in this example).

   If you need to reinstall a font later, you can drag it back from the new window to the Fonts window.

9. Free up additional disk space.

   For information about freeing up disk space, see "I've Run Out of Space on My Hard Disk," on page 130.

10. Defragment your hard disk by right-clicking the disk in My Computer, clicking Properties on the shortcut menu, and clicking Defragment Now on the Tools tab in the Properties dialog box.

Analyzing the boot log in Windows 95 or Windows 98

Every time you start Windows 95 or Windows 98, a file is created on your hard disk that contains a log of all the activities that occur when Windows starts. Windows Me doesn't make such a file. You can analyze this log file by obtaining Boot Log Analyzer, a helpful utility you can download from *www.vision4.dial.pipex.com*.

Boot Log Analyzer analyzes the log file and shows the duration of each event that occurred during Windows startup. ▶

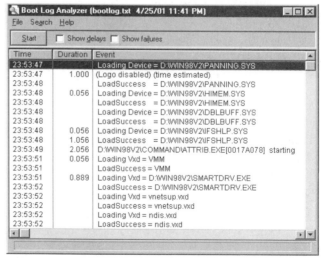

Look for an event that has an unusually long duration and see which hardware device (such as a network card) or software program is associated with that event. Then try removing and reinstalling the device or software program. If that doesn't work, check the hardware or software manufacturer's Web site to see whether you can download and install a new driver or an update file that might solve the problem.

The same windows open whenever Windows starts

Source of the problem

Windows remembers how your screen looks whenever it shuts down so that it can offer you the same open windows the next time you start the computer. This is a convenience, but sometimes these same windows get stuck, opening every time you start Windows.

To keep windows from reopening, you can stop Windows from remembering settings for each window, as described below. To prevent this problem from happening again, you can adopt a few practices to follow when you shut down Windows.

How to fix it

1. Click Start, point to Settings, and click Control Panel.

2. In Control Panel, double-click Tweak UI. (In Windows Me, you might need to click View All Control Panel Options to see the Tweak UI option.)

   If you do not have Tweak UI installed, see "Where Do I Get Tweak UI?," on page 33.

3. On the Explorer tab in the Tweak UI dialog box, clear the Save Explorer Window Settings check box. ▶

4. Click OK to close the Tweak UI dialog box.

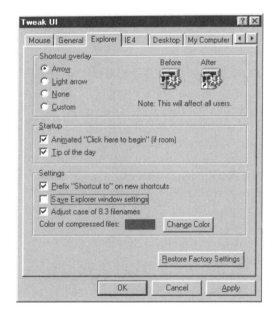

How to prevent it

If you'd rather avoid having Tweak UI wipe out the settings of all Windows Explorer windows, make sure you follow these rules whenever you shut down your computer:

● Be sure to close all open windows—both Windows Explorer windows and My Computer (folder) windows—before you click Shut Down on the Start menu.

● Wait to turn off the computer until you see a message that says *It is now safe to turn off your computer.*

The modem dials whenever Windows starts

Source of the problem

If your Web browser or e-mail program starts whenever you start Windows, it can push the modem into trying to connect to the Internet because it wants to retrieve a Web page or an e-mail message.

If you'd rather maintain tighter control of your modem and phone line and prevent Internet Explorer or your e-mail program from dialing a Dial-Up Networking connection whenever it starts, follow these steps.

How to fix it

- If your Internet service provider (ISP) or online service has provided software that establishes a connection, look in the software's options for an autodial feature and disable it.

If you're using Dial-Up Networking to connect to an ISP, follow these steps:

1. Start Internet Explorer, and on the View menu (in Internet Explorer 4) or the Tools menu (in Internet Explorer 5), click Internet Options.

2. In Internet Explorer 4, select the Connect To The Internet Using A Local Area network check box on the Connection tab in the Internet Options dialog box.

   On the Connections tab in the Internet Options dialog box in Internet Explorer 5, click Never Dial A Connection and click OK. ▶

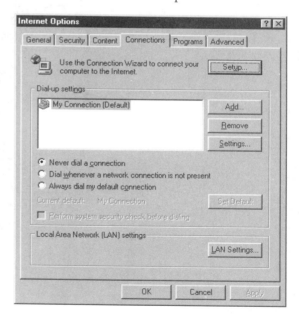

3. See "Outlook Express Automatically Dials My ISP," on page 68, for information about preventing Outlook Express from dialing your ISP whenever it starts.

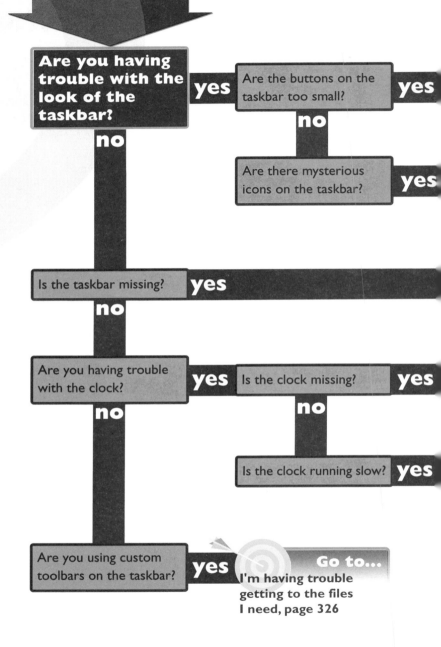

Are you having trouble with the look of the taskbar?

yes → Are the buttons on the taskbar too small? **yes**

no ↓

Are there mysterious icons on the taskbar? **yes**

no ↓

Is the taskbar missing? **yes**

no ↓

Are you having trouble with the clock? **yes** Is the clock missing? **yes**

no ↓ **no** ↓

Is the clock running slow? **yes**

Are you using custom toolbars on the taskbar? **yes**

Go to...
I'm having trouble getting to the files I need, page 326

The taskbar

Go to...
The taskbar buttons
are too small, page 322

Go to...
The end of the taskbar
near the clock shows
mysterious icons,
page 324

Go to...
The taskbar is missing
or in the wrong place,
page 320

Quick fix

The clock is always located at the far right of the taskbar, or at the bottom if the taskbar is on the left or right edge of the desktop. To get it back if it's missing, follow these steps:

1. Right-click the taskbar, and click Properties on the shortcut menu.

2. Select the Show Clock check box.

3. Click OK.

Go to...
The clock loses time,
page 327

If your solution isn't here

Check these related chapters:

The desktop, page 14

Folders, page 106

The screen, page 264

The Start menu, 292

Or see the general troubleshooting tips on page xiii

The taskbar is missing or in the wrong place

Source of the problem

It's an unnerving feeling to look down and find that the taskbar you've come to rely on is gone. Although the taskbar normally stays in its own space at the bottom of the screen, not covered by windows, you can set the taskbar so that it allows other windows to use the entire screen, even if that means covering the taskbar. And while the taskbar is usually tall enough to display one row of icons and buttons, you can also inadvertently resize the taskbar so that it's flatter than a pancake, making it impossible to see. The taskbar might even be set to automatically hide itself until you move the mouse pointer to it, when it pops up ready for action. If you can't find the taskbar, you should track it down by following these steps:

How to fix it

1. Press Ctrl+Esc to open the Start menu and display the taskbar.

2. Right-click the taskbar, and click Properties on the shortcut menu.
   Alternatively, you can click Start, point to Settings, and click Taskbar & Start Menu or Taskbar And Start Menu (in Windows Me).

3. On the Taskbar Options tab in the Taskbar Properties dialog box or on the General tab in the Taskbar And Start Menu Properties dialog box (in Windows Me), select the Always On Top check box. ▶

4. Clear the Auto Hide check box if it's selected.

5. Click OK.

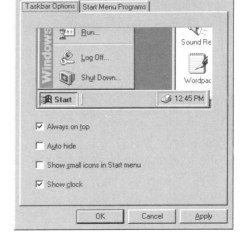

If the taskbar is still missing when the Start menu opens, it's been resized down to a thin strip that's very hard to see. To restore the taskbar to full size, follow these steps:

1. Click the Minimize button in the upper-right corner of every window you have open.
   Normally you could just click Show Desktop on the taskbar to minimize all windows, but that trick won't help you this time!

---

2. Move the mouse pointer to the edge of the screen where the taskbar appeared when you pressed Ctrl+Esc, until the pointer changes to a two-headed arrow.

3. Drag the edge of the taskbar until the taskbar is the height you want (or width, if the taskbar is along the side of the screen). ▶

Usually the taskbar has room for just one row or column of buttons, but you can make it any height or width you want using this method.

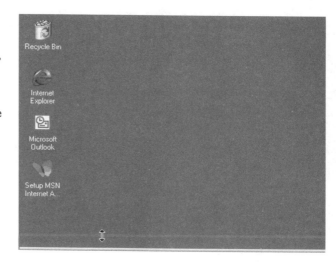

What if my taskbar has moved?

In Windows, it's not all that hard to dislodge the taskbar from its normal location by accident. While you won't actually lose the taskbar by moving it (unless of course you also somehow resize it so that it's flat), you might end up scratching your head wondering why the taskbar is now standing vertically along the side of the screen rather than lying neatly along the bottom. ▶

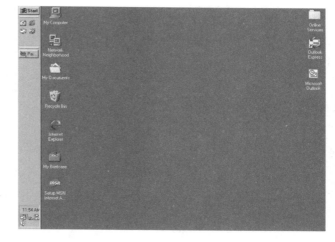

To get the taskbar back where you want it, position the mouse pointer in any empty area on the taskbar and drag the taskbar back to the bottom of the screen. If you can't seem to get ahold of the taskbar, you're probably grabbing it by one of its toolbars—reposition the mouse pointer and try again.

The only toolbar that's almost always on the taskbar is the Quick Launch toolbar, which is usually located immediately to the right of the Start menu (although it can be repositioned). You might have other toolbars on the taskbar, however. To configure which toolbars are open, right-click the taskbar and point to Toolbars. Select a toolbar on the shortcut menu to display the toolbar.

Tip
To learn more about adding custom toolbars to the taskbar that can simplify access to your favorite submenus on the Start menu or folders that you frequently access, see "I'm Having Trouble Getting to the Files I Need" on page 326.

The taskbar buttons are too small

Source of the problem

The icon on each taskbar button identifies the program that's open, but the text description next to the icon gives you more useful information, such as the name of the folder or document that's open. But as more and more buttons occupy the limited real estate of the taskbar, the text description on each button gets shorter and shorter, eventually becoming useless.

If the taskbar is crowded with buttons, you can increase the space for buttons on the taskbar, which in turn increases the width of the text area in each button. Another option is to increase the size of the buttons, which provides more space for text and icons. To try out these alternatives, follow these steps.

How to fix it

1. Position the mouse pointer on the handle at the left end of the row of taskbar buttons (at the top if the taskbar is oriented vertically). ▶

2. Drag the handle to the left (or up if the taskbar is oriented vertically). ▶
   This expansion might encroach on the Quick Launch toolbar if it's displayed, but you'll have more room for the taskbar buttons.

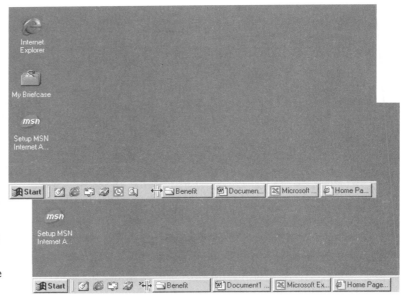

If you want still more room on the taskbar, you can remove the Quick Launch toolbar:

1. Right-click anywhere on the taskbar where there's not a button or an icon.

2. On the shortcut menu, point to Toolbars, and click Quick Launch.

If you want still more room, you can increase the height or width of the taskbar as follows:

1. Move the mouse pointer to the top edge of the taskbar (or the right or left edge if the taskbar is vertical).

2. Drag the edge of the taskbar up (or to the right or left) so that the taskbar becomes twice the width or height.

   If you find that you're unable to resize the taskbar in Windows Me, right-click the taskbar, click Properties, click the Advanced tab, and in the Start Menu And Taskbar list, select the Enable Moving And Resizing check box under Taskbar. Then click OK.

Tip

To have Windows display the entire text for any button on the toolbar, just hold the mouse pointer over the button for a second or two. A pop-up description will appear that gives you information about the file, folder, or Web page that's open and the name of the program in which it's open.

To further maximize the button area, you can remove some of the icons in the system tray at the end of the taskbar, near the clock. For more information, see "The End of the Taskbar Near the Clock Shows Mysterious Icons," on the next page.

If instead you want to make the text in buttons more readable by increasing the size of the text, follow these steps.

1. Right-click the desktop, and click Properties on the shortcut menu.

2. On the Appearance tab in the Display Properties dialog box, click the Item down arrow, and click Active Title Bar in the list. ▶

3. Make a note of the current setting for the active title bar's font and text size so that you can reset the buttons to their original state if you need to.

4. Click the Size down arrow next to Font, and click a size that's larger than the current size by 2 or 3.

   This number represent size in *points* (a unit of measurement in typography).

5. Click Apply, and take a look at the taskbar to see the change.

   Try different settings until you find the one you want. Keep in mind that changes you make here will also affect the title bar of each window. Also, you might find that you'll want to increase the size of the taskbar as you enlarge the buttons.

6. Click OK to close the Display Properties dialog box.

The end of the taskbar near the clock shows mysterious icons

Source of the problem

If you've had your computer for a while, you've probably noticed a slow buildup of icons next to the clock as you've installed programs and utilities. If you want to rid the taskbar of icon clutter, you need to identify and get rid of those icons you don't need.

You can often discover what the icons do from their shortcut menus. Sometimes you can even use the shortcut menus to remove the icons. Alternatively, you can often find shortcuts in Control Panel to configure the applications that show icons on the taskbar. To remove the icons on the taskbar, follow these steps.

How to fix it

1. Right-click an icon to open its shortcut menu.

2. Review the options on the shortcut menu to identify the program and determine what it does. If you decide you don't need the program, continue to step 3.

3. If you see a Properties command on the shortcut menu, or another command that lets you adjust the program's options, click it and look for an option in the Properties dialog box named something like Show Icon On The Taskbar. Clear this option, and click OK.

If there is no command on the shortcut menu that leads to a Properties dialog box, look for a Close or Exit command to click on the shortcut menu. After you click Close or Exit, follow the instructions on the screen to quit the program.

Remember, quitting a program might not prevent the same program from starting again the next time you start Windows.

If you can't find a Properties, Close, or Exit command on the shortcut menu, look in Control Panel for an icon for the program:

1. On the Start menu, point to Settings, and then click Control Panel.

2. In Control Panel, double-click the icon that's associated with the program you want to remove. (In Windows Me, you might have to click View All Control Panel Options to see the icon.)

   - To remove the Volume Control icon, which looks like a speaker, double-click Multimedia, and on the Audio tab in the Multimedia Properties dialog box, clear the Show Volume

Control On The Taskbar check box. (In Windows Me, double-click Sounds And Multimedia, and clear the same check box on the Sounds tab.) Click OK.

- To remove the Power Management icon, which looks like a power plug or a battery, double-click Power Management, and on the Advanced tab in the Properties dialog box, clear the Always Show Icon On The Taskbar check box. (In Windows Me, double-click Power Options instead.)

- To remove the Infrared icon, double-click Infrared Monitor, and on the Preferences tab in the Properties dialog box, clear the Display The Infrared Monitor Icon On The Taskbar check box.

- To remove a language indicator icon from the taskbar if you have two or more keyboard languages installed, double-click Keyboard, and on the Language tab in the Keyboard Properties dialog box, clear the Enable Indicator On Taskbar check box.

- To remove the PC Card icon from the taskbar if you have a portable computer with a PC card slot, double-click PC Card (PCMCIA), and on the Socket Status tab in the Properties dialog box, clear the Show Control On Taskbar check box.

Deciding which icons to remove

Most icons on the taskbar are there to remind you that a program is running and to give you a convenient way to access their features. Be sure to explore an icon's benefits before removing it—you might find it's worth keeping. Also, think twice before you disable a service just to get rid of the icon, and make sure you know how to start the service again. Even if you disable a program to rid yourself of its icon, a shortcut to the program might still be in your StartUp folder and the icon might reappear when you next start Windows. For more information about the StartUp folder, see "Programs Start Automatically, Without My Approval," on page 312.

> **Tip**
> If an icon you removed appears again after you restart your computer, you can disable the program to keep it from starting the next time you reboot. Click Run on the Start menu, type **msconfig** in the Open box in the Run dialog box, and click OK. Then click the Startup tab in the System Configuration Utility, clear the check box next to the program, and click OK. But be careful not to disable the wrong program!

Disabling the Task Scheduler

You can remove the Task Scheduler icon only if you shut down the Task Scheduler. To do this, double-click the Task Scheduler icon on the taskbar (in Windows Me, double-click the Scheduled Tasks icon in Control Panel), and on the Advanced menu in the Scheduled Tasks window, click Stop Using Task Scheduler. You won't find any Properties dialog box for this service in Control Panel. To turn the Task Scheduler back on, double-click My Computer and double-click Scheduled Tasks (in Windows Me, double-click the Scheduled Tasks icon in Control Panel), and click Start Using Task Scheduler on the Advanced menu.

I'm having trouble getting to the files I need

Source of the problem

The folder system neatly organizes files on your hard disk, but it doesn't always provide quick access to your files, especially when they're buried several folder levels deep. You can solve this problem, gaining quick access to files without having to open folder after folder, by creating a custom toolbar for a folder and its subfolders on the taskbar. To quickly open a file in the folder, you can click its button on the toolbar. You can also create custom toolbars for Control Panel options, printer options, and scheduled tasks—all by following these steps.

How to fix it

1. Right-click the taskbar, point to Toolbars on the shortcut menu, and click New Toolbar.

2. In the New Toolbar dialog box, navigate to the folder you want to show as a toolbar. ▶

   You can select a disk drive or Control Panel and show these items as custom toolbars too. You can also select Printers, Dial-Up Networking, and Scheduled Tasks.

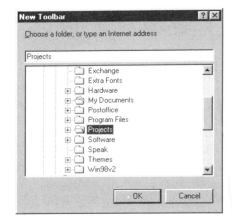

3. Click OK.

   There's usually room for only one or two buttons on the new toolbar. To see the entire contents of the toolbar, click the double-arrow button (>>) at the right end of the toolbar. ▶

Tip

To use the taskbar efficiently, drag the toolbar handle to the left of the new toolbar name to the right until just the toolbar name is visible. Now you can click the double-arrow button (>>) when you need to open the toolbar.

New toolbar

The clock loses time

Source of the problem

Your computer is a marvel of modern technology, but if you've found that a cheap wristwatch keeps better time than the clock on the taskbar, you're probably wondering why.

Believe it or not, your computer's hardware is actually keeping very good time. It's just that the clock on the taskbar becomes out of sync with the clock built into the computer from time to time.

You can keep the Windows clock on track and on time by understanding when it's likely to lose time so that you can readjust it when necessary. To do so, follow these steps.

How to fix it

● If you occasionally open the Date/Time Properties dialog box to set the time or date, watch the clock as you navigate. When you change the day or month, you'll see a loss of a second or so. When you change the year, the clock actually stops until you click OK or Apply. The clock stops even if you immediately change the setting back to the current year, but in this case, it stops for as long as you have the Date/Time Properties dialog box open. ▶

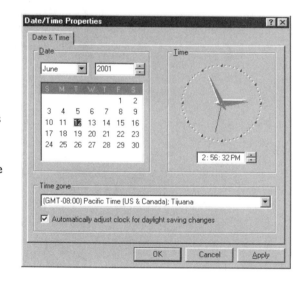

To open the Date/Time Properties dialog box, follow these steps:

1. Right-click the clock in the taskbar.
2. Click Adjust Date/Time on the shortcut menu.

● If you leave your computer on all the time, consider restarting it occasionally if you see the time drifting. When the computer reboots, it synchronizes the clock with the computer hardware BIOS, which keeps the correct time.

Tip
To obtain the correct time, contact the U.S. Naval Observatory, at *tycho.usno. navy.mil/what.html.*

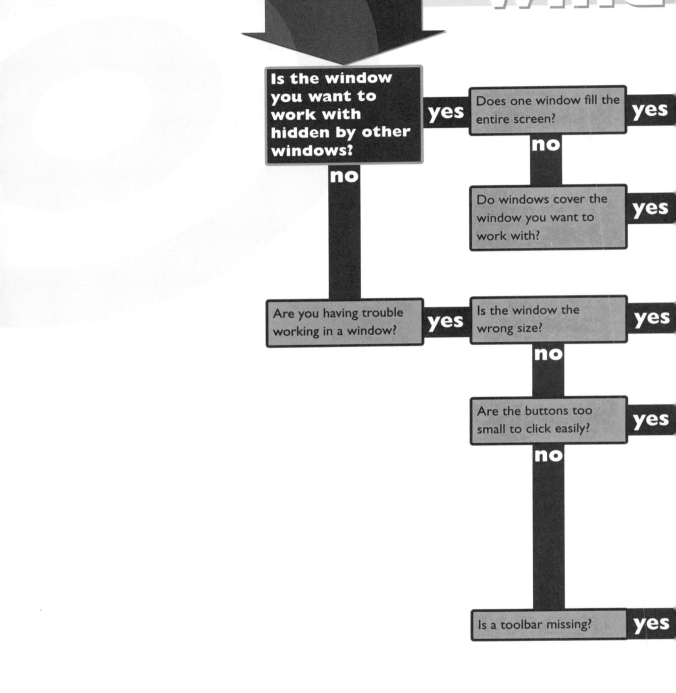

Is the window you want to work with hidden by other windows?

yes → Does one window fill the entire screen? → **yes**

no ↓

Do windows cover the window you want to work with? → **yes**

no ↓

Are you having trouble working in a window?

yes → Is the window the wrong size? → **yes**

no ↓

Are the buttons too small to click easily? → **yes**

no ↓

Is a toolbar missing? → **yes**

Go to...
One window covers all
the others, page 334

Go to...
The window I want is
behind other windows,
page 330

Go to...
A window is too large
or too small, page 335

Quick fix
If the buttons on the title bar are too small to click easily, you can
increase their size by following these steps:

1. Right-click the desktop, and click Properties on the shortcut menu.

2. On the Appearance tab in the Display Properties dialog box, click the
   Item down arrow and click Active Title Bar in the list.

3. Click the up arrow in the Size box to increase the size of the title bar
   and the buttons on it. The preview area in the dialog box shows the
   size of the buttons as you increase the size of the title bar.

Go to...
I can't find a toolbar,
page 332

If your solution isn't here
Check these related chapters:
Or see the general troubleshooting tips on page xiii

The window I want is behind other windows

Source of the problem

Opening multiple programs, each in its own window, lets you switch between programs quickly and easily copy information from one file to another. When you open two documents in two windows, for example, you can copy text in one window, switch to the other window, and then paste the text. But if the window you want to work in is buried under other windows, you can excavate it using one of the following methods.

How to fix it

● Click any visible part of the window you want to bring to the foreground. If another window covers the window you want, drag its title bar to move it aside. ▶

  If another window is maximized so that it fills the entire screen, you won't be able to move its title bar. Instead, try the following approach.

● Click the Minimize button of the window in front (the leftmost of the three buttons in the upper-right corner of the window). ▶ below

  Minimizing a window shrinks it to a button on the taskbar.

Because the taskbar is usually visible, clicking a button on the taskbar is a convenient way to bring a window to the foreground. If you can't find the taskbar, see "The Taskbar Is Missing or in the Wrong Place," on page 320.

Minimize button

● On the taskbar, click the button for the window you want. If a taskbar button is too small to display the complete names of the window it represents, position the mouse pointer on the button and pause without clicking until a description appears.

To use the keyboard to quickly shuffle through all the windows until you find the one you want, press and hold down the Alt key and press the Tab key repeatedly until you see the name of the program and document you want to open in the window that pops up. Release the Alt key.

Tiling and cascading windows

Another way to quickly access any window is to tile or cascade the windows that are open. Windows that are *tiled* are arranged in a grid on the screen so that they don't overlap. Windows that are *cascaded* are arranged in an overlapping pattern so that you can see each of their title bars. ▶

Only windows that are open are tiled or cascaded. Windows that are minimized to buttons on the taskbar remain minimized. Whether you tile or cascade the windows that are open, you can then click an individual window's Maximize button to have it fill the screen.

To tile the windows on the screen, follow these steps:

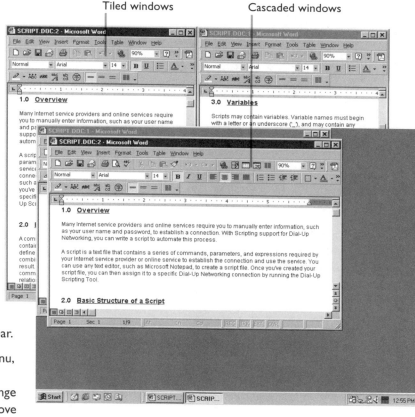

Tiled windows   Cascaded windows

1. Right-click the taskbar.

2. On the shortcut menu, click Tile Windows Horizontally to arrange the windows one above the other, or click Tile Windows Vertically to arrange the windows side by side.

After you tile windows, you can restore them to their original positions by right-clicking the taskbar again and clicking Undo Tile.

To cascade the windows on the screen, follow these steps:

1. Right-click the taskbar.

2. On the shortcut menu, click Cascade Windows.

After you cascade windows, you can restore them to their original positions by right-clicking the taskbar again and clicking Undo Cascade.

Tip

If you're having difficulty finding your program on the taskbar because the taskbar buttons are too small, see "The Taskbar Buttons Are Too Small," on page 322, for solutions to this problem.

I can't find a toolbar

Source of the problem

A toolbar is supposed to make hard-to-find menu commands easy to reach. But that's not what you get when the toolbar itself is missing. Toolbars can seem to vanish if you inadvertently move or disable them.

If a toolbar drops out of sight, you probably dragged it out of position while trying to move something else on the screen. But if you still can't find a toolbar after carefully searching the screen, you probably disabled the toolbar without realizing it. Here's how to determine whether a toolbar that's missing is actually disabled and how to put a disabled toolbar back in action.

How to fix it

1. On the View menu of a window that's missing a toolbar, point to Toolbars, and locate the name of the toolbar you're looking for. ▶

2. If there's no check mark next to the toolbar name, click the toolbar name to enable the toolbar.

If a check mark appears next to the toolbar name, the toolbar is already enabled and it's open somewhere on the screen. You need to find the toolbar and drag it back where it belongs.

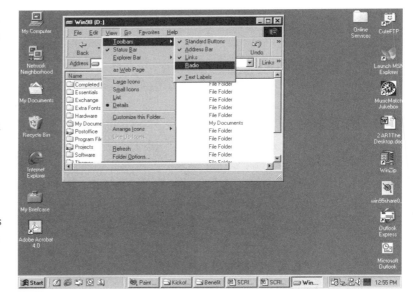

1. Carefully check the screen again for the toolbar.

    The toolbar might be pushed almost completely off the side or bottom of the screen. ▶

2. Position the mouse pointer on the narrow bar that appears at the left end of a horizontal toolbar or at the top of a vertical toolbar.

    If the toolbar has become a floating window somewhere on the screen, position the mouse pointer on the window's title bar.

3. Drag the toolbar where you want it.

    Other toolbars in the vicinity of the spot to which you drag the toolbar are automatically readjusted to accommodate the new arrival, but if you drag a toolbar to the wrong spot (next to another toolbar rather than above or below it, for example), you can drag the toolbar's handle (the narrow bar) to fine-tune the position of the toolbar.

Customizing toolbars

Although you can turn on toolbars or turn them off in My Computer and Windows Explorer windows, you can't add or remove buttons. But in programs such as Microsoft Office applications, if you don't find your favorite command on one of the stock toolbars, you can usually customize the toolbar, adding new commands that are available on menus. Creating a custom toolbar is like hanging your favorite tools where you'll always find them.

Tip

In addition to turning on a toolbar using the Toolbars menu, you can also right-click a different toolbar and then select the toolbar you want on the shortcut menu.

Missing toolbar

> ### Discovering new toolbars
>
> Although Windows has standard toolbars that appear in all My Computer and Windows Explorer windows, many programs have special toolbars that contain buttons for the commands that you're most likely to need. One day, when you have some free time, go through your favorite program's toolbars one by one. You might discover toolbars that you'll want to display because they contain easy-to-use buttons for commands that you frequently choose.
>
> To browse through a program's toolbars, point to Toolbars on the View menu, and then click each toolbar name to enable it. After you display a toolbar, you can usually learn the purpose of its buttons by resting the mouse pointer on each button without clicking to see a pop-up description.

One window covers all the others

Source of the problem

When one window hogs the entire screen, it's most likely maximized. When a window is maximized, you can't move it or change its size, so you can't drag its title bar and you don't see its border—the thin frame surrounding the window that you can drag to resize the window. (If you do see a window's border, the window is sized to fill the screen, but it's not maximized. To resize such a window, see "A Window Is Too Large or Too Small," on the facing page.)

When a window is maximized and it covers all the other windows you need, you have three options: you can minimize the window to shrink it to a button on the taskbar, you can restore it to its original size so that it no longer fills the screen, or you can close it. Here's how.

How to fix it

- To minimize a window, click the Minimize button (the leftmost of the three buttons in the upper-right corner of the window).

    The window shrinks to a button on the taskbar. You can click this button to reopen the window, or you can press Alt+Tab to cycle through the programs that are running, regardless of whether they're open in windows or minimized to buttons on the taskbar.

- To restore the window to its original size, click the Restore button (the middle button in the upper-right corner of the window).

A maximized window fills the screen.

You can also double-click the window's title bar, or right-click the window's title bar and click Restore on the shortcut menu. If the middle button shows a single box instead of a set of overlapped windows, the window has already been restored.

A window is too large or too small

Source of the problem

No matter how large your screen, you can never have enough space for the windows you want to open. Working in Windows requires frequently readjusting windows. Windows that are too large can crowd out other windows, and Windows that are too small might not show enough of your work. Here's how to make each window the exact size you want.

How to fix it

1. Position the mouse pointer on a corner of a window.

   The mouse pointer becomes a diagonal double-headed arrow. ▶

   If the mouse pointer doesn't change to a diagonal double-headed arrow, click the Restore button (the middle of the three buttons in the upper-right corner of the window) and try again.

2. Hold down the mouse button, and drag the corner to resize the window.

3. Release the mouse button when the window is the size you want.

You can stretch a window vertically or horizontally by following these steps:

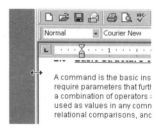

1. Position the mouse pointer on the border of the window so that it becomes a double-headed arrow. ▶

   Use the top or bottom border to resize the window vertically, and use the left or right border to resize the window horizontally.

2. Hold down the mouse button and drag the border to resize the window.

3. Release the mouse button when the window is the size you want.

Tip

To minimize all open windows, click the Show Desktop button on the Quick Launch toolbar next to the Start button.

Index

Microsoft Backup (*continued*)
  installing, 3
  interim backups, 6
  media, 5
  protecting Windows with,
    10
  recovering backups without
    Windows, 8
  registry, backing up, 5
  removable disks, 5
  restoring files, 12
  routines, 6
  schemes for using, 6
  selecting files, 4
  Windows Me, installing in,
    4
Microsoft Exchange, 90
Microsoft Fax. *See* faxing
Microsoft File Information,
  263
Microsoft Internet Referral
  Service, 166
Microsoft Mail, 91
Microsoft Management
  Console, 263
Microsoft Office, 87, 90, 93,
  101, 333
Microsoft Outlook, 50, 90,
  93, 187
  Contacts list, 87
Microsoft Paint, 18, 19
  resizing Wallpaper in, 19
Microsoft PhotoDraw, 17,
  18
Microsoft Registry Checker,
  305
Microsoft System Recovery, 8
Microsoft Virtual Machine,
  230
Microsoft Windiff, 263
Microsoft Windows 2000
  server, 225
Microsoft Windows NT, 225
MIDI, 285
mirrors, 64
Modem Properties dialog
  box, 43
modems
  56K, 239

modems (*continued*)
  cable, 86, 167
  call waiting, 126, 175
  Class 2, 97
  diagnostics, 169
  dialing automatically, 43
  dialing properties, 169
  dialing speed, 165
  dialing whenever Windows
    starts, 317
  DSL, 86
  error control, 169
  external, 240
  flow control, 169
  international adapters, 185
  laptop, 184
  line noise, 126
  modem savers, 184
  modulation type, 169
  Outlook Express
    disconnects, 67
  performance, 239
  preventing Outlook Express
    from dialing, 68
  settings, 169, 240
  V.34, 239
  V.90, 239
  Winmodems, 127
monitor. *See* screen
motherboards, 118, 284
mouse
  additional options, 193
  buttons, backwards, 193
  cleaning, 191
  double-click speed, 195
  double-clicking doesn't
    work, 194
  gunk, 191
  Microsoft, 193
  mouse pads, 191
  moving erratically, 191
  pointers, 105
  pointers, and desktop
    themes, 189
  pointers, finding, 193
  pointers, hard to see, 192
  pointers, moving too fast or
    slow, 189
  pointers, won't move, 190

mouse (*continued*)
  sensitivity, 189, 195
  switching the buttons, 193
moving files, 104
.mp3 files, 286. *See also* sound
MS-DOS, 114
  CD-ROM drivers, 275
  startup files, 274
MS-DOS Compatibility
  Mode, 139, 235, 237
Mscdex.exe, 275
msconfig. *See* System
    Configuration Utility
Mscreate.dir files, 106
Msgsrv32, 255
MSHOME workgroup name,
  125
MSN, 26, 79, 155, 167
  MSN Messenger, 241
  Online File Cabinets, 81,
    186
  Setup MSN Internet Access
    icon, 26
multimedia, 154
  previewing, 113
multiplayer
  Internet games, 117
  network games, 124
multiple monitors, 270
  display adapters compatible
    with, 270
  moving windows between,
    271
  using, 271
multiple users. *See* user
    profiles
music. *See also* sound
  CD-ROM drive won't play,
    284
  CDs, 290
MusicMatch Jukebox, 290
My Computer
  column widths, 109
  columns overlapping, 98
  converting to Windows
    Explorer, 111
  moving, 108
  opening folders in same
    window, 110

About the author

Steve Sagman is the author of more than 20 books on the subjects of graphics, Microsoft Windows, business applications, and online communications, and he has contributed to several more. For Microsoft Press, he has also written *Running PowerPoint*, now in its fourth edition, *Microsoft PhotoDraw 2000 At a Glance*, and *The Official Microsoft Image Composer Book*. His book *Traveling The Microsoft Network*, also published by Microsoft Press, was the recipient of the Award of Excellence from the Society of Technical Communication. His books have sold well over a million copies worldwide, and they have been translated into Chinese, Dutch, German, Greek, Hebrew, Japanese, Portuguese, Russian, Spanish, and Thai.

When he's not writing books, Steve runs Studioserv (www.studioserv.com), a technical communications company that offers book editing and production, creation of user documentation, software training, and user interface design.

And when he's not writing or running his business, Steve plays jazz piano, sails his boat, Offline, and toils in the fertile loam of his garden. He can be reached by e-mail at steves@studioserv.com.

The manuscript for this book was prepared and galleyed by Studioserv (www.studioserv.com) using Microsoft Word 2000. Pages were composed using Adobe PageMaker 6.52 for Windows, with text in ACaslon Regular and display type in Gill Sans. Composed pages were delivered to the printer as electronic prepress files.

Cover designer

Landor Associates

Interior graphic designer

James D. Kramer

Principal compositor

Sharon Bell, Presentation Desktop Publications

Principal proofreader

Tom Speeches

Indexer

Audrey Marr

Proof of Purchase

0-7356-1166-1

Do not send this card with your registration.
Use this card as proof of purchase if participating in a promotion or rebate offer on *Troubleshooting Microsoft® Windows®*. Card must be used in conjunction with other proof(s) of payment such as your dated sales receipt—see offer details.

Troubleshooting Microsoft® Windows®

WHERE DID YOU PURCHASE THIS PRODUCT?

CUSTOMER NAME

Microsoft®

mspress.microsoft.com

Microsoft Press, PO Box 97017, Redmond, WA 98073-9830

OWNER REGISTRATION CARD

Register Today!

0-7356-1166-1

Return the bottom portion of this card to register today.

Troubleshooting Microsoft® Windows®

FIRST NAME | MIDDLE INITIAL | LAST NAME

INSTITUTION OR COMPANY NAME

ADDRESS

CITY | STATE | ZIP

E-MAIL ADDRESS | ( ) PHONE NUMBER

U.S. and Canada addresses only. Fill in information above and mail postage-free.
Please mail only the bottom half of this page.

For information about Microsoft Press® products, visit our Web site at **mspress.microsoft.com**